FRESH START
MOMENTS

True Stories to Ignite
Passion & Purpose

I would like to thank the following authors for permission to include these stories in this anthology:

Riding Fences by David McCumber. Adapted from *The Cowboy Way: Seasons of a Montana Ranch* by David Mccumber, ©1999 Avon Books

Salute by Gary Greenfield. Adapted from *Life's Ride or Fall ... You Make the Call* by Gary Greenfield, ©2008 AuthorHouse

Published by Danzig Insight Services
www.BobDanzig.com

ISBN 978-0-9858039-1-9 (Paperback)
ISBN 978-0-9858039-4-0 (Hardcover)
ISBN 978-0-9858039-5-7 (eBook)

Publisher's Cataloging-in-Publication Data

Danzig, Robert J., 1932-
    Fresh start moments : true stories to ignite passion & purpose / written and compiled by Bob Danzig.
    pages cm
    ISBN 978-0-9858039-4-0

1. Inspiration. 2. Conduct of life. 3. Hope. 4. Self-actualization (Psychology). 5. Career changes. 6. Change (Psychology)--Case studies. 7. Success in business. I. Fresh start moments : true stories to ignite passion and purpose. II. Title.

BF637.S4 D365 2015
158/.1 –dc23   2015953190

FRESH START
MOMENTS

True Stories to Ignite
Passion & Purpose

Written & Compiled by
Bob Danzig

Danzig Insight Services

Dedication

To my dear wife, Dianne, a model of COURAGE, whose life affirms the ability to grab on to "fresh start moments." In her case, she went from having no skills for employment following a painful divorce – to raising three daughters – while working full-time at a hospital and putting herself through college and graduate school.

In Dianne's professional life as a mental health therapist, she is quick to admit that none of this could have happened were she not open to embracing those fresh start moments. What a privilege to call her "my wife."

Acknowledgements

How delicious and varied are the true stories I am about to share with you. A hearty bow of gratitude goes to each writer who contributed to this inspiring anthology. Your personal stories demonstrate what can happen when we are open and receptive to opportunities that invite choice and action. My appreciation also goes to the talented and able Kira Rosner, who guided this book to reality.

Contents

2. BLAZING LIGHTS

5. MY FRESH START MOMENTS

REFLECTIONS

Preface

Reflecting on the privilege of occupying space on this wondrous planet, it seems to me that life is a series of chapters – each rich in the invitation to add dimension, purpose and passion to our lives.

As one peruses these pages, you will discover a variety of *fresh start moments*. There are stories about confidence and leadership; receptivity, courage and perseverance; education, business and career choices; adventures and soul-searching; finding your calling; adventure and taking risks; transformation and discovery; facing fears and overcoming obstacles; marriage, divorce and renewal; parenting and caregiving; loss, aging and acceptance; persecution and inner strength; hardships, illness, addiction and healing; and faith and salvation – all situations and qualities that reflect the human condition. Finally, there are stories about people from various walks of life whose words and actions influenced others, becoming part of their fresh start moments.

All these stories are sincere and forthright. Some are lighthearted; a few are gritty. Despite their differences, they each share a noble purpose – a defining moment where the writer's willingness to move forward in his or her life paved the way for change.

Reading this marvelous collection triggered memories of my own fresh start moments and inspired me to include several personal stories in the final chapter.

My hope is that every reader draws strength from these shared experiences. May they serve to remind each of you how valuable you are – and how following the quiet whispers of your heart will help you identify and achieve your joy path in life.

Opportunities for fresh start moments are always available. All we need to do is keep an open mind and a ready "finger on the start button."

Introduction

A Father's Pride

FRESH STARTS TAKE COURAGE
by Darcy Plunkett, MSW, LISW

"What is your fresh start?" When asked this question by my sweet dad and reflecting upon my answer, it is clear to me that I have had a LOT of fresh starts in my life. I have always looked at this as a "weakness," as I don't seem to stick with things for long. This tendency has made me question my decisions and myself. Why am I so unclear about my direction? Did I study the wrong thing in college? Maybe I should have gone the corporate route. Maybe I should have taken that job....

I have come to realize that I am an evolving being, constantly growing and changing and becoming. I now embrace all of my life experiences and look at them as outward manifestations of where I was at that particular time in my internal life.

The jobs I've had don't define who I am as a person. What defines me are values, which allow me to continue to grow and work toward being a vessel of light in this world.

When in the throes of fresh starts, one can become despondent. At least, I know I can. When things don't go as planned, or I look back on my life with regret, the negativity inside me can seep out and run the show. So, rather than being a vessel of light, I'm quite the opposite.

Most recently, I launched a magazine for moms called *Chic Mom*. It was my baby. I was extremely passionate about it, as were my readers. The premise was to grow through the experience of motherhood, while continuing to embrace and evolve the woman inside. I felt like I was riding a creative wave and could not fail.

But, I did fail. I couldn't materialize it into a profitable business in print or online. Even with help and support from others, it was too much work for one woman, especially a busy, devoted mother. I lived with feelings of failure, regret and sadness that my baby didn't materialize like I SO believed she could. I also lived with jealousy about how other mompreneurs took off and were making their ideas work while balancing their families. I had some dark, ugly times around it.

After finally accepting that it wasn't going to pan out as I had hoped, I made the decision to re-enter my prior field. I had been a social worker/psychotherapist but was a little rusty. Volunteering at a women's counseling center two days a week quickly turned into a part-time job. I worked there for one-and-a-half years to get comfortable in the therapist's chair again. Then, I went into private practice with a close friend and fellow professional counselor.

It wasn't easy! It is a big responsibility to hold space for someone in deep emotional pain, give him or her the safety to freely express themselves and help them heal from some painful life experiences. There were times when I would ask, "Why am I doing this? My husband makes a good living. I can just go to the gym and work out! Or pick up a hobby!"

But the part of me that has gifts to share and has experienced pain and loss wanted to be connected to something bigger – a higher purpose.

I believe great change can come about from all pain, loss and suffering. Once worked through and healed, we discover how things could be better for others struggling with similar issues. I have gained such confidence in my ability to create a safe environment for others to heal. The one theme that has occurred over and over in my life is COURAGE.

I realize now that I had it all backwards. I spent too much time focusing and even ruminating on the "negative" experiences I wished were different. I even white-knuckled through decisions and life changes that should have made things alright, until I really started looking at the fact that I had the courage to actually start a magazine; publish six issues; begin, run and operate a website; re-enter a profession and actually sit with women and help them through their own emotional work and healing. Wow! My courage is a huge gift in my life.

I have also witnessed the incredible courage of people who come to therapy to do the often painful work that will allow them to grow and flourish in new ways. All of this has inspired me to get certified as a life coach and launch a website and coaching program that offers packages to people who want to heal and emerge transformed and more connected to their authentic selves. Do you know what it is called? *Courageously You.*

Beautifully, it is the culmination of my past experiences and what I've learned in all of my jobs. Little did I know that really, I am an entrepreneur at heart. Perhaps that is the reason I didn't settle for a specific career with one company. Now, I will be offering coaching sessions to people online and on the phone using the skills I learned about technology;

and I will write a blog to deeply connect with others. It is the magazine and my training combined.

So, here's to fresh starts! If we can embrace them, feel the feelings that accompany them, be open and allow them, they can be the very best things that happen to us.

Chapter One

Guiding Lights

"Learn to recognize and value the nurturers in your life.
When you are open, those people will find you."
– Bob Danzig

It seems to me that the magic of the brain includes our capacity to be open-minded or close-minded. When we choose the former, it allows new sunlight to brighten our paths. Those tiny rays of light can be subtle or vivid; they can influence our day or our entire lives. What is key is the fact that experience is a guiding light when we choose to stay open-minded.

The following stories highlight people who have been influenced by others, either directly or indirectly, and the power of receptivity.

INSPIRATION
by Gil Eagles

This is a story of a boy born in 1940 to Polish parents on the island of Cyprus. Because of circumstances of the war, all Jews were ordered by the British government to evacuate the island in 24 hours. The young parents, carrying two suitcases and their five-month-old baby, boarded a British oil tanker headed for Palestine. Upon arriving, the couple was given a choice to either stay or continue to an undetermined location. They chose to continue and eventually found themselves in a refugee camp for Jews in a remote part of Tanganyika (now Tanzania), East Africa.

In this remote part of Tanganyika in 1941 there weren't any modern facilities. There was no plumbing or electricity, certainly no radio, books or any kind of reading material. There were also no other European children for the little boy to play with. The local native children became his friends. He grew up speaking Swahili fluently and learning the ways of the natives.

It so happened that European big game hunters would occasionally pass through. On one of these occasions, one of the hunters saw the young white boy, now 7 years old, running wild. He told his parents, "You'd better send your child to school."

The only school available for European children in 1947 was a British boarding school located a two-day train and bus ride away. His parents told the young boy arrangements had been made and that he was going to go to school. Since he had no familiarity with schools, the young boy had absolutely no idea what they were talking about. Nonetheless, he very much enjoyed the two-day train and bus ride, but he was in for a shock.

He didn't realize they were taking him to a boarding school, and his parents were going to leave him there. All of a sudden, he found himself in a very strange, and what seemed to him, a very hostile place. Almost all of the children were British Colonials. They, of course, spoke English. He spoke only Swahili and a little Yiddish. The other children already knew how to read and write. The little boy had never seen a book and didn't even know the alphabet. To make matters worse, his name was different. Since the others came from the British Isles, they had familiar names such as Smith, Jones, Murphy and MacDonald. His Polish name was Igal Zyskowicz.

Young children can be cruel and tend to tease those who are different from them. Zyskowicz soon became Zysko-witch and Zysko-bitch. The little boy cried himself to sleep at night and could not understand why the other children were teasing and bullying him. He wondered whether his parents were ever coming back to rescue him.

His initiation at school was so traumatic that he developed a stutter. It became so severe he couldn't say a single sentence without stammering. Because of his embarrassment, he stopped speaking. He didn't say very much for the next seven years. Due to his silence and his inability to read and write, the teachers thought he had a learning disability. At the age of 15, he was permanently sent home with a letter saying, "Your child needs 'special help,' which we cannot give him here." The young boy never returned to a formal school again.

Fast forward to 1958. Igal, his parents and his younger sister immigrated to the United States. Imagine coming from primitive Africa to New York City. Here again was another major adjustment for the now young man who was, for all intents and purposes, still illiterate and had a debilitating stutter. That little boy was me.

On the second day, my uncle, the one who sponsored us to come to America, took us out to a dinner. I vividly remember my embarrassment that day because I couldn't read the menu.

With the help of my uncle, my father and I managed to secure jobs in a pizza concession on the beachside boardwalk in Far Rockaway, New York. I was a strong, strapping young man who was well suited for the heavy manual duties of the job. I remember carrying 100 lb. bags of flour for the pizza baker. In those early days, soda came in glass bottles. Part of my job was to unload the crates from the delivery truck, stack them in the basement and continually replenish the water cooler. That's how we kept soda cold.

The store's Lost and Found department was atop the refrigerated display case behind the counter. Common forgotten items were beach paraphernalia such as towels, Frisbees, sunglasses, suntan lotion, etc. At the end of the season, one of the items that were not claimed was a small record. These small 45 rpm records with the large hole in the center were quite popular in the '60s and '70s. They were frequently used in the old-style jukeboxes.

Since no one else wanted the record, I took it home to the small cold-water bungalow my family rented nearby. It so happened that as part of the sparse furnishings there was an old record player. Fully expecting music, I was surprised to find that it was a talking record.

Although I still couldn't read and didn't know what the label said, nonetheless, after all those years in British boarding school, I understood English. So I could understand what was being said. It was a motivational message delivered by Paul J. Meyer of Waco, Texas. And since we did not have a television or radio in the bungalow, the record became my entertainment.

I listened to it often. One day I realized the person on the record was actually speaking to me. He said that by changing my thoughts, I could change my life. The message began to get through to me. The notion that I could change my life by merely changing my thoughts was something I had never heard or knew before then. I still vividly recall the words spoken on that record these 50 years later. I remember Paul saying, "That which you vividly imagine, sincerely believe and ardently pursue, will invariably come to pass." Wow!

The one thing I wanted more than anything else was to speak. Not to be a professional public speaker, which I eventually became, but not to stutter so that I could feel comfortable speaking, especially to girls. I was 19 years old, had never been on a date and worked at a beach resort where bikini-clad gals were everywhere. Girls sure became a strong motivation to quit stuttering.

Following Paul J. Myer's suggestion, I began to vividly imagine what I wanted. I recall walking alone on the beach (by now the season was over) imagining myself speaking fluently to girls. I began to practice out loud, "Hello my name is Igal, I come from Africa, do you want to go out?" I haven't stopped speaking since. As far as the dating part, I made up for lost time. Actually, I have been happily married to my princess for 39 years.

I also recall buying simple children's books and teaching myself to read. As my reading improved, I became obsessed with improving my vocabulary.

As a result of finding that small, lost record, which no one else wanted, my life took a dramatic turn. No one knows what little thing can make a "fresh start moment" and a big difference in one's life. I count my blessings every day.

MY FIRST SPEAKING ENGAGEMENT
by Barry Roberts

Has it been 20 years already? My good friend and speaking mentor, Gil Eagles, encouraged me to begin my speaking career before I knew what it was all about. Gil advised me that the way I personally dealt with day-to-day stress was something worth sharing with others. Not realizing that I was doing anything extraordinary, I began to extensively research this subject area, as I continue to do even today. After several years of inquiry and study, months of writing and rewriting, hours of rehearsal and preparation, I was ready!

My first public performance of the material and my presentation, then titled, *Fun With Stress, Using Our Sense of Humor to Minimize Day-to-Day Stress*, would be for a local, joint meeting of a Men's Association and Ladies Auxiliary. Until this time, I had only shared the program with my immediate family. They were honest with me; they liked it, and I believed it was very good. I was just a little nervous. I had been singing and entertaining in nightclubs for many years at this point, but this was very new to me.

Mailings were sent to all members of both groups, and advertising posters with my photo were posted all over town. At last, the big night arrived and it seemed that everyone had shown up; I observed an equal number of friends, family and unfamiliar faces.

While the room was filling up, I found a quiet corner of the corridor. There really was no backstage or private area for me to collect my thoughts. Today, I enjoy "working the room" and meeting the audience members prior to speaking; on that day, I just wanted some alone time to review my notes. Friends and well-wishers found me to offer encouragement and to tell me how eager they were to hear my presentation.

With about five minutes to go, a middle-aged woman I did not know approached me, rather slowly. "Excuse me," she said, "are you the speaker?"

"Yes I am," I replied, with a big smile on my face.

She nodded her head slowly for a moment. As she looked me directly in the eye she said, "My son died two months ago and was sick for a very long time before that. So, just how are you going to make me laugh?"

I was stunned. I couldn't speak. My stomach sank, and my heart was in my throat. I saw the anguish on her face and felt incredibly sorry for this woman. I didn't know what to say and honestly don't remember what I eventually did say. I do remember thinking, "Oh my goodness, this is horrible and not what I need right now." I felt selfish thinking that and yet, somehow, we finished our conversation as she walked into the auditorium.

I gave myself a pep talk; I knew I had to shake this off and deliver an outstanding presentation. Hearing my introduction, my energy level was up. "And so ladies and gentleman, let's welcome Barry Roberts!"

I walked onto the stage to a nice round of applause and began my program. Throughout my years of stage experience, I always made a point of making direct eye contact with various, individual audience members. This helped them make a more personal connection with me, and as I saw smiling faces, it became very soothing and built my confidence.

Ninety seconds into the program, I made eye contact with "the woman," sitting rather glum faced right there in the center of the fourth row. I was rattled for the moment and quickly decided that if I were to stay composed, to stay upbeat, I had to avoid eye contact with her again. If I couldn't see that she was accepting of my philosophy on using our sense of humor to minimize stress, it would destroy me.

As the evening went on, the attendees laughed and nodded approval at all the right places. They were truly "up" during the audience participation segments, and I finished to sincere, enthusiastic applause. Friends, family and many of those unfamiliar faces rushed me afterwards to tell me how much they enjoyed and appreciated all I had to say. I was thrilled, and at the back of the crowd was "the woman," waiting to talk to me after everyone else had gone.

"Barry?" she said.

"Yes, um … thank you for staying."

"Barry, I'm sorry to have told you all of that before your program, and now I want you to know that for the first time in two-and-a-half years, you taught me that it's okay to laugh again. It's okay to live my life and have a good time. Thank you for that … thank you very much." And she reached out and gave me a hug.

I understood at that moment what it was to make a positive difference in someone's life. I realized that this was what I wanted to continue to do. I feel blessed to have had and continue to have the opportunity to do just that!

A BELIEF CHANGE
by Brenda Gill

My move to the East Village was supposed to be the first act of a new play starring a better version of me; yet I felt haunted, empty, unsure and unsettled. I was unwilling to trust others and unable to trust myself, when I encountered a Master choreographer at the Nuyorican Poets Café who showed me the way back to myself with dance.

When you enter the Café, the exposed brick infuses the environment with an earthiness that mingles with the poet's painting of words spoken to the beat of the conga. Miguel Algarin, the co-founder of the Café, would entreat the poets to speak their truth opening with, "taca, dun, dun, dun; taca, dun, dun, dun," mimicking the clave beat.

I felt right at home in this bohemian bar. It was the Salsa dancing that kept me coming back. My mother and father met Salsa dancing. I guess you could say I was conceived by the horizontal completion of the vertical expression of intimacy.

One night while dancing at the Café, someone interrupted my revelry.

"Miguel wants you to come upstairs."

"Why?" I asked, not wanting to stop.

"I dunno. He said it's important."

"Alright."

I climbed the stairs of the Café where I was confronted by Miguel and a dance legend – Alvin Ailey. Alvin had on jeans and a simple shirt, but he was ablaze with energy.

Miguel said, "Alvin wants to give you a scholarship to his school."

Me? A girl who first studied dance by reading library books on ballet, holding on to her bureau, assuming the five ballet positions while trying to mold her body to match this French dance dialect.

"But first Alvin wants to ask you some questions," Miguel said.

Alvin approached, scrutinizing my body. "I need to see your facility."

He asked me to raise my leg and stretched it forward to see how high it would go. He seemed pleased when it went over my head. After some contemplation and further assessment, he said, "OK," and I realized I'd been dismissed.

That marked the beginning of my brief but transformative tutelage under Alvin Ailey. He saw something special in me – even when I was having a hard time believing that I had anything special to offer the world.

During that same time period, I had been cast in the play *Nuyorican Nights*, and Alvin Ailey was the play's artistic director. I had such anxiety and fear when I was around him. It wasn't because of the bottles he threw at the cast, which he threw to shatter our complacency, but because I had a fear of failing him, of not measuring up. I was the dance captain of the play and had been given a scholarship to his school, which meant I was subject to greater scrutiny by Alvin. While other actors could rest during breaks, Alvin would have me run dance drills, as he sat on one of the Café bar stools critiquing my every move.

"Longer. Straighten those legs on the jeté."

"Yes, Alvin."

"Now, pique turns. Feel yourself high up on your arch as you spot the back wall."

Alvin watched me leap and pirouette, responding to the music using my height and flexibility to its full advantage.

Just then, Alvin got off the bar stool and started to dance with me. I was awestruck. *Could this be happening? Was I really dancing with the Alvin Ailey?* Before I knew it, I was in a lift over his head. His creative energy leaped into my soul, instantly quieting my mind. I was in the moment, dancing interpretively with Alvin. He was the pilot soaring above the clouds, taking me and my technique along for the ride, reaching a higher plane – craft on top of technique, on top of soul, covered by music. That day, the sound waves from the music acted like the ping of an airplane's black box helping me to locate and awaken my soul.

Alvin believed in me in a way that hadn't happened before. Growing up, I wasn't told that I could do anything, be anything. My parents were both alcoholics – troubled. They spent more time focusing on themselves and their past, than on me and my future. Life had stolen my innocence, my sense of wonder and my belief in myself. But when someone you admire and respect believes in you, it makes you believe in yourself. You start to think that maybe, just maybe, you have something to offer the world.

When the play ended, I began my scholarship at Ailey's. Following that, I had a brief career as an actress, singer and dancer before becoming an attorney. During that notoriously difficult first year of law school, I would close my eyes and remember Alvin. His belief in me is with me still, showing me the way through dance and through life.

MY OCEAN JOURNEY:
COUSTEAU TO CLIMATE CHANGE
by John Englander

The Undersea World of Jacques Cousteau was a long-running series of television specials in the 1960s and '70s. It seemed like everyone watched them – not too surprising, as we only had about a half dozen TV channels in that era. It was more than that though. Captain Jacques-Yves Cousteau, the charismatic Frenchman, and his crew aboard the research vessel *Calypso* showed all of us the hidden world beneath the waves.

Cousteau was a very real influence on my teenage fascination with the ocean, which became my focus for sport and career. He started a nonprofit organization, The Cousteau Society, the first major environmental group in the world. I became a dues-paying member, joining more than 100,000 others. Like millions of divers and tens of thousands of oceanographers, I traced my start directly to his pioneering efforts. *Time* magazine listed him among the 100 most influential people of the 20th Century.

Thus, it was rather surreal three decades later in January 1997, when Captain Cousteau joined me in Orlando, Florida to help raise awareness for a small dive-industry environmental program that had elected me as chairman. He literally was the co-inventor of the scuba gear we still use today, a device he named the "Aqua Lung."

JYC, as friends called him, (pronounced ZHEEK) was 86 years old, still very sharp, demonstrating encyclopedic recall. The visit gave me the opportunity to spend some quality time with him over a period of several days. Starting on our ride from the airport, he confided that his nonprofit organization had declined to about half its peak size and could use a "fresh start." While I was generally aware of that, it was poignant to hear it from him.

The next afternoon, during one of our extensive private talks in his hotel suite, he complimented me on what I was doing in the diving industry and my grasp of larger ocean issues. Then, *out of the blue*, he asked if I would consider "joining his team," quickly making it clear that he wanted me to become CEO of the Cousteau Society. I struggled to calmly consider what he was proposing, but it was as if the air had been sucked out of the room.

Even though it was almost two decades ago, I remember my thought process clearly. Doing as he was suggesting would require me to quickly sell my majority ownership of a very large scuba diving operation in the Bahamas where I had lived for 25 years and probably move to be near one of their offices: New York, Virginia or possibly Paris. Was this realistic? Would my wife think I was crazy to get out of a successful business to run a declining nonprofit that was largely based on one larger-than-life individual, who was very old and had a complicated family structure? I tried to consider it all rationally but sensed this was one of those unexpected moments in life where you just have to *take the plunge*.

Cousteau was still standing just in front of me, making it obvious that only a few seconds had actually elapsed since the question. I slowly nodded and said, "It would be an honor," realizing I had no idea where this would lead.

Within weeks we had worked out the basic arrangements. It was incredibly exciting to have this new career at age 46. After some phone calls with the Captain and lots of discussion with many in my network, a plan of action was starting to take shape. Unfortunately, by the time I started work as CEO in April, Cousteau was in the hospital, though initially with a good prognosis. As I feverishly worked to create a plan to revitalize the organization, his condition deteriorated.

By the end of June, I was sitting in the front row at his memorial service in Notre Dame Cathedral with the crowds overflowing into the streets of Paris. It was nearly a state funeral with the old crew of *The Calypso* as the pallbearers – definitely another surreal experience. He was the best known and loved person in France, with an amazing global following as well.

With his untimely death, his widow decided to buy out my contract and run things herself. This was not the fresh start I had in mind. I flew back to our rented house in Virginia. Without anything to do, I often stared at the sea, contemplating my future. For months I was lost, not knowing what would have meaning compared to my inspiring mission of the last few months. It was a depression of sorts.

Over the next several years, I found some interesting opportunities that helped get me back on my feet. I also now had a young daughter. Becoming a father at age 50 was another fresh start, adding an entirely new dimension and perspective.

In 2004 a small but influential marine organization was looking for new leadership. The Cousteau item on my resume added a strong credential, landing me the job as CEO. The International SeaKeepers Society was mostly comprised of owners of "mega yachts." They had invented a clever system, enabling almost any substantial ship to continuously gather oceanic and atmospheric data and transmit it via satellite for scientists to use.

Some of them wanted to understand the issue of climate change. So, in 2007 I organized a small group of our members to go to Greenland, "ground zero" for the melting ice, the dominant force driving the sea to rise beyond the levels of the last 100,000 years.

Having had a strong environmental interest since college, I had become somewhat obsessed about understanding the factors regarding climate change and then finding a way to communicate them. Standing there with my group on the rocky shore of this huge, mostly ice covered Arctic island, I suddenly had an epiphany. As the ice on land melted, raising sea level, it would move the shoreline farther inland for millennia.

Recalling my study of ancient sea level as part of my geology major in college, I thought I could research the facts and write a book that would translate the science into terms anyone could understand. If I could put the new phenomenon of changing sea level in the context of the natural ice age cycles, it might help to reduce the climate confusion, given the very visible and tangible way that higher sea level would destroy real estate and infrastructure, with profound economic impact on individuals, businesses and communities.

The following day we were scheduled to explore the vast ice sheet and some of the myriad glaciers that were melting and calving into icebergs, causing the sea level to rise. We learned that the Jakobshavn Glacier we were visiting had been identified as the likely source of the iceberg that sank the Titanic. Points like that could help explain the facts in an interesting way.

Researching and writing the book was much harder than I expected. By mid-2009 I had resigned from the nonprofit to work full-time on the book, never expecting it would take four more years. I was *connecting the dots* about the ocean-land boundary in a way that no one had ever done.

It was my first book. Naively, I imagined it could soon be a bestseller, that climate change would be well understood, and that I would find something else to do, without any idea what that might be.

High Tide On Main Street: Rising Sea Level and the Coming Coastal Crisis was published on Monday morning, October 22, 2012, though without any announcement. We planned to start the promotion in mid-November, after the upcoming U.S. presidential election was over, possibly allowing me a chance to get some media attention for the book.

After the years of research, writing and rewriting, I was in a relaxed mode that afternoon. I noticed the news about a tropical disturbance forming south of Jamaica. Living in Florida we are always alert for these, but on the 22nd this one seemed unremarkable. Within 24 hours, it had strengthened to the threshold for getting a name.

"Sandy" did not directly hit Florida. Nonetheless, it did a lot of damage to our coast by Thursday. By then, all eyes were on its projected path to hit the mid-Atlantic area of the U.S., perhaps around New Jersey and New York. Like so many people, my wife and I were now following the storm's track, particularly since we each had grown up in the Northeast. She still had family in the area.

On Tuesday the 30th, it felt like we joined the entire world in watching morning television, showing the New Jersey shore and Manhattan awash and underwater, seemingly out of a disaster movie. My book was far from my mind, until Linda noted that one version of the manuscript she had read described the scenario of a storm hitting that area. She was right, but I had to look to see what was actually in the final edited version as it was published. To avoid using the word *surreal* again, I will call it *eerie*. On page 121, there was my description of a superstorm on "Sandy's" exact track, hitting Atlantic City and devastating Manhattan.

Soon, I had a call from a producer at SKY News television in London, who had discovered my new book on Amazon, asking to interview me live on their *Sunrise* program the following morning. During the six minutes on-air, anchor host Eamonn Holmes asked me how I wrote about "Sandy" one week *before* it happened. I answered honestly that the timing was as spooky to me as it was to him. That unexpected event and interview gave me a new fresh start.

The last two years of presentations and briefings to communities, governmental agencies, business groups and investors were quite unplanned. I had almost stumbled into becoming a leading expert about the facts, forecasts and impacts of rising sea level. For example, as I write this account in the fall of 2014, two years later, I am returning from explaining rising sea level to the government in Hong Kong. The prior week I was in Savannah, Georgia giving a presentation to 2,000 people concerned with the protection of historic buildings. In a few days, I will be the program speaker for the Miami Chamber of Commerce, helping business leaders understand the problem posed by long term rising sea level.

Given the nature of this topic and the challenge to communicate it to diverse audiences, it seems that I may not need to find another fresh start. I founded the Rising Seas Group consulting firm where I work with organizations and government agencies helping them understand their risks from rising sea level and what they must do to adapt. My schedule is busy, plus I have started to write a sequel book, which explains the impact of rising sea levels and gives many more examples of what businesses, communities and individuals must do now to prepare and protect their assets.

We rarely can see what is coming "around the corner" or even how apparent disasters such as Cousteau's untimely death, making my time at the helm of that organization short-lived, actually positioned me for a fresh start in ways I was unable to see at the time.

Like all the other restarts and new directions, this part of my career and life developed because I was willing to take a risk, maintained a good network and was open to new opportunities.

A CAREER IN COMICS
by Brendan Burford

I've been lucky. But I don't think I am an exception. I think we're all lucky – we just have to be perceptive enough to identify those opportunities and fearlessly dive into them. I'm guessing any "fresh start" begins with an individual identifying an opportune moment and doing something about it.

I was fortunate right out of the gate for being given parents who were blindly supportive of my quirky childhood interests – they didn't seem to measure my future prospects in direct relationship to the viability of my interests. As a kid, one of my biggest passions was comics. Comic books, comic strips, cartoon illustration – it all fell into the same vast pool for me, and I was deeply immersed.

It was an intense hobby, but even at a very young age I was certain I wanted to make comics into a career. There's no real road map on how to go about doing this, and my parents never seemed concerned that I was following such an uncertain path. I think they were just happy that I had latched on to something so passionately, and they decided they would simply stand out of the way.

Initially, I wanted to be a cartoonist. I was always a good cartoonist growing up, and I was known for being that kid who could draw. Early in my childhood and all through art school and my early professional career, I was on track to becoming a cartoonist. I had my cartoons published in various publications, and I ran my own small publishing company, where I created an anthology that included my own work. At one point, Random House came calling wanting to publish a book of my comics. But over time, my *own* cartooning work was becoming less important to me.

The more I studied comics, the more I began to think of them critically. And my expectations of what comics could be or should be exceeded my opinion of my own work. Everyone is self-critical, but in my case I was increasingly uncomfortable with the idea that I couldn't meet my own expectations. I realized that being a part of the process was equally, if not more rewarding than slaving away on my own comics work. I was good at helping other artists see a path to a higher level of achievement – I could help them accentuate their strengths and beat their weaknesses. Even if they had bad habits, I could help them re-position those habits to serve them better.

Today, I'm the Editor of King Features Syndicate. At King Features, we sell daily comic strips like *Blondie, Hagar the Horrible* and *Mutts*, along with dozens of other wonderful features, many of them household names. I'm lucky to work at King Features, which is a unit of Hearst Corporation. I've worked at this company for nearly 15 years. And my arrival at King Features was helped along by a lucky little detail.

It was 1999, and I was working at DC Comics, bouncing from project to project as an editorial assistant. I had spent about a year working there, but it was uncertain if I would wind up staying beyond each project I was assigned. I knew I wanted to find something more permanent in the comics business, and I wasn't sure if DC was the place for that, so I reached out to a couple of different comics companies to see what opportunities were available.

King Features was one of the companies I reached out to. I wrote a letter to the editor, Jay Kennedy, and hoped for the best. A few days after I sent that letter, Jay called me. I recall being amazed by the simplicity of it. I wrote him a letter and he called. My expectations probably prepared me to hear from some anonymous human resources person, only to be thrown into a pool of applicants for a job that didn't even exist.

Shortly into the conversation, Jay revealed that he was, indeed, looking for an editorial assistant, but that he had some specific criteria for that position. The thing he was most interested in was whether or not I could write. Of course, I told him I could write. I was shocked at how simple a thing was at the top of his list of criteria, but he quickly elaborated by explaining that most people *think* they can write, but they really can't. He saw it as a key litmus test of a person's larger set of skills. Still, I assured him I wouldn't disappoint. However, deep inside, I had a moment of panic. I knew I was a capable writer, or at least I *thought* I was. But what if he measured these things by a very different set of criteria than I could imagine?

He asked me to prove that I could write by giving me a simple assignment. He requested that I write a 600-word press release about a retrospective gallery exhibit featuring the cartoon art of Roy Crane at the Society of Illustrators – King Features would be sponsoring the exhibit. This was fictional. There wasn't actually going to be a Roy Crane show at the Society of Illustrators. Jay just wanted to give me an assignment that would show an ability to not only write a formal press release but would also show my ability to write with historic perspective on an important cartoonist.

What Jay didn't know (how could he?) is that I was then, and remain now, absolutely enamored of Roy Crane and his cartooning career – he's one of my very favorite cartoonists of all time. What luck! It would be a breeze to write passionately about Roy Crane. So, I did. And I sent it to Jay a day later. Within 30 minutes of sending the piece, he called me back and requested that I come in to meet with him to discuss a job opportunity.

I went to work for Jay for over seven years. He was a great mentor and friend. He opened doors for me and taught me many things. In March of 2007 Jay died quite unexpectedly. The earth stopped for me and for our company – Jay's death was a shocking loss. After he was gone, I was faced with a very different sort of fresh start. Filling his shoes would be the biggest challenge of my life to that point. But that is another story.

THE CALLING
by Ron Herman

I knew from a very early age that film and television production was my calling. My love of the production side of the business began as early as junior high. As a ninth grader, the local high school was looking for assistance in building its radio station. I immediately volunteered.

I was hooked from the start. How exciting was it to have the power of communications at my fingertips? There was only one problem; radio is not a visual medium. Watching records spinning on a turntable just wasn't going to cut it!

Early in tenth grade, the local PBS station came in to ask students to volunteer for its first annual auction. The positions they were trying to fill were for haulers and schleppers, pushing carts of donated product on to various sets. I volunteered, and from the minute I arrived on location and saw the lights, the cameras and the production truck, I knew that this was going to be my future.

I met an extraordinary lady in the eleventh grade, who would later become my wife. She was a theater major. She wanted to do shows – she wanted to be in the spotlight. I wanted to make major motion pictures and television shows. We would often sit in restaurants and dream of movies, plays and television shows.

That same year, I was hired by the PBS station as a production technician. In this role, I learned how to operate cameras, lighting, audio and the equipment in TV studio control rooms. When the auction came around again, I was on staff. I was called *"the teen"*! My future wife even got involved. She was running the character generator and was called "the teen's chick"!

I had a four-year run at the PBS station, and then I was left to complete my degree in broadcast and cinema. Between my junior and senior years, my girlfriend, Sharon, became my wife.

During my senior year, Sharon was the breadwinner. She worked as a full-charge bookkeeper at a local retailer. Upon my graduation, we decided to follow the advice of Horace Greeley, "Go West, young man."

It was May of 1974, and with $2,000 in the bank and my wife's new Chevrolet Camaro, we decided to move to Los Angeles. I had been given the names of a few contacts from friends and relatives and began "banging" on the start button.

Sharon immediately was hired as a bookkeeper. I quickly exhausted all of the contacts that friends and relatives had given me. A bit frustrated, I found myself playing bridge around the pool with the ladies in the apartment complex where we lived. My wife told me, in no uncertain terms, that I needed to get a job and stop playing cards.

I was so disappointed by the lack of results in my job search that I applied for a job at the retailer, The May Company. I had experience in selling cameras and much to my chagrin, I got offered the position. I was supposed to start at the mall the following Monday. I had less than a week to find a job in the industry. One more chance, albeit slight, to kick-start my career.

I drove to Hollywood to try one more time. On that eventful day, I found myself driving down Cahuenga Blvd. I passed the Technicolor building, and when I arrived at the corner where Willoughby crosses Cahuenga, a sign on a building screamed, "VIDTRONICS – The Greatest Name in Videotape."

Dressed to the nines, or in my case maybe the eights, I parked and walked into the lobby. The receptionist asked me what I needed. I told her: "A job." At that exact moment, a very large, teddy bear of a man with a white beard entered the lobby from the corporate suites. The receptionist continued, "The only job opening we have is for a clerk/typist." I responded, "I don't know what a clerk does, and I don't type very well, but I'll take the job."

The man laughed and asked who I was. He invited me into his office, and within an hour he offered me the position of assistant operations manager. That moment, and because of that man, my career began in earnest. His name was Burt Lippman, and he became my mentor and my friend. He taught me the business of the business. To this day I rely on his teachings in my professional and personal life.

This was the start button push I needed! I was able to spend the next 40 years working on some of the very highest profile television, film and commercial projects.

I now live in Charlotte, North Carolina and still accept projects, when I am not on the golf course.

I'VE NEVER WORKED A DAY IN MY LIFE
by Brian D. Sather

All I ever wanted to be (or so I thought) was a professional musician. I dreamed about it, planned for it and practiced from my teen years on. In 1983 I met one of my best friends, Greg. I had just switched high schools and as fate would have it, the change led me to Greg. He played guitar, me drums. From the first meeting, we knew we were two musical souls who had found each other. Our tastes in music were similar, and our love of all things rock-and-roll was also compatible.

Our pursuit continued through our sophomore, junior and senior years in high school. It led to us creating a band, recruiting friends to join us and planning and playing gigs, including a party at a friend's house on a hayrack, complete with a homemade light kit. Truth be told, we even convinced the high school to allow us to create our own study hall option – an hour in the music department's practice facility jamming and writing music.

When we both graduated, we went to separate universities, but vowed we'd keep pursuing the dream and hopefully find our way back to our mission. Little did I know that life was about to present me a new "start" button. I had no idea what was waiting, and that it would change the course of my life and create a career that has now spanned nearly three decades.

My college of choice was in Sioux Falls, South Dakota. It wasn't necessarily my first choice but it proved to be the catalyst for what has turned into an amazing career. I was offered a music scholarship, and I had family connections at the school. I declared my major before day one. Music Education. I believed that this major would give me the best chance to bridge a life between broke musician and fame. While I worked to make it big, I would teach to make money – or at least that's what I thought. I loved music, and this seemed like the best way to do what I wanted. So much for 18-year-old wisdom.

Enter my college roommate, Mike. He and I, like most freshmen, were thrust together through some random process, where the college decides who you're going to room with. As it turned out, their choice proved prescient. Mike and I never really discussed our majors much. Our discussions mostly centered around the typical college freshman subjects – girls, traveling home to visit and what we were planning to do Friday night.

My first few weeks were challenging. I was taking Music Theory and frankly, hating it. One night while I was doing schoolwork (I can't recall which class it was for) Mike was getting ready to leave. This was the middle of the week, and our conversations hadn't disclosed any great parties or events, so naturally I was curious. I asked Mike where he was going. He informed me he was going to the college radio station for his three-hour shift as a disc jockey. When I prepared to attend college, I had not even considered this as a profession I'd pursue. It was intriguing to say the least. I wanted to know more. Mike told me I could tag along some time and watch. OK, count me in. Anything to get me out of homework.

I joined Mike one night in the studio as he prepared for his shift. This place was downright cool. The people working there were cool. It was a radio station run almost entirely by college students. The formats during the days were jazz, but in the late afternoons and into the evenings it changed to rock. The only rules for the DJ, other than following the log and format, were that you couldn't play music currently on local top-40 radio stations. So, as an example, if U2 had a new album out, and one of the songs was being played on a local radio station, you couldn't play that song, but you could play anything else on the album.

This was back in the days of real vinyl albums, and the radio station had thousands, spanning as much as 30 years of history. Mike sat down at his post and began his shift and introduced song after song after song from groups I loved. On this night, he was playing Van Halen, Huey Lewis and the News, Bruce Springsteen and more. I was mesmerized. Now this looked like fun. He would provide weather updates, create unique segues between songs, and in general, he was in charge. I was enthralled.

The next day, I decided to switch my major. I wanted to be a broadcaster. Period. No question. I muddled my way through the rest of my music education curriculum for the semester, but by the time December rolled around, I had my own on-air shift at the radio station and was on my way.

This ability to have my finger on the start button allowed me to jump at a passion and a love that was lit in me on that autumn day. However, if that was the end of the story, I don't think it would fully illustrate the power of this start. When I pushed start that day, I thought I was going to be an on-air radio professional. I changed my major in January and began what I believe the school called a Bachelor of Arts in Mass Communication or Speech Communication. My classes were interesting and theoretical, but the practice of working at a radio station was where it was for me.

Before long, this led to moving into a management role as the station's traffic director and eventually, I was promoted to program director. Mike and I would sit around our dorm talking radio. There was a whole group like us. I would describe us as "radio geeks." We'd make aircheck tapes, critique each other's work, talk about music and new artists, and dream about the future. I always said that if someday I could get paid for this, it would be gravy – because I loved it so much I'd do it for free.

Eventually, Mike and I were in our sophomore year and looking forward to our future as radio broadcasters. We were struck by the realization that while our major gave us some general knowledge in a lot of different facets of communication, the only area the school could give us any practical knowledge was radio. We were immediately hit by a concern for what we'd do if the only jobs we could get after school were in television. How would we be able to succeed? This conversation led us to pursue part-time jobs at a local television station. Yes, just like that we decided – we needed some television experience to round things out. Just in case.

When we both applied to KELO-TV, we had no idea what we were doing. My job was advertised as a production assistant position. I thought I was going to interview for a job in the department that made television commercials. That sounded fun and exciting. I guess I should've gotten the clue when I interviewed with an executive producer in the news department. Regardless of my naiveté, they hired me for the job. As it turned out, I would be an assistant in the newsroom working Monday through Friday from 5:00 a.m. to 8:30 a.m. I had no idea what I would be doing, but I was going to be trained.

I edited videotape, organized graphics (and back then it was slides they put in a machine), put information in the Chyron and ran a teleprompter. In a week, I knew that radio with pictures was way better than radio. I was hooked for good. In fact, within a month, I knew that someday I wanted to run a television station.

Within four months, the station saw my interest in learning and assigned me other tasks. I would come in on Friday and Saturday nights and enter scores into the system for the sports department. My counterpart, who worked the 3:00 to 6:30 p.m. shift resigned, and I had the opportunity to move. This is when having my finger on the start button really took on its first real test.

To take the advancement opportunity and put myself in the position to really pursue this as a career, I had a choice to make. In order to have my music scholarship, I was required to participate in an ensemble and take private lessons. There were three ensembles, and mine was concert band. Every afternoon they rehearsed at 4 p.m.. My shift at work wouldn't allow me to be in an ensemble. Therefore, I'd have to give up my scholarship.

The following day, I made an appointment with my conductor and my advisor. I told him my choice. I was quitting the band, giving up my scholarship and pursuing my dream. He challenged me and really asked me to think about this. It was a life-changing choice, and he had seen my growth as a musician and wanted me to be sure. I told him I was. When I stood up and walked out of that office, I was completely at peace. I knew I was making the right decision, but had no idea where this new fork in the road would lead me.

It has meant everything. The move to afternoons, while not overly significant, exposed me to more people at the TV station. Eventually, I was offered opportunities to shoot video. In my junior year I was promoted to a full-time photojournalist position. A few years later, I moved into sales at another station. Now, 28 years later, my career has led me to run two television stations for Hearst Television – a division of the Hearst Corporation.

What's the lesson? I think there are three important points. First, when you have your finger on the start button and are ready to push it, this might only be the beginning of a greater plan for your life. Make no mistake though, had I not pressed it that night in the fall of 1985, I wouldn't be running one of America's great TV stations – KCCI in Des Moines, Iowa. I was ready. But I had no idea the trajectory that decision would put me on.

Secondly, you must also believe in the path the start button puts you on. I didn't know where this would all go, and there have been plenty of other opportunities along the way. But the first button I pushed, which led to all the others, was a challenge. I had to have the conviction to let it play out.

Lastly, be thankful for the people who introduce you to the start button. I will forever be grateful for my friend Mike. He and I reconnected through Facebook a few years ago. I am so glad we did. I've had the chance to thank him for introducing me to this career path through that little, student-run college radio station. If he had not presented me with that first start button, I don't know what I would be doing today.

I tell people all the time that I haven't worked a day in my life. I mean it. One of my first loves was the broadcasting business, and to this day it remains so. I love what we do and what we stand for. Pushing start, and more importantly being prepared to push start, was the impetus.

A DAD'S HAND
by Dan T. Joerres

It was April of 1998. I was working as an account executive
selling ads for six radio stations in Madison, Wisconsin. I
was fresh out of the University of Minnesota, "killing time" as
Annemarie, my bride-to-be, was finishing her undergraduate
degree in nutrition at the University of Wisconsin. Radio
was in my blood ... my father was the general manger of
five very successful radio stations in the Milwaukee area. I
spent my entire childhood around these stations, but for me,
selling radio in Madison was just a pit stop. Annemarie and
I were set to be married later that summer, and I knew that
Madison was only a stepping-stone.

That spring, Annemarie was accepted into an internship
program in Milwaukee and landed a job at Children's Hospital of Wisconsin as a pediatric dietician. So, Madison was
in the rearview mirror as I placed a phone call to my father,
"Where can I get a job in Milwaukee?" I did not want to
work for him, and I did not want to sell radio against him. So
my options were limited.

I found myself with two interviews at competing television stations. WTMJ was the dominant local NBC affiliate
with hit shows like *Friends, ER, Seinfeld,* etc. The interview
went well, but there was no immediate opening for an account executive position; the only available opportunity was
in research. I thought to myself, a job is a job. I would take it.

In the meantime, I had another interview scheduled
at the local Hearst-owned ABC affiliate, WISN-TV. This
was an interview that I almost canceled because I had this

gig at WTMJ that really excited me. With a good family name in town, I could not cancel, so I showed up for a breakfast meeting at a local diner, called Miss Katie's.

I had heard of Miss Katie's before, but I'd never had the chance to dine at this establishment. The diner was in the heart of Marquette University, within walking distance of WISN-TV. Miss Katie's was known to play host to everyone from Marquette Basketball Coaches to U.S. Presidents. Being all of 23 years old, I showed-up for the interview that almost did not happen – chewing gum, no less! Little did I know that morning, my finger was on the ultimate "start button!"

My meeting was with a gentleman named Pete Monfre. Pete was the general sales manager and a "coach" in the truest sense of the word. I went from thinking about the opportunity at the competition to sheer excitement about the chance of working for Pete. He spoke about advertising sales and what he expected out of his team. He indicated that he did not have a "list" available but the station was thinking about expanding the staff. The list they would have available was none other than the Yellow Pages. I was offered $2,000 per month and a "chance."

In exchange, Pete asked for a two-year commitment. It was a gentlemen's agreement. My father was my guide through this process. I remember him saying, "Dan, Hearst is a great company. You are very lucky to have this opportunity. Marry this company and make a commitment." And so I said, "Yes." It was a summer of, "I do's!"

On June 15, 1998, I awoke eager and excited. I drove my pristine 1987 Grand-Am to 759 N 19th St. and entered WISN-TV as the newest member of the team. I was staring at another start button as I pressed "Enter" on the security door at the station.

My first three months at WISN-TV were challenging. I was struggling and felt as though I was in trouble. I made a lot of sales calls and thought my first sale was going to come through any day. Finally, in October of that year, I made my first sale – and it was a big one. It was the start of the dot-com boom, and I found an Internet start-up in Chicago that wanted to expand to Milwaukee. They agreed to sponsor the previously unsold *Tech-12* segment. The wind was at my back, and I was on a roll.

That ultimate start button led to more start button moments at WISN-TV. In 2002, Frank Biancuzzo was named the General Manager of WISN-TV. With Frank's support, Pete promoted me to National Sales Manager and eventually Local Sales Manager. Little did I know that working under Frank Biancuzzo for 5 years was a glimpse into my future – a future I could never have predicted.

In retrospect, it is fascinating how short the segments of life are and how fast start buttons appear. By 2008, the sky was the limit and the pace of my life had increased exponentially. Annemarie and I had four children by that time: an eight-year-old son, a four year-old son and one-year-old twins.

The next start button came, but this time it was in North Carolina. As life-long Wisconsinites, moving to North Carolina was a tough putt. The opportunity was with our sister station in Winston-Salem. This was a chance to let our family experience a different part of the country, the opportunity to work for one of the best general managers in the country, to be a general sales manager, and to grow within the greatest media company on the planet. We hit the start button as a family, packed our bags and moved south, knowing we could always move home if things didn't work out. We had the security blanket of a rock-solid family, as well as a great company behind us.

So, on April 28, 2008, I started as the General Sales Manager at WXII in Winston-Salem, North Carolina. The excitement that came with a fresh start was exhilarating, but I was already looking ahead. After all, I had two marriages going ... one to my wife of 10 years and one to a company that I am fiercely loyal to. My plan was to learn under General Manager Hank Price for a few years and then earn a chance at moving back to WISN-TV in Milwaukee as the President and General Manager. You see, Hearst Television owns 29 stations all over the United States. My dream was to run WISN-TV and eventually, earn an opportunity to run the first station Hearst ever purchased – WBAL-TV in Baltimore!

My time in Winston-Salem flew by. We had a tremendous run, increasing our share of business in the market and hiring new people who would become future leaders for our company. To say that I was having fun was an understatement.

In the summer of 2010, I was invited to participate in an Executive MBA-type program through the National Association of Broadcasters called the "Broadcast Leadership Training Program." This was an intense 10-month program that focused on teaching individuals how to run and/or own media properties. I would be traveling to the NAB Headquarters in Washington D.C. once a month for three-four days of classes, typically Friday through Sunday.

It was in November of 2010, while headed to Washington D.C., that I received a call on my cell phone from the Assistant to David Barrett, the Chairman and CEO of Hearst Television. "This is Linda Lange calling from David Barrett's office; I have David on the line for you."

I was caught off guard by the call ... David picked-up the phone and informed me that he was passing through Greensboro in a couple of weeks and wanted to meet with me to talk about the "next step." I was infused with excitement thinking that I might finally have my chance at running WISN-TV! David and I were set to meet on December 16, 2010. This was an easy date to remember, as it was my parents' wedding anniversary.

I remember that day vividly because we received an ice storm in North Carolina, an ice storm on the most important day in my career to that point! The roads were glazed over. I was in disbelief. I called David as I tried to navigate my way to our meeting. I indicated that I would be late for our 9 a.m. breakfast due to road conditions.

David, being the caring individual that he is, said, "Take your time and call me if you do not think you can make it." Not making this meeting was not an option … I'm from Wisconsin … ice and snow does not stop me! If I needed to walk the 20-mile distance, I would! I made the meeting, albeit 10 minutes behind schedule. We met for almost three hours and discussed many opportunities that were about to become available within the company. We left each other with an agreement that we would talk about the next steps at the beginning of the New Year.

On January 4th of 2011, the "start button" of a lifetime was presented to me during my follow-up conversation with David. "Dan, on January 14th, I want you to meet me in Baltimore, where we will introduce you as the new President and General Manager of WBAL-TV." WOW! The opportunity of a lifetime, both personally and professionally!

Once again, I find myself working under Frank Biancuzzo, who is now a Senior Vice President with Hearst Television, as I manage the first television station that William Randolph Hearst purchased. It is an honor and a privilege to be at the helm of WBAL-TV. A privilege all due to the result of an interview at Miss Katie's. A start button that has given me opportunities beyond my wildest dreams!

"YOU CAN DO THIS"
FOUR WORDS AND ONE UNFORGETTABLE WOMAN
by Walter Anderson

Barry Williams was my best friend when I was growing up in White Plains. In many ways, our lives were completely different. He lived in a two-story clapboard with a backyard; my family occupied a railroad flat in a tenement building. My home life was troubled; his seemed serene. He was black; I'm white. I dropped out of high school; he went on to Harvard. But what we had in common, what made all the difference in the world to me – was Barry's mother, Mrs. Williams.

I didn't even know her first name. She was always Mrs. Williams, the tall, dignified schoolteacher across the street who was rearing three sons on her own.

Sometimes Mrs. Williams told us stories. "A long time ago, in the marsh country of England, there lived an orphan boy named Pip," she might say. "One bleak evening he was visiting the graves of his parents. The sky darkened, and the wind blew, and the boy, afraid, started crying. Suddenly a deep voice roared, 'Keep still or I'll cut your throat!' and a terrible figure rose from among the tombstones."

"Then what happened?" I asked enthralled.

"If you would like to know," she answered, smiling, "read the book *Great Expectations* by Charles Dickens." She made me want to go to the library.

Other times Barry and I would be out in the driveway on a Saturday shooting hoops, and his mother would say, "Boys, could you come and give me a hand?" The next thing we knew, we would be helping her with a student she was tutoring. I felt proud that Mrs. Williams valued my help. I didn't realize until much later that by teaching someone else, Barry and I were learning too.

Mrs. Williams made sure Barry and his brothers did their homework, and if I happened to be visiting, she watched while I did mine. Usually Barry and I studied at the kitchen table. Mrs. Williams stayed nearby, in case we had a question. At home I lived in fear of my father's alcoholic rages, and I wasn't used to that kind of discipline – or attention.

Her favorite words of encouragement were: "You can do this." I heard them often because I was impatient and easily frustrated. When a math problem refused to yield its secret or an essay confounded me, I gave up and slammed my pencil on the table. Calmly, Mrs. Williams took a seat beside me and talked me through the assignment step-by-step. Something about her quiet reassurance, "You can do this, Walter," settled me down, and I managed to finish my work.

Barry and his brothers went to private schools, an expense that must have strained Mrs. Williams' budget, and she worried about the quality of my education. One day she took me to a local parochial school, had me tested, then persuaded my parents to let me change schools.

I attended for a while, but I was told not to return after an angry exchange with a teacher. Unperturbed, Mrs. Williams took me to another school, had me tested again, made sure I would receive the necessary financial assistance, then convinced my parents that it was important for my future. I made it through two grades in one year.

When we were ready for high school, Barry applied to boarding schools. Mrs. Williams believed that would be the best thing for me as well. Anything to get me away from the streets where she saw too many kids getting into trouble.

I was accepted into a prep school and again awarded a scholarship. But when I saw the other students – kids in pressed shirts and blazers – all my old insecurities came rushing back. I could not do it. I entered the high school in town. A year-and-a-half later, failing nearly every subject, I dropped out.

One of the hardest things I have ever had to do was tell Mrs. Williams about it. She gazed at me with her cool brown eyes and said nothing. "I'm going into the Marines," I said shrugging, "I won't need high school."

"Okay, Walter." Her voice was quiet. "I don't agree with you but you are old enough to make your own decisions."

Six months later, in the Marines, I realized how right she was. In three-and-a-half years I would be out of the service, a 21-year-old with no diploma. What sort of future would I have? *Dear Lord,* I prayed, *please give me another chance.*

The next morning, I went to the first sergeant and said, "I want to go to school." The first step was to take an exam for a high school equivalency diploma. I must have done well because after seeing my scores the Marines enrolled me in a special electronics program.

Again, I felt out of my league. *Dear God,* I prayed, *let me pass just one course.* The instructor began his lecture. I started taking notes, but there was so much I didn't know; so much I was afraid I would never know. "There's no way I'll get through this class," I thought, putting my pen down. "I should just walk out the door right now."

All at once, I heard a familiar voice inside my head, warm and reassuring: "Don't give up Walter. You can do this." I wasn't so sure, but I owed it to Mrs. Williams and to myself to try. Taking a deep breath, I picked up my pen and concentrated on my instructor's lecture. I graduated seventh in a class of 24. It was the biggest thrill of my life.

"I can't wait to tell Mrs. Williams," I thought. But by the time I made it back home the Williams's were not living across the street anymore. They had moved, and no one knew their new address.

After the Marines, I went on to receive my bachelor's degree. By the age of 26, I was well into a career in journalism. I became a newspaper editor and eventually Editor-in-Chief of *Parade* magazine.

Several years ago when I spoke at a dinner, I told the audience, "All the successful people I've ever known have one thing in common. In their childhood, there was someone who said, 'I believe in you.' For me, that was my best friend's mother, Mrs. Williams." It was gratifying to give her credit. Still, I longed to tell her how she had changed my life and thank her for all she had done for me.

Some time later, I spoke to *Parade's* senior investigative reporter about Mrs. Williams. "I wish I could get in touch with her," I said.

"I can find her," he declared.

A few days later he called. "Walter, Mrs. Williams lives a few miles away from you. She has retired from teaching, and her son Barry is a successful attorney."

Mrs. Williams and I had a reunion at my house. All I could do at first was thank her over and over again. Then the words spilled out in a rush. I told her about everything I had accomplished, eager to make her proud. "I graduated college as valedictorian. Then I got into journalism, and today I'm the editor-in-chief of a magazine."

She smiled. "Of course, you are, Walter," she said, her voice as full of assurance as it had been so many years ago.

Ilza Louise Berry Williams never doubted for a moment I could accomplish anything I set my mind to. It just took me awhile to believe it for myself.

"YOU'LL BE THAT MUCH OLDER ANYWAY"
by Kathleen Sanders

Lucy was my very special maiden aunt, my mentor and
inspiration, especially during my confusing teen years in
the '50s. She was born in Connecticut, the oldest daughter
of immigrant Sicilian parents. My father, her only brother,
was the middle child. Aunt Lisa was the youngest, though
there was a younger son, who was killed by a trolley car
(witnessed by my father), when they all were young children.

Despite coming to America at the turn of the century
without much schooling and little knowledge of the English
language, Grandma and Grandpa wanted their family to be
educated, productive Americans who could make a significant contribution to society. Lucy and my Dad acquired a
number of degrees between them from institutions such as
Pratt Institute, St. Joseph's College, Southern Connecticut,
Yale and Columbia universities.

Dad, a metallurgist, made many contributions in his
lifetime, as did Lucy, who started her career as a teacher,
became a principal of an elementary school and then the
first selectman (mayor) of her town in the Naugatuck Valley
of southern Connecticut. Unlike my Dad, she never married or had children of her own. Had Lucy not started her
political career so late in life, our family and friends feel that
she would have been destined for state and national politics.

As Lucy's oldest niece, I should have focused on an institution of higher learning immediately after high school,
but I was detoured by the rebel in me and eventual marriage
to someone my father thought was the perfect match for

his (sometime) non-conforming daughter. I did take some college classes throughout my late teens, 20s and 30s, while having a fairly nice life with my successful husband, lots of big homes, lots of moving around and travel abroad. I also had two beautiful children, the unconditional loves of my life.

Then, my life changed drastically in the '70s and '80s. Gone were the husband, the "cushy" lifestyle and many of the accoutrements.

Lucy was still there, not quite as strong as in her earlier years, but still able to argue politics with anyone who listened. At family gatherings, she was still the matriarch, still had that presence about her and was still much loved by one and all. When we had our special moments together, she often reminded me that, "You'll be that much older anyway," which I interpreted to mean to get back to school and get my degree. With higher education, I knew I would have better opportunities for employment.

In the '90s, I finally listened to my weakened, though still special, Lucy and walked across the stage at Lesley University with my Bachelor of Science degree in Human Services in my hand. Though Lucy was unable to be there to witness the ceremony, I heard later that a smile crossed her face when she heard the news.

She passed away a few years later, and as the funeral procession drove by the school where she taught for so many years (and now bears her name), the children were outside on the sidewalk waving American flags.

Again and again, I have said with my eyes to the sky, "Thank you Lucy." Thank you for being my inspiration, my very special aunt and a person loved by all who knew you.

HINDSIGHT
by John Chang

As I reflect on my life experience thus far, it is filled with "fresh start moments," often identifiable only through the lens of hindsight. Sometimes the decisions to move forward with a fresh start at the time it presented were easy; sometimes they were difficult – but all were important experiences in the mosaic of life. Often it was a part of my life journey where I could identify a wonderful mentor.

Believe it or not, my first recollection of a fresh start moment presented itself to me in the sixth grade. I was interested in helping fellow students when I entered middle school and decided to run for a student council officer position. I can remember how nervous I was, holding my note cards for my campaign speech in front of the entire student body at an assembly. I was the lone sixth grader running. As you can imagine, most candidates were eighth graders. My strength came from the unwavering support I received from my social studies teacher who taught me the lessons learned from campaigns past. Miraculously, I won the election that year for student council secretary. If I had not pressed the start button here, I would have certainly missed my first opportunity to lead.

In high school, while I was strongly interested in math, science and computers, my freshman English teacher gave me a fresh start in haiku and poetry that led to my involvement with the literary magazine and school newspaper. She mentored me and encouraged me for four years to become a section editor, and eventually I became a member of *Quill and Scroll.* This experience provided me with some lifelong editorial skills that I have used throughout life and even today as I oversee the production of clinical content for care guidance.

During my junior year in college, I met my independent study mentor in chemistry. This was my first serious endeavor into research. My mentor gave me the freedoms and responsibilities of a graduate student. This enabled me to be a good steward of the resources I needed to carry out important experiments. I had full access to the laboratory stockroom. I could order all the necessary starting materials for my experiments. He made a commitment to meet with me weekly. With every successful experiment were many failed experiments but each with important lessons learned, the challenges of generating "new" knowledge. The week before graduation, after 18 months of hard work and five lab notebooks of data, I had finally synthesized the "active" compound I had set out to make, 400 micrograms of "pure" compound as verified by nuclear magnetic resonance (NMR) and gas chromatography (GC). Six months later, a graduate student continued my work and validated that I had indeed developed a methodology that worked, and we published our results in the *Journal of the American Chemical Society.*

I applied to medical school thinking I was going to be a pediatrician. After all, I had loved volunteering all four years of college at the children's hospital. Little did I know, I would find a mentor during my first year of medical school who would guide me toward an interest in internal medicine with a special focus on geriatrics. My mentor gave me the opportunity to conduct my second serious research project on chronic obstructive pulmonary disease in the elderly. He let me run with the research, allowed me to be the first author of the journal article in *Chest,* and he allowed me to present the research at pulmonary grand rounds and at a national scientific meeting. Had it not been for his mentorship, I may not have pursued my future interests in internal medicine, chronic disease epidemiology, and health policy and management.

During residency, I focused on internal medicine and had the opportunity to be mentored by the chairman of the department, who later became the director of the U.S. Agency for Healthcare Research and Quality, and who also helped develop my interest in health policy and management.

After residency, I wanted to get a taste of a career in academic medicine, so I started a fellowship in primary care research. It was my fresh start that allowed me to maintain the privilege of caring for patients, teaching medical students and residents, and developing and implementing research projects. In the second year of my fellowship, a mentor encouraged me to pursue a Ph.D. program in health policy and management, while continuing to develop as a junior faculty member. I focused on a wide range of topics and applications, including quality improvement, quality measurement, operations management, meta-analysis methodology and preventing falls in the elderly. I learned many lessons in project planning and implementation, grant writing, budget development and human resource management – lessons that I still reflect on today.

After completing my Ph.D., I had my most recent fresh start by joining Zynx Health and Hearst, which has allowed me to take my interest in improving the quality of healthcare and care guidance to a national and global scale. It has been an exciting journey, applying all of my previous experiences towards innovative, scalable and sustainable care guidance solutions.

With so many fresh starts, I look forward with my eyes wide open for the next fresh start to come.

IMPACT OF A MENTORING MOMENT
by Charlie Swift

I have had many great mentors in my life and career but none so impactful as my freshman year linear algebra professor. The irony of it all is that I hardly had a relationship with this man, and I couldn't even recall his name if you asked me. The most memorable feature I remember was that he wore the same maroon sweater in every class I ever had with him. So, the question must be asked, why do I reflect back and still classify him as one of my great mentors? The answer is simple. He was the one who gave me permission in life to create "fresh starts" for myself. It was a moment of transition for me. One where I realized the importance of being able to take control of one's life, both in terms of career and family. In the midst of all the numbers and theories flying around the classroom, he took one memorable hour in the middle of the semester to share his thoughts on life, and I continue to pass them along today. In many ways, as our world keeps changing faster and faster, what he said has become more important to me every day.

Here are the two pieces of wisdom he shared with us: First, was the statement that what he was currently teaching us in that class would effectively be irrelevant in 10 years. Technology and the advancement in our understanding of the world would evolve past where we were now. Our goal was simply to learn how to think rationally and continue to learn. The world of possibilities in whatever path we chose would continue to unveil itself, and our passion and curiosity to learn would be a critical barometer of our long term success in life, however we defined success. The moment we stopped learning was the moment we stopped participating in the world.

As the world evolves, this investment I try to make in myself continues to be a fundamental driver in my overall happiness in life. Even today, I challenge myself to ask the questions: "What did I learn today? Where did I learn this from?"

I recognize that the method of learning comes in many forms and that we should always be open to new ways of thinking. In this age of social media, Google and "big data," the access to information is greater than ever before, and I recognize now how much more I don't know.

The second statement made was, in many ways, even more empowering. To move forward in life successfully frequently requires that one takes risks. Everyone has his or her own individual level of comfort with risk, but it is critical that we understand what our level is up front. Once we understand that, we should make sure we have put enough money aside to be able to get up and walk away from any job at any moment.

You cannot tell off "The Man" if you are afraid for your security in life. You will be hard challenged to break free and follow your chosen path in life if you are beholden to others. Happiness in life is driven by the freedom to do what you want to and explore the areas of the world that inspire you. More importantly, true leaders set their own path.

As simple as it sounds, this lesson has served me well over the years. It has allowed me twice in my life to walk away from jobs that were no longer satisfying and find new opportunities and new careers that have led me to the fulfilling career I have now. It has guided my long term financial planning, forced me to reflect on what is truly critical to survival and ultimately allowed me to better appreciate all the things in life I can afford to do now.

So to my freshman linear algebra professor from 29 years ago, I say, "Thank you." You were right that I would probably not remember or use that calculation on vector analysis. And you were right that the passion to learn and freedom to walk away would ultimately guide my long term happiness and success. Your class was the first fresh start of my independent adult life. It also enabled many of the fresh starts that followed.

TICKETS TO TOMORROW
by Lawrence Feldman

After almost three years at the University of Wisconsin, I found myself having gone through several majors and well on my way to being a well-educated, unemployed, potential graduate. In 1960, much like today, this was not an unusual circumstance. I must admit, I was getting slightly nervous, but had been a zoology major since the middle of my junior year. This choice of zoology was made of necessity, since I had to select a major that would enable me to accumulate 30 credits in a concentration over the next three semesters.

One day in February of my senior year, as I was plodding through the deep and slippery Madison snow, while at the same time trying to figure out how to get a date with a beautiful coed, I happened to look down so as to prevent myself from falling. There, lying in the snow was a clean white envelope that I did not realize was the path to my future.

Picking up the envelope and opening it, I discovered two tickets to the Minneapolis Symphony Orchestra, which was going to perform several days hence at the Student Union Theater. Turning to my companion, the girl of my dreams, I recognized my entrée into the much-desired date, and out of my mouth came, "Would you like to go with me to the symphony?" Barbara enthusiastically said, "Yes," and I glided home in a very happy state.

When I got home and reflected on my good fortune, I had an abrupt shock upon turning the envelope over and seeing the typed letters reading "Dr. P. W. Wilson." It was the name of my professor in the bacteriology course. I could immediately see myself sitting at the concert with my date; my professor, who somehow remembered his seats and got his tickets replaced; and my course grade going down the drain. This called for drastic action. I called my date, explained the situation and we did something less memorable (alas, no romance).

The next day, I returned the tickets to Dr. Wilson, who related that his wife so looked forward to the Minneapolis Symphony that performed each year in Madison, and he had no idea what had happened to his tickets. He thanked me profusely; I took my next exam and managed to get an excellent grade.

To my great surprise, Dr. Wilson approached me and asked what I planned to do after graduation. I knew I wanted to pursue my education, but I told him that I had no idea in what field. He said, "You are doing very high-level work in my course. Why not think about bacteriology?"

"That sounds like a good idea," I replied.

After class three weeks later, Dr. Wilson asked if I had time to chat with him in his office. He told me he was so impressed with me that he took the liberty of calling some colleagues of his and had obtained admission for me in several programs at other universities with full assistantships. I went on to obtain my doctorate degree, eventually becoming a faculty member and ultimately, a Senior Associate Dean and Vice President at the University of Medicine and Dentistry of New Jersey.

What I didn't know was that Dr. Wilson was a past president of the American Society of Microbiology and a world famous bacterial physiologist. He knew professors all over the world, and my honesty and success in his course impressed him so much that he led me into my productive and satisfying career.

The lesson I learned was honesty is always a good policy, and one should always be alert to "fresh start moments." Who knows when seemingly random events can produce unimagined opportunities?

MR. BROWN
by Andrew C. Jackson

The yellow school bus chugged south along 117ᵗʰ Avenue. It was only 7:30 in the morning, but already the temperature was above 90 degrees and the humidity at 85 percent. I could feel a thin film of moisture on the back of my neck as the damp, green vinyl of the bus's seats slipped and slid under my thighs. The bus lurched forward down the hot, two-lane road and crossed a low, concrete bridge. In the water below us, gar fish, alligators and bluegills swam lazily in the canal that served as south west Miami's "railroad tracks" – a barrier separating the rapidly expanding, mostly white housing tract of Pine Meadows from the working-class African American community of Lincoln Heights.

Once over the bridge – and out of our comfort zone – the busload of white sixth-graders could look out the right side of the bus across a long, flat expanse of green. Cane fields stretched out for miles, right up to the edge of the Everglades. Out the left side of the bus, adjacent to the canal, a wide field filled with high-tension power lines served as a further buffer zone between Pine Meadows and our destination of Lincoln Heights. More precisely, we were on our way to school at D. L. Norton Elementary. A busload of 50 white sixth-graders headed to school in an all black neighborhood.

In Miami, sweat is a constant companion if you aren't inside an air-conditioned space. Where we were heading, we wouldn't feel a breath of that cool, clean air all day. At D. L. Norton a faint, humid breeze that blew through open jalousie windows and a mouthful of rusty-tasting water from an old drinking fountain would have to do. On that hot October morning in 1975, I did not know this day would alter the trajectory of my life forever.

For each of us, there are moments on which our futures turn. Something flint-like inside us is charged and ready to spark. When the force of an idea or the breath of some Holy Spirit strikes that flint, our lives can ignite with a new beginning. I had a moment like that when I was 11 years old, and I can see and relive it as if it happened yesterday. A tall, thin, black man without much of an agenda and probably no recollection of the moment I am about to describe, was the force that sparked in me a lifetime of learning. The first true fresh start moment of my young life was waiting to happen. I just needed to be open to it – and fortunately, this day I was.

School integration in the 1970s was designed to give African American students access to the same quality of education as their white counterparts in neighborhoods with higher tax bases, more political clout and better schools. School integration wasn't designed to give white kids exposure to traditional, teacher-in-the-front classrooms with effective, no nonsense curriculums. But in my case that's exactly what school integration did. It changed my life and for the better. And it happened at a poor, underfunded school in a neighborhood on the wrong side of the tracks. The catalyst was simple: a few words of encouragement from my teacher, an African-American man – Mr. Brown. But there would have been no D. L. Norton Elementary School and no Mr. Brown teaching there if it weren't for Dwight Norton.

On an uncharacteristically cool February morning in early 1952, Captain Dwight Lindsay Norton felt a freshening breeze from the north and pulled his collar up around the back of his neck. Jamming his hands into the pockets of his khaki pants, he shivered a little as he looked out over the palmetto scrub and pine forest in front of him. As a white, veteran pilot of the Second World War, he knew how it felt to return home to a country that was thankful for his service. He, himself, had much to be thankful for. He had his life, his livelihood and a dream that he could not only see but touch, as he ran his hand along the rough edge of a saw-palmetto bush. Captain Norton had just purchased the 3,000 acres of pine forest and fallow fields that he now surveyed. But his dream wasn't so much about profit as payback.

The Tuskegee Airmen, a group of African-American military pilots, who formed the 332nd Fighter Group and the 447th Bombardment Group of the United States Army Air Forces, had one of the most outstanding combat records of the war. They'd flown nearly 1,600 combat missions protecting Allied bombers and lost only 27 aircraft, compared to an average of 46 among other 15AF P-51 groups. They destroyed nearly 300 enemy aircraft and damaged another 150.

With the purchase he had just made, Captain Norton had the vision to develop a sub-division he would call Lincoln Heights. It would be a new community for a new era. His dream was to provide housing for returning African American veterans, including members of the Tuskegee Airmen. He had served along-side black soldiers in combat and felt great admiration and respect for their fighting spirit and ability to overcome the many obstacles created by both war and racial prejudice. Lincoln Heights would be a neighborhood for these men and their families. A neighborhood made up of prim houses, parks, and in the middle of it all, a school of its very own.

A generation later, as part of the effort to integrate schools in Miami during the 1970s, Lincoln Heights' D. L. Norton

Elementary School became a "sixth-grade center," bussing in sixth-grade students from the surrounding, mostly white communities. This social experiment of school integration wound up saving me from a failing academic career conducted under the auspices of another social experiment of the 1970s – the "open-classroom."

The open-classroom movement, which originated in Britain following the Second World War, was once viewed as the answer to all of America's problems – both educational and societal. The concept was to do away with formal lessons and testing and for students to learn independently "by doing." This resonated with those who believed that America's formal, teacher-led classrooms were trampling creativity and crushing students' individuality. Following the counter-culture movements of the 1960s, when traditional authority was questioned at every level, the open-classroom concept seemed to point the way forward for America's schools.

One of the main aspects of the open classroom was that there were no desks for students or teachers – the classroom was structured as a large, open space or workshop. Students moved independently from workstation to workstation in small groups or on their own – at their own directive. Sounds great, right? Well, if your motivation as an 8-year-old student is to get away with doing as little as possible, and oversight is to be avoided at all costs, it is truly amazing.

When my family emigrated from the industrial north of England in 1972 to Miami, Florida, there was a lot for us to learn. Two cultures separated by a common language, indeed. By the time I started second grade at Greenwood Elementary School, I'd just about figured out how to talk so that people in America could understand what I was saying. A strong teacher presence and a structured classroom would have probably been helpful from the start – at least someone would have noticed how out of place I felt.

Greenwood was designed and built from the ground up as the quintessential open-classroom school of the 1970s. It was a brand new school, in a brand new neighborhood – and for us – in a brand new country.

At Greenwood they called each of the large open-spaces a "pod." Rather than being in a class, you were part of a pod. Walking into Greenwood on the first day of second grade, I felt like a pale lima bean stuck in a pod full of green peas. It was an inauspicious start to say the least. Dressed in long Bermuda shorts, a shirt and tie, and most unfortunate of all, knee-high, white cotton socks, I did make an impression on my pod mates. Not the one my mother had hoped for, but from that memorably humiliating experience I began to learn quickly. My real mission at Greenwood was to try to fit in.

I listened carefully to how my friends and classmates spoke American. I'd repeat the words they said and try to make my broad vowels sound like theirs. The R's got harder and the T's in the middle of words became D's. To my young mind there was absolutely nothing cool about the British accent. When we'd gather as a family to record cassette tapes of our U.S. experiences for our family back home in England, we'd always listen back to the recording before sending it off. I would cringe when I heard my odd sounding Lancashire accent. I wanted to be an American.

As second and third grade progressed, I did okay at school. The bar was low, I was a newcomer, and I soon began to learn my way around the pod system. One thing that became obvious early on was that if you gave the impression of doing work, it was just about as good as actually doing work. I got very good at that. There were no formal tests, no sitting down at a desk in front of the teacher and so no real monitoring of what we were doing. Not only was this style of teaching and learning new, but the school itself was brand new. One gets the impression that the well-intentioned educators were, more or less, making this all up as they went along. Many of today's academics say that they were.

There were group projects, the creative exploration of ideas and lots of free, unsupervised hours of self-directed goofing off. Looking back now, I know that I did get something positive from the creative time, but I wasn't learning the basics and began to realize that I wasn't doing very well on the self-graded quizzes. I began to feel pretty smart at playing the system, but dumb at and incapable of doing the actual schoolwork. We were never sat down in front of a teacher, and it must have been very difficult for the teachers to gauge how we were really doing.

By the second half of fourth grade, and especially in fifth grade, the wheels began to come off. I'd forgotten how to learn. The goal was now simply not to get caught. Notes went home to my parents but didn't make it back to the teacher. I forged my mother's signature on several of these notes. When she was finally called in for a meeting with the teachers and shown the forged correspondence, she cried her eyes out right there in front of everyone. That was a low point in my young life, a low point even now. It was a feeling of failure and shame that I never wanted to experience again. As fifth grade came to a close and my time at Greenwood Elementary ended, I truly believed that I wasn't smart and that I wasn't ever going to be.

So, on that hot October morning as the school bus turned left onto Boggs Drive, and the ancient vehicle's pneumatic brakes wheezed in protest, my expectations for the beginning of my second month of sixth grade at D. L. Norton were about as low as the day's barometric pressure.

Unlike the new and sparklingly clean pods of Greenwood, D. L. Norton was a bit of a dump. I'd never actually seen a school like this one. It was typical of most elementary schools built in the 1950s. Four long rows of low buildings set side-by-side and divided into four classrooms each. A small patch of grass separated the buildings, and at one end of the campus was the cafeteria.

D. L. Norton's cafeteria had the distinctive décor of a couple thousand spitballs permanently attached to the white asbestos tiles of the dining hall's ceiling. They were testament to several generations of small-time juvenile delinquents' considerable lung power. Though located in the middle of an all-black neighborhood, the school's students were now predominantly white, but there were many African-American and Latino students as well. It was a good cross-section of Miami's population at that time.

I was in Mr. Brown's class. We were special. Apparently, we had been identified as having had some "issues" at our prior schools, and so we did not go from classroom to classroom for subjects like social studies and art. In the interest of behavior monitoring, we stayed put in Mr. Brown's class all day. He taught all our subjects. This was kind of amazing. For me, compared to Greenwood's pod system it was like stepping back in time. Having always been fascinated by the past as a kid (and even now), I actually kind of liked it.

Mr. Brown was a tall, rail-thin man, who had the smallest ears I've ever seen on an adult. He had the kind of personal style that only a black man in 1975 could embody; smooth, unflappable, proud and a bit of a badass – in a very real and respectable way. Polyester slacks set high on the waist, nicely polished shoes and form-fitting shirts with wide collars were the order of the day for Mr. Brown.

My friend David Blackwell's athletic ability made him a favorite of our teacher. I wasn't much of an athlete so didn't get the ball thrown to me when Mr. Brown conducted recess. David did, and I wished I had Brown's respect the way he did.

For many of us, sixth grade is when the first hormones of puberty begin pumping through our veins, and suddenly the opposite sex becomes intriguing in ways we couldn't have imagined even six months before. That hormone cocktail is even more potent when you are surrounded by a school full of other 11-year-olds and only 11-year-olds. There has probably never been anything like D. L. Norton's integrated "sixth grade center" before or since.

My first kiss would come later that year – a coordinated bathroom pass excursion during class-time meant the halls would be empty, and a quick but heart-pumping peck could be accomplished. That's another memory – and another story. But the kids weren't the only ones stealing kisses that year. The teacher in the classroom next door was a bouffant blond who would often slip into our classroom when the lights were down for one of the films we'd watch during history or social studies. The clackety-clack of the old-fashioned 16 mm projector banged out a steady rhythm as Mr. Brown and his paramour stood very close to each other in the back of the classroom. I definitely saw my own teacher's hand slyly slip along Ms. Bouffant's backside on more than one occasion. It was 1975 after all. So, to my young and aspiring mind there were at least a few reasons to respect Mr. Brown and to want to earn his respect in return.

In those early months in Mr. Brown's class, I did the work that was assigned because I simply had no other choice. There we were – in five rows of desks facing the front of the classroom and (unless we were watching one of those films) constantly under our teacher's gaze. What a concept, accountability.

So, I did what was asked as best I could, but I honestly didn't know how I was really doing. Math was never easy, but creative writing was really fun. I was finishing assignments because Mr. Brown made sure we did, and I guess on some level I wanted to impress this man.

I had no particular expectations as our bus pulled up in front of the school that morning, other than dealing with the oppressive heat. I strolled through the classroom door just as the bell rang, sat down in my seat, second from the front in the row closest to the door, and rooted around in the compartment below my flip-top desk for a notebook and pencil. Mr. Brown started the day like any other. We listened to the national anthem over the crackling loudspeaker. I can still hear the popping and snapping of the phonograph record that dutifully played America's theme song, morning after morning. We said the pledge of allegiance, sat down to start the day, and then something truly amazing, unforgettable and life changing happened. As I sat there dumbly looking up at Mr. Brown, he pulled a piece of paper out of a folder with a bit of a flourish. He held it up for the entire class to see and then said those six amazing words I'll never forget, "You should all be more like Jackson...."

I really and truly couldn't believe what I was hearing because no teacher had ever said anything remotely like that. That's mostly because I hadn't ever done anything to deserve hearing those words. It was one of those moments when you're so surprised by what's being said that you doubt you're actually hearing it. I was confused, yet amazed, and so awestruck by the moment that I can't remember the exact words that followed. But those first six I can still hear echoing right now – all these years later.

Mr. Brown went on to praise me for both diligence and effort and for having not only turned in my assignment on time, but for delivering a piece of work that delighted him. To be honest, today I'm not even sure what the subject of that paper he waved around was. It doesn't even matter. At that moment, I knew for the first time in my life that I could be successful if I just did the work and did my best. From then on, for the most part, I would do both of those things – do the work and do my best. Put that to work in your life, and with a bit of luck you'll do pretty fine.

That afternoon I got off the bus at the corner of 108th Avenue and 118th Street, just a block and a half from my house, and my 11-year-old legs started moving all on their own. As you do at that age, I just started to run. Running home, running toward the rest of my life and not running away from anything. I felt as if I wasn't moving across the Earth, but rather that the Earth was turning beneath my feet – like a giant ball that I alone was moving with the force of my own two legs.

FINDING MY WAY
by Theresa Crone

There are times, when looking back on my life, I relive memories so painful that I wish I could forget the constant abuse and neglect I had to endure growing up. It is amazing to me how children can grow up in the worst situations, not realizing just how bad things really are, until something happens when they suddenly see the past for what it is and find that ray of hope for the future.

Yes, I was subjected to serious child abuse – the kind that burns into your brain for the rest of your life and comes from a person you love – someone who was also seriously abused – causing you to think that only if you are mistreated, you are loved. Naturally, my self-esteem was always low. So just getting through life was a challenge. All any of us really want is to love and be loved, but some of us get it in ways that cause great pain, as I did. Difficult as this is to recount now, I feel I must, in order to give just a little background for this story.

My mother was a product of horrible abuse growing up. Always sick from years of liver and kidney disease and fighting cancer, she considered me a "punishment" in her life. My father wanted a second child after having my sister, but my mother did not. For the rest of her life, she never forgave me or forgot to remind me of that fact.

Just imagine being told on your sweet sixteenth birthday, "I hate you and wish you had never been born. I am going to make you suffer the rest of your life for having to have you!"

Mother was always telling me I was stupid and fat and that no one would ever love me. She blamed me for her sickness, even though I didn't have anything to do with it. Of course, I learned to blame myself for this, too.

My father worked hard and loved my mother very much. He did not go against her wishes out of fear that she would leave him if he did. He and I always had a loving relationship, but he never stood between my mother and me. I am not sure he really knew the extent of my abuse when he wasn't home to see it.

Ironically, my mother wore the pants in our family, even though she was always sick and unable to manage the household herself. My sister didn't have it easy either, but over the years it was clear that I took the brunt of mother's physical and emotional abuse, since my sister got to go out and have fun and do all the normal things I was never allowed to do. I was forced to stay home to do all the household chores.

From the time I was in third grade, school faculty knew that there was something wrong at home, so they secretly put me in a counseling program throughout my schooling. However, back then there wasn't much they could do to help me except to try and listen to what I had to say. School became my only refuge and was the one comfort I had in life.

By high school I ran with a tough crowd, had very low grades and felt that I wasn't smart enough to do anything. I felt like I wasn't even smart enough to graduate. During my first years in high school, I got mostly C's and D's, except my favorite subjects of Choir and English, in which I always received A's or B's.

Then something happened at the end of my junior year that would change my life. One day I was called into my choir director's office. Though I knew I did well in class, I was afraid I had done something wrong. When I arrived, he sat me down and said he knew that I was a lot smarter than I let on. He and the other teachers had been discussing my situation, and they felt I was not living up to my potential. He proposed that if I got straight A's throughout my senior year, he would give me the key to the music room so that I could practice every day. I was so excited. For the first time in my life, I felt I could do anything and succeed.

All through summer while school was out, I couldn't wait for the first day of school, determined that nothing would stop me from achieving my goal. On the first day of school, Mr. White approached and gave me the key to the music room. It was like receiving a diamond and more thrilling than any other thing that had ever happened to me. Every morning, I would go to my first class, find out the assignments and listen to the lecture, then go straight to the music room to practice. My grades improved to straight A's. It was unbelievable how one person's faith could change my whole life!

For the first time ever, I knew I was smart and could succeed. My mother did not believe what was happening and thought I was cheating, so she went to the school and talked to the principal. He told her that it was true, and if I managed to get on the honors list I would have a four-year scholarship to the University of Washington.

Knowing that Mr. White believed in me, I worked hard and studied every moment I could. Living on a farm there were a lot of chores for me to do each morning and each night after school. There was also the fear I would find my mother laying unconscious on the floor or in a coma. Plus, there were dinners to prepare, dishes to do, chores in the house, feeding the animals, and collecting and candling the eggs. At night, as the rest of the house slept, I did my homework in peace.

By the end of my senior year, I was on the honor roll for the first time in my life. Though my parents did not allow me to go to college, as my sister had, I was still proud of my accomplishments. I found out after my mother died that she must have been proud too, as she had saved and hidden my graduation announcement in *The Columbian* newspaper.

Mr. White's faith in me inspired me to work harder to prove myself and made me a stronger person. I was eventually able to overcome my eating disorder and learned to better respect myself later in life.

I never got to really thank Mr. White, but he was the greatest person I have ever had the pleasure of knowing. Without him believing in me, I would not have understood just how smart I really am, or that if you truly believe in yourself you can accomplish anything.

I am living proof that the loving kindness of one person can truly impact another's life for the better – a gift I have never forgotten.

REMINDER TO BREATHE
by Kira Rosner

During a casual phone conversation, a friend mentions she is taking an exercise class she likes. *I feel like I have been hit over the head with a frying pan. Like I've been jettisoned back in time and then fast-forwarded to the present.*

"Can you get me your teacher's phone number?" I ask in a loud whisper.

"Sure," she says, "Are you okay?"

"I think so," I reply, recalling something I read about our souls choosing our life paths before we incarnate and setting up vibratory guideposts along the way.

She calls back with her teacher's number. A friendly voice answers when I call.

"My girlfriend is taking a class from you," I say. "Can you give me a phone number for where you trained?"

I call the number intending to ask if any classes are being offered close to where I live. Instead I hear myself say, "How can I train to teach what you teach?"

"The Nia technique has a martial arts influence. It's taught in belt levels," the woman says. "We offer a training program in Portland, Oregon."

"Nia." It is the first time I hear the name.

After she explains their course schedule, I say, "Is it possible to organize a course of my own and have a teacher fly to the Midwest?"

"That can be arranged," she replies. "You will have to get a certain number of students, rent a studio with hardwood floors and host the teacher."

The details don't concern me. Things seem to fall into place when I follow my inner guidance.

"Do you have a video I can buy to show others?"

"Of course."

When the tape arrives, I rent the local ballet studio in town and invite my friends to join me. One brings a small TV that plays videos.

A handsome couple appears on the screen. Their movements are fluid, balanced, engaging. My girlfriends and I all try to follow along. We are in our 40s and a bit hesitant. My mother Bea joins us; she is in her 70s and dances freely with abandon.

The next day I receive a call from a Nia teacher named Winalee Zeeb. Her voice is musical. "I will come to the Midwest to teach a White Belt training if you sign up at least five students," she says.

Several of my friends have never taken a dance class and have no intention of teaching one. Yet, they rally around me and agree to spend the money and take time out from their busy schedules to take the course. I trust my intuition and they trust me. Humbling.

A few days later, a woman from the Midwest calls the Nia office in Portland looking for a White Belt closer to her home. They give her my number. I now have six students.

The perfect location manifests. A building five minutes away from where I live with a spacious room with lots of windows, hardwood floors, a kitchen, bathroom and plenty of parking.

After we do the preliminary work, Winalee arrives with a laptop, a Bose CD player and a suitcase full of sunshine. (I know that sounds sugary. You might think otherwise if you met Winalee. She is one of the happiest and most genuine people I have ever known.)

Winalee asks us to bring items to class that have special meaning: a favorite memento, pictures of friends and family, etc. She contributes stuffed dolphins.

We enter our airy classroom and form a circle on the floor with our treasures in the middle. Winalee's voice is animated and soothing. She pours her heart into her teaching, and we listen attentively.

As the week progresses, we learn movements from different modalities that have been harmonically blended by Debbie Rosas and Carlos AyaRosas, the visionary founders of this doorway to heaven.

Winalee reminds us to breathe. I feel lighter, more comfortable in my own skin. We all do. She reminds us to remind our students to breathe too.

What living creatures need to be reminded to breathe? The answer is – women who steel themselves to function in a world where being sensitive is misunderstood. The answer is – men who are afraid to expose their vulnerability so they hide in plain sight, convinced others will only see what they show them.

Nia is a map that leads the willing home, and Winalee is our captain. She will laugh if I call her that; she will laugh if I don't.

The week is blissful. Winalee's portable CD player fills the air with empowering music by Jana Stanfield. As we sail around the sunlit room barefoot, I beg the big wall clock to slow down.

The night after graduation, Winalee and I go to a dance at a local college. Halloween is approaching and many of the students are in costume. The dance floor (where I later teach Nia) is crowded and the music is loud, just the way we like it. We arrive home after midnight and sit on my kitchen floor eating peanut butter ice cream.

The day of Winalee's departure arrives, and she flies off to return to her cherished husband and a busy international teaching schedule.

My friend Jacquelina and I offer our first class through a local community college called Indian Hills. They provide us with a large gymnasium. (A cement floor is not ideal for Nia, but we manage.) The space seems adequate until the students arrive. The room is so packed, we stand inches from the wall!

I go on to teach Nia to students ranging from 5 to 90 years old, sometimes in the same class! Age is insignificant when you encourage each individual to move at his or her own pace.

I teach a group of home-schooled children who like to watch each other dance; we take turns being the star. I teach seniors who tire easily; I give the entire class seated in chairs. I organize benefits for a woman's peace group and a crisis center; we dance beyond our differences, and judgment takes a back seat to acceptance. In the light of recognition, we sink into our roots and meet ourselves.

Reflections

Mentoring is a two-way street. One direction is being open and welcoming when someone crosses our path who is ready and willing to guide us to new possibilities. The other invites us to reach out and open the window of fresh tomorrows for others.

I decided from a young age to seek the positive and be open to learning from the people around me. Because it served me so well, I found myself quite comfortable years later becoming a teacher and sharing my insights with those who came to me for counsel.

Later on in the book I will discuss how I became a speaker and what led me to talking openly about my own difficult childhood. To this day, it continues to amaze me how something so painful has given strength to others. That said, it is both gratifying and humbling to include the following stories.

I WANT TO BE A JOURNALIST
by Kelli Parker

As I sat there in the Drewry Room of the College of Journalism at the University of Georgia, I clung to every word Bob Danzig said, as if he were only speaking to me and not the other 50 or so people in the room. Captivating. That is the only word I can think of to describe him that day. This man was telling my story – only it was his own. He had come from the same less-than-perfect background I had. Yet, there he was, the vice president of a world-renowned publishing company telling me that I could do the same thing. "You are talented," he said. Me? Talented? Sure, I know how to survive and how to work hard to get everything I want, but I never considered that talent. Bob made it sound believable, and I was sold. The more I listened to him, the more I wanted to hear. I wanted him to keep telling me how far in my life I could go.

There was a reason he was so enthralling, but I did not realize it until later. Immediately after his speech, I went up to him and he grabbed me – I mean he physically put his arm around me and pulled me close to him. And it wasn't just with me; he was like that with everyone who came up to talk to him. Normally, I would have felt threatened, but with him, I was totally comfortable, as if I'd known him for a long time.

"What do you want your life to be?" he asked.

Stunned, I stammered, "I want to be a journalist." At the time I thought I could have come up with something better to say. Without missing a beat, Bob said, "You can do it, you will do it, because you are who you are and you are wonderful." That just made my day. I walked away from that room floating on his words and repeating them over and over in my head. Graduation was fast approaching, and I was feeling less than confident about my chances of getting a job right out of college. Bob's words took away my worries.

I know people who think the power of positive affirmation is imaginary, but I can argue that point all day. Thinking positively has taken me a long way, and I thank Bob for becoming not only a friend that day but also a "thread in my personal tapestry," as he is fond of saying.

Soon after meeting Bob, I accepted a summer magazine internship in New York. I decided to take a chance and write Bob, explaining who I was, how he had spiritually enlightened me, and that I'd like a chance to "do lunch" when I arrived in Manhattan. Honestly, I never expected him to respond. After all, being a high-powered executive with a budding motivational speaking career doesn't leave much time for mentoring, I thought. But to my delight, he called and said he would love to meet with me. Even more surprising, the day after I arrived in New York, the internship coordinator handed me a message from him. He had tracked me down before I'd had a chance to get in touch with him! Amazing.

A few weeks later, we met for lunch and he beamed when he saw me. I didn't think he would remember me, but he grabbed me again and hugged me like we were old friends. Over lunch, I did most of the talking. He wanted to know everything about me – my childhood, why I chose the University of Georgia, what I wanted out of my summer in New York and so on.

Bob adopted me that summer. He said he wanted to be my mentor and that he was going to make sure I had the best time I could in the city. He made good on his promise, and I saw the theater, the ballet and many other things I'd never had the opportunity to experience. Having grown up on the streets of New Jersey, these kinds of luxuries offered a whole new world to me.

I grew up the product of a broken home. My father left when I was 4 years old. My mother fled her duties soon after, and my brother and I became my grandmother's responsibility. When my grandmother was diagnosed with a brain tumor in 1989, we siblings became wards of the state of New Jersey. My brother and I were separated and moved from one foster home to the next. A wonderful family, who told me I could be anything I wanted despite my humble beginnings, eventually adopted me. I learned that hard work and focus were all I needed to succeed. I could have become another foster home statistic, but I didn't want that to be my future. I finished college and now have a job at a newspaper doing exactly what I want to do with my career. And champions in my life like Bob have ensured that I stay on a path to a lifetime of success.

ILLUMINATE YOUR SOUL TO SHOW THE WAY
by Brenda Gill

"I was shuffled around from foster home to foster home. One of my first jobs was as a newspaper office boy. Then after the Navy and college, I became the publisher of that newspaper. Seven years later, I became the President of Hearst Newspapers nationwide."

Did Bob Danzig just say what I thought he did? Here at this multinational corporation? Did he publicly disclose that he was a foster kid?

Bob was the guest speaker being interviewed by Chris Perry for a one-on-one conversation about success and leadership. The talk was held in the company's premier event space with sweeping views of Times Square.

When Bob made that statement, linking his early adversity in foster homes to his capacity for perseverance, I was stunned by his candor and transparency because I had been struggling with my own past.

In 2002 I spoke to some special needs kids at a public high school about my past, but I told my story in the third person, talking about how this "girl" had overcome great adversity. I ended the story saying, "I share the story of this girl with you because she is me and I am you."

The numerous Thank-You letters I received weeks after the event showed me how impactful my words were to these young people. It gnawed at me because there was clearly more I could do. But what was holding me back?

After I pored over the many letters, I realized that I was not ready to expose myself in that way and definitely not to corporate America. Yet, here I was listening to Bob Danzig, former President of Hearst Newspapers, openly discuss his foster care experience. Somewhere in the back of my mind I thought, "Well he can do it, but I certainly can't."

I agreed with Bob that the conversion from "survival" to "perseverance" could be a *hidden* advantage in advancing one's career. But for me the emphasis was on hidden. I took pride in not showing the "survival" scars of my youth. I took comfort in the fact that people assumed that I had an average upbringing with caring parents, along with an extensive support system that guided me through and into adulthood, culminating in a highly successful legal career. Nothing could be further from the truth in my case.

Haunted by the voices of those public school students, I continued to struggle with this idea of revealing myself to the world. There were glimpses of recognition of the unassailable truth of Bob's statement; like the time I answered a question for my *NV Magazine* Movers & Shakers interview about the hardest lesson I've learned. I replied that the hardest lesson was "learning to accept the past and stop living thinking about *if only*." I said that, "I had succeeded in spite of or because of my past. Either way, staying focused on the *now* seemed to produce the greatest success." Deep down I knew the truth.

Most everything Bob said resonated with me. I knew I would have to find a few minutes after the speech to chat with him.

When the talk was concluded with a standing ovation, Bob stepped down from the platform and headed towards the back. As is usual for these types of events, there were many people who wanted to meet him, congratulate him and touch base with him. I picked up a glass of wine and waited for a free moment to grab his attention.

"Hi, I'm Brenda Gill. I want to thank you so much for your speech today. It was quite inspiring," I said, shaking his hand while simultaneously thanking him.

"I'm glad you enjoyed it," Bob said.

"I especially enjoyed your candor in sharing that you were in the foster care system. We have that in common, as I too was in the foster care system."

"Really, how was that for you?"

"It wasn't particularly good, and I served on the board of the Door in an effort to help address some of the challenges with the foster care system."

"That's great. I do the same thing."

"I know, and my hope is to one day follow in your footsteps, writing and speaking about my experiences and being in a place where I can share them with a larger audience."

"That's admirable. Do you have a business card on you?"

"Yes, here you go."

"Thanks. It was nice speaking with you."

"The pleasure was all mine, Bob."

That night I thought long and hard about how I would ever be able to replicate Bob's model. I mean, I'm not a president and don't have an extensive network like Bob. I decided that I would table those thoughts for the time being and get back to focusing on my legal job.

About three weeks later, I received a surprise gift box from Bob Danzig with a copy of every book and CD that he had in circulation at that time, each one personally autographed and a cover letter from Bob saying, "I hope you find some inspiration by reading these books and listening to these CDs. Best of luck to you, Bob." I immediately crafted a handwritten Thank You note and sent that off to him. The timing was perfect as this was just what I needed. I was and am eternally grateful to Bob for his generous gesture.

That night and for each night thereafter, I read every one of his books and listened to all of his CDs. I knew that this was what I ultimately wanted to do. To replicate this model where I could take my life lessons and use them to benefit others. By illuminating his soul, Bob was showing me the way. I am hopeful that in time I will do the same.

THANKSGIVING
by Agne Kevelaitiene

I met Bob Danzig on Thanksgiving Day. Although we only had a brief moment to talk, I brought home a lot of inspiration from that meeting and still carry it with me.

Right now, I am in the middle of reading Bob's book, *The Leader Within You*. I find it quite a page-turner, full of precious nuggets of wisdom and useful insights, not only for leaders, but also for everyone walking on a spirit-lifting way to self-fulfillment. *Shakespeare Lives on Cape Cod* is also on my Kindle and the next book I plan to dive into.

All of Bob's insights echo my own aspirations. As part of my profession, I lead new manager training and integration initiatives. To help my colleagues advance, I continuously search for ways to convey leadership concepts. Bob's expertise and the examples he provided offer a new angle and very clear messages to lean on.

I am facing a challenging time in my personal journey after winning a green card and settling in the USA. This is a life-changing experience for me. Amid an ocean of uncertainty and haste, Bob's timely encouragement, advice and wisdom is helping me find a peaceful balance in my soul and mind.

Meeting Bob when I did is one of those divine whispers. Maybe it is no coincidence it happened on Thanksgiving. My "fresh start" moment created an enduring thread in the tapestry of my experience.

"Change is an opportunity."

Chapter Two

Blazing Lights

"Change is an opportunity to experience something new.
The way we handle it determines the direction our lives take."
– Bob Danzig

The inner promptings that seed our choices rely on how aggressively we listen and are willing to step forward. Do we just hear, or do we permit those impulses to enhance our momentum?

The writers in this chapter have generously shared how their listening linked to action.

YOUR JOB IS TO BE YOU
by Huggy Rao

One afternoon in the fall of 2004, when I was on the faculty of the Kellogg School of Management, I received a call from my Stanford colleague Chip Heath. He informed me that Stanford Business School was seeking to hire a senior professor in organizations and asked for my recommendations. I suggested three people. He then told me that all three had urged that I be offered the position, and he asked me what I thought about it. I said I was happy at Kellogg but would consider it.

In December 2004 I went to India and was in Rajasthan. After the New Year, I checked my email to find that Stanford had unanimously voted to offer me a job. I was amazed – I had not visited Stanford for a job talk or interviews. In any event, after I came back to Chicago, I could only go to Stanford in March in view of my teaching schedule at Kellogg.

Before I went, I consulted Michael Tushman, a professor at the Harvard Business School. He urged me to negotiate my role as a senior professor. I was aghast. I had not even thought of it! I thought my job was to research and teach.

When I visited Stanford, I spent time with Jeff Pfeffer, a phenomenal researcher, scholar and teacher who was a star when I was beginning my career. I asked Jeff, rather pompously I thought, as to what my role would be. My hope was that this would be grist for my conversations with the deans.

Jeff's response floored me and liberated me. He said, "Huggy, your job is to be you. That is why we want you." Still astonished, I said "Really?" When he chuckled and said yes, and asked me if I could be myself, I said, "I have a comparative advantage in being me – yes, I can do it."

Jeff's reply was the most liberating definition of a job I have ever heard. "Be you!" It also told me that Stanford, as an excellent organization, had a simple norm: "If you are yourself, you will do a great job."

That conversation with Jeff was a door opener for me. Since 2005, after I moved to Stanford, I use that to figure out what I like to do and what I won't do. I don't do things that require me to be a different person than I am!

RIDING FENCES
by David McCumber

This is not a famous mountain. It's not big enough, and it's in the wrong place. You can see it from downtown White Sulphur Springs, Montana, but even from that remote vantage it doesn't stand out from its neighboring peaks, some shorter, some taller. It is not quite 8,000 feet at the summit. No wisps of smoke threaten lava. No pitches or crevasses hold the bones of those who failed to conquer it, though death visits often enough. No sleeping bags or ski poles or stainless steel watches or amusement-park rides have been named for this mountain, and you can't take a ski lift to the top, which is a good thing, though I can remember days when I would have been pleased for a ride.

People do not generally make pilgrimages to this mountain, although I did.

On Birch Creek Ranch this mountain is called Tucker – not even Mount Tucker, just Tucker. It is a lesser peak in an obscure range called the Big Belt Mountains, which is in turn a tiny section of that enormous upthrust of granite and dime-novel romance called the Rocky Mountains.

The fact that it is a flyspeck in the scale of big country – the rest of this ranch, central Montana, the flatlanders' fantasy called the West – does not alter the fact that this mountain changed my life.

I came here for reasons of my own: Journalistic curiosity about a lifestyle glorified to the point of religion in our culture – what is the Marlboro Man if not an icon, squinting down, square-jawed at the mortals on Sunset Boulevard? – and other, deeper reasons, having to do with letting go of one life to find another and taking a measure of myself in a new way.

I had signed on to Birch Creek as a grey-headed green-horn, proposing to make my living out of doors, with my body as well as my brain. Twenty years behind a desk in a newsroom, or rather nine newsrooms, had left me searching for more. The search took me from corporate striving and urban living in California, back toward the beginnings of my family, to cleaner country, to something both smaller and bigger. Which is a way of saying I quit my comfortable management job, started writing for a living again, and moved to a little town in Montana, near where my grandfather started the twentieth century. For me, cowboying on and around this mountain completed a rather thoroughgoing midlife metamorphosis.

Sometimes, in the mornings of the succeeding year, watching the sun rise over Tucker from the window of the old blue trailer that served as a bunkhouse, I would think about the cowboys of my childhood. There was Roy Rogers, who would shoot the gun out of the bad guy's hand every week on our little black-and-white TV. The Cisco Kid and Wyatt Earp and the Lone Ranger. None of them ever saw the business end of a cow, as far as I could tell.

Some of those first February subzero mornings I would wonder why I was spending my forty-fourth year busting truck tires and hosing out cattle trucks and shoveling out another man's barn. It was hard to see, through that grimy little window, just where that kind of work fit into the great legend of the West.

I would discover that I hadn't done enough of that kind of work yet to be trusted doing anything else, or even to realize that privation and sweat and cold and danger and manure-shoveling were all part of the price of the ticket. The payoff came on days like this, up on the mountain, just you and the cows and the grass and, if you were lucky, a horse.

I hadn't spent enough time on the mountain yet to know the profound satisfaction of working on a piece of ground long enough to know it, of seeing the animals under your care thrive and grow.

I came to this mountain that February, trying to save the calves that started life there in blowing snow and 30 below. We saved quite a few and lost too many. In March I took a harrowing ride down the mountain in drifted snow, rescuing a pickup with no clutch or brakes. In April I came proposing to fix the fence that runs up the face of the mountain, and the mountain laughed and showed me great stretches of wire still under six-feet of snow.

In May I came back to fence again, through brush so thick two hundred yards of fence took an entire afternoon. In June I watered hayfields in the shadow of this east face, and in July and August I helped to bring in the hay the cows would eat the next winter. In September I fixed more fence than I thought possible. For three glorious days in October, riding some of the best horses a man could put his legs around, I rousted cows from the same brush. And in November, at five degrees in a ground blizzard, I chased renegade cows on foot through dense pine timber, and just thinking about that makes all the work I've done since then seem luxuriously simple. As I closed the last gate that day, I thought about the huge gate that opened for me, on this mountain. About what it did for my self-esteem and my soul to do honest work with my hands, and to relearn what it means to be at the bottom of the pecking order in any organization.

I've since gone back to riding a desk in a tall building, wrangling my words and those of others, but the lessons

Tucker taught me about myself keep me coming back here, once a year, to remember.

Each of our new starts feeds the next – as this mountain feeds each new adventure in my life. I will treasure it, as long as I'm alive.

TAKE THE LEAP
by Debra Janssen

Keeping my finger on the "start button" began in 1998, when I made a leap to a new role after 14 successful years at a large financial services processor. I had started as a buyer in the Purchasing department and left as CIO. It was fun working with a growing company, which presented opportunities to try new roles in the days when companies took more chances on individuals who weren't an exact fit for the job. My motto was – right place, right time, right attitude. I thought that I could push a lot of start buttons! I figured if I failed, I didn't have very far to fall, so why not raise my hand to gain new experiences?

My leap to the new role was to another financial services processor, who hadn't made money for three years and needed help digging into issues to find ways to achieve profitability. In week three, it was announced that the CEO was leaving, and I was quite furious as I was working for him and had just joined the company. I voiced my concern and pushed my start button. Soon, I was in front of the chairman of the parent company and laid out a proposal detailing what I thought was needed and asked him to give me six months to gain traction and provide results. If he didn't care for my work at the end of six months or if I didn't care for the job, we would part ways with no hard feelings. The next thing I knew, lunch was being delivered to his office. I took this as a good sign, and he offered me the role of Interim CEO for six months! I did my best not to pass out, thanked him countless times and was off and running.

The announcement of my interim role stunned many, and the betting odds on my success weren't good as I was the third CEO in three years. I didn't think about that at all and just got to work and started pressing every start button that I could identify. First, I traded out members of my team swiftly and only accepted individuals who were willing to believe that we could succeed, even in challenging waters. Second, I quickly visited as many customers as possible to ask for their support in giving me time to make changes, promising that they would see a difference quickly. And third, I held many employee meetings to talk to about the need to change, or we would all be without jobs.

Within a year, we had swung the company results from a $13M loss to a profit of $1.5M. We were all stoked and a bit amazed that focus, urgency and passion could drive results that quickly. By the way, the "Interim" CEO was changed to CEO after just six weeks into the assignment. I ended up staying with the company for three years in that role.

I have always said that this job was the most memorable job in my career, as it was leadership during the middle of surgery, and we didn't know whether we would live or die, so decisions and start buttons had to be triggered quickly. It involved hard work and some sleepless nights, but it was a ton of fun and rewarding at the same time.

I learned a lot about myself in this role. I realized that when start buttons show up, you need to view them as opportunities and push them. Sometimes the path to what you will achieve is visible; sometimes the path is an exciting unknown. I have no doubt that my ability to push the start button early on in my career played a big role in getting me additional CEO roles – and that pushing many start buttons positioned me as an individual who has seen the movie in six different languages and is capable of managing multiple challenges and opportunities.

Needless to say, it's been a fantastic ride. I achieved much more than I ever thought would have been possible. So, what are you waiting for? Get busy and push your start buttons. You never know where it will lead you....

TAKING RISKS
by Patricia Haegele

When I married my first husband, an Attorney/FBI Agent, we were required to move from his first assigned office in Atlanta to Cocoa Beach, Florida. Not exactly a move I was looking forward to, particularly since I was interested in beginning my own career.

I discovered that the top employers in Cocoa Beach were the Kennedy Space Center, Patrick Air Force Base and the *Florida Today* newspaper. I was offered and accepted a position as the Administrative Assistant to the Advertising Director of *Cocoa Today*. Within a year, I was promoted to the sales force and before long, I was recognized as the top sales person. During the same time period, I got an opportunity to meet and work with Vince Spezzano, the Publisher of *Cocoa Today* and also Al Neuharth, the CEO of Gannett, the company that owned *Cocoa Today*.

Fast-forward to some years later. Gannett was launching the national *USA Today* newspaper, which would be headquartered in Washington, D.C., with the national sales team headquartered in New York City. At that time, I was working at the *Washington Post* as a National Sales Director. Vince Spezzano was named the first President of *USA Today*. During this time, I had changed jobs but not careers, going from *Cocoa Today*, to the *Tampa Tribune*, to the *Washington Post*. Vince offered me a position as a Sales Director in New York City.

I considered this a substantial risk, particularly leaving the *Washington Post* as one of the top female sales managers to take a position with a startup newspaper. However, I took the risk, made the move and never looked back. Within one whirlwind year, I was named the VP of Advertising for *USA Today*.

That same year, Al Neuharth hired Cathie Black as President and Publisher of *USA Today*. The advertising sales weren't doing as well as projected. When Cathie took over the reins everything changed. Cathie needed someone immediately who was a leader, knew how to sell and could hit the ground running. Al Neuharth and Vince Spezzano informed Cathie that they knew exactly the person for the job, someone who possessed all of those attributes, in addition to selling advertising when no one else could. They suggested that Cathie talk with me, and she did.

From that time, Cathie became my mentor. Later on, Cathie was instrumental in my selection as the first President of the Newspaper National Network and was the primary decision maker for my selection as the first woman Publisher of *Good Housekeeping* magazine.

MATTERS OF THE HEART
by Gloria Ricks Taylor

For years and years, I had hoped to be recruited by one particular New York-based communications company. Eventually, my dream became a reality and I was ecstatic. My career path in public relations and my sense of accomplishment had taken a major leap forward. I was working with a smart group of executives, many of whom I had known for years. An office and new department space was renovated and decorated to my specifications. I hired a competent staff of my choosing. I was elected a vice president in the days when women rarely held that title. Life was good, but …

… the love of my life lived in London. He or I commuted every weekend for months on end. I would leave my office on Friday afternoon, head to JFK for the long flight to the UK and return to New York on Sunday evening. He would make the reverse trip the next weekend. Eventually we realized we couldn't continue to live in such a manner. Life was too fragmented, too disjointed and we were tired of saying goodbye. Together we decided that I would resign my dream job after just six months and relocate to London. (He was the chairman of a company that had just been floated on the London Stock Exchange.)

I was on *cloud nine* that I was moving abroad, yet very sad that I was leaving my ideal job. Resigning was traumatic, to put it mildly. I was letting down the man who had hired me and whom I greatly respected; he was gracious, but I knew I was a big disappointment and perhaps an embarrassment. He said, and I paraphrase: "If you had told me you were leaving for another company, I would be highly disappointed, but in matters of the heart 'I step aside.'"

Two months later, I was living a carefree life in London.

Two months after that, I had lunch with the managing director of the UK subsidiary of the company from which I had resigned.

Two months after that, I was employed by the subsidiary as a full-time consultant to create a corporate communications department. I was walking on air and went on to experience some of the best times of my life.

Seven years later, my husband (then retired) and I relocated to New York when I was appointed to an even bigger role at the parent company that I had left under *less than ideal* circumstances.

Twenty plus years later, though no longer working full-time, I continue as a consultant.

Had I not made the big, scary choice, I would have always wondered *what if*. Instead, my life was enriched, my world was expanded and my experiences and friendships will forever be cherished. Sadly, my beloved husband has since died, making my decision to choose him over a career even more meaningful.

MAKING IT UP
by Eliot Kaplan

When people ask how I got this cool job, I tell them the truth: I made it up.

Flash back 15 years. I had been a successful magazine editor my whole working life, 20+ years. Yet things were going badly at that moment. I like to say that we had creative differences, the bosses and I – I was creative; they were different. But it was more than that and not all their fault. Despite awards and accolades, my time was simply running out there and everyone knew it.

So I stepped back for a minute and evaluated – and I advise anyone in a similar position to do the same. Instead of just moving to another editor position, which would have probably meant uprooting my young family, I thought, "What is it about being an editor that I like and that I'm good at, and which parts are not my strength and my passion?" I broke it down to: (1) I love working with writers and stories, and (2) I love discovering and placing talented people in the right spot.

Our business is a small one, maybe all businesses are. When somebody leaves a magazine you immediately call your editor friends and say, "Whom should I hire?" I took a million of those calls myself. And I suddenly realized: "This knowledge is worth something to someone. Perhaps I can have a more stable and fulfilling career moving people rather than words around, and leave more of a legacy, which is important to me."

So in May 1999, I met with Cathie Black, then the President of Hearst Magazines. I made my pitch (nothing like being unemployed to really focus you on making a great pitch). My timing was good, too. It was the height of the first dot-com boom and print companies were losing talent to "we promise to make you rich by sundown" startups like catfood.com.

Three weeks later I was named Editorial Talent Director of Hearst Magazines, the first such position in our industry. Fifteen years later, I have a fancier title but my job at its core remains the same–find the world's best editors and art directors for our 21 magazine brands. When I walk through our gleaming café in the morning, I see people I've brought here, people whose lives I have changed as they get a chance to pursue their dreams. Talk about a legacy!

One of my favorite movies is a little gem from 1982, *Diner*. Near the end, a wiser, older fellow says to the scruffy, malcontent played by Mickey Rourke, "Always a dreamer, eh?" Rourke replies, "If you don't have good dreams, you've got nightmares."

Dream on.

FINDING YOUR NEXT ADVENTURE!
by Ann Shoket

It is my mission in life to help young women feel so confident that they can walk into any room and *own* it! And
as the Editor-in-Chief of *Seventeen* for seven years, I had the
privilege of being able to put that mission into real-life action
by talking to millions of young women each month. Even
when I was a teen, I remember wanting all the girls around
me to be brave and strong. In junior high, I started a club
with a few friends, and we called ourselves W.O.W.: Women
of the World. Talk about confidence! I don't know where that
bravado came from, but back then I knew that there was so
much more out there in the world than I could see from my
bedroom window in Littleton, Colorado.

That's the feeling I have tried to carry with me every day
in my job – and in my life. It's what I love about teenagers
and young women: At this moment you are pure potential.
You can do or be anything. The possibilities for your future
are endless! When you're looking back on your own teen
years, it can be hard to remember ever feeling so unencum-
bered by ideas of who we *should* be or what we *should* do with
our lives. But when you reconnect with your inner 16-year-
old, you find that buzzy feeling of *freedom* – the ultimate
fresh start!

Before *Seventeen*, I ran a leadership campaign at another
teen magazine, where I had the opportunity to interview the
most powerful women in America: entrepreneurs, senators,
CEOs, and even an astronaut! But my proudest moment came
when I had the chance to interview my idol, Barbara Walters.

We sat in her well-decorated dressing room backstage at *The View*. It was all soft tones and pretty patterns – just as you'd expect from such a legend. Barbara graciously answered my questions, and then at the end of our time together, I asked her: "What's the one thing you wish you had known when you were a teenager that you didn't figure out until later in life?" Barbara got very quiet – it was a literally a dramatic pause – and then, with great gravitas, she said: "Don't imagine that your life now is the way that it's always going to be. You have no idea the adventures that are in store for you."

This is such a crucial message for young women who are just figuring out who they are and imagining what they can be. But it's also an important message for people of all ages to remember: Be open to every opportunity. Don't pigeonhole yourself into one idea of who you are or what you still can be. And *never* stop looking for the next adventure.

WORKING WELL
by Blair Schlumbom

I began my working life when I moved to Los Angeles to work at the Ritz Carlton, Huntington Hotel after I graduated college. This was another time I kept my finger on the "start button" and jumped at an opportunity in a new and unknown place, but I feel that every young graduate must make this big leap as they start pursuing their career. I worked at the hotel in sales and worked in two different departments. It was exciting work, and I was learning so much. I worked with a young group of professionals for one of the great Ritz-Carlton general managers.

He was a very experienced and a notoriously hard driving executive. We worked six to seven days a week and from very early until very late. After three years, I was doing quite well and had been promoted. It was at this time that there were discussions that I might be promoted again and moved to another property in a different city (which is the way with hotel management). I liked my job but was not a fan of living in LA. The prospect of moving to a city that was more undesirable was even less interesting to me.

I had always loved magazines and thought of getting into the publishing business, but the opportunity at the Ritz-Carlton came first. In my current job, I was calling on the Midwest territory and had fallen in love with Chicago. One day, I decided that if it wasn't now, it was not going to be, ever. So, going against my family and my hotel management's strong advice not to leave what was becoming a successful career, I quit my job and moved to Chicago to make my way in a career that I was passionate about in a city where I wanted to live.

It was there that I began meeting with the senior managers at all the top magazines in hopes of finding a magazine sales rep job. One after the other told me that I needed more experience, needed to go work for an advertising agency (I was a sales person, not a media planner), that it was far too competitive. Within a few months, I got my dream job. I became the Midwest Manager at Adweek Magazines. It was the perfect job in publishing that helped me not only get publishing sales experience, but in a category that helped me to gain valuable knowledge about our industry.

I ended up living and working in Chicago for six years and was eventually promoted and moved to New York City. I worked for many different top brands in senior positions in New York. In one role, the midwest manager who had told me that he couldn't hire me before I went to work at an agency, actually reported to me.

My working and personal life is so rich and full. It's the result of hard work, passion, and most of all, always keeping my finger on the start button and never letting anyone or anything get in the way of my dreams.

POETRY LIFTS
by Candy Altman

Imagine a warm August day in upstate New York. I was a newly minted freshman at Cortland State, a college I chose for a number of reasons: I grew up in New York City and wanted an experience as different as possible from my urban life in the Bronx and the privileged kids I grew up with in Riverdale; I was the child of two educators and Cortland had a great teachers college; it was a small school, and having come from a large high school, small felt right.

It's funny how we gravitate towards what we know, isn't it? I grew up surrounded by educators, and my parents believed teaching was a great career for a woman because you could "fall back on it" when you had children (AKA, be home by 3 p.m. each day. It was 1973). It seemed reasonable, but there was something else in my head and my heart – something about which I had no point of reference. Journalism.

I am a child of Watergate, the Vietnam War and the Civil Rights movement. I was a gentle protagonist. An obedient rebel, who wanted to change the world but didn't want to offend my parents. So, I planned to major in elementary education.

But something happened on my second day at Cortland. I was drawn up the hill to the second floor of Brockway Hall. There, down a dimly lit hall, was a small door that said WCSU-AM. I turned the handle tentatively and walked in.

And so it began, the path that would lead me to a career in journalism. The path that would let me tell stories that could change the world in small ways. I had to push my way towards the news side because the station managers wanted me in traffic, a woman's role at that time. Despite that, I worked my way up to news director and chairman of the lecture board.

Yes, I did major in elementary ed, but I minored in history and went to graduate school for journalism at the University of Missouri. And believe it or not, with 40 years hindsight, the elementary ed degree has come in handy as I've managed teams and worked with all kinds of personalities.

I have a favorite poet and a favorite poem. Robert Frost and *The Road Not Taken*. It spoke to me as a child, and it speaks to me today: "I took the road less traveled by/ and that has made all the difference."

I followed what I loved and found my way, taking a path that wasn't conventional. I risked the known for the unknown. The turning point came on that fateful day in Brockway Hall, looking down that dimly lit hall. It made all the difference.

WHAT I FOUND IN THE BASEMENT
by David Niven, PhD

I was in the basement of the psychology library at Ohio State University. It's in one of those stately academic buildings, the kind that makes you think you should put on a tweed jacket with elbow patches before you go inside. Spread out on the big oak table before me were my notes for a study I was doing on the effects of optimism on decision making.

In a few weeks, after I finished writing up the results, I would be submitting the paper to an academic journal. It would have to pass muster with the editor and make it through the review process, but I was, appropriately enough, pretty optimistic about it being accepted and published.

I thought about what that meant. My paper would look awfully handsome all laid out and typeset. The title in bold and my name in all caps underneath. It would likely be a respected journal, too, which would look really good on my resume. And, if I was lucky, my paper might be read by up-wards of 23 people.

I'm not kidding. Academics fuss and sweat over the ideas and analysis of a topic for months and months, sometimes years and years, all the while trying to reach a microscopic audience of hyper-specialized scholars with a common inter-est – all of whom are themselves laboring on their own studies in the hopes that I and a handful of others might read their next paper.

Looking up from the library table, I was surrounded by shelves filled with academic research reports. They towered over me, lining the walls and halls, and blocking out what little natural light might seep down into the library through the tiny basement windows. I thought about all the work that went into those reports. And, I thought about all the people who would never read them.

There were reports on life satisfaction, relationships, prosperity, parenting and all manner of good things. But no regular person was ever going to come to the basement of the psychology library to read about how they could make their lives better. And if they did, they would find the reports filled with jargon produced by academics writing to impress other academics. In academic journals, plain English is viewed as undignified.

Sitting there thinking about the absurd math of it all, I asked myself a question that changed the way I did research and really changed the way I did everything. What if I tried to make what I'm doing more useful?

From that question, I reimagined how I work. I started a new project that would take these research results that I thought were important and almost translate them into words and a format that anyone could understand and use. The project was published – and reached an audience many thousands of times bigger than any of my traditional academic writing ever did. My "fresh start" came by not judging what I was doing by the standards that are commonly used but instead by standards that are useful. Though it hardly seems revolutionary, asking how you can make what you are doing more useful can change everything you do.

THE BIGGEST STAR
by Bill Fine

Eighteen-year-olds are not normally fully prepared to make one of the most major and important decisions impacting their lives. Choosing the right college, then major and ultimately career path, should best be left until you are at least 19; at least for me. It took one year in college to find my "start button" along the banks of the Rio Grande River – making a decision to reset and immediately begin a path and vocation that I have followed for the past 40 years.

Although I didn't know it at the time, none other than President Gerald Ford charted my current career path. Early in his presidency, as part of an overall energy policy, Ford embraced a silly notion that by closing the nation's colleges and universities during the cold winter months of January and February, the U.S. would save a substantial amount of energy. Students would stay at home and make up the lost coursework in the spring. His vision was, of course, a fallacy – a mere drop in the bucket required to tackle the worldwide energy crisis that led to cars lining up for blocks just waiting to get filled up.

Dickinson College, home for my freshman year, fell for the president's request hook, line and sinker. After taking most of the winter off, we would return to a six-day schedule in late February. In the midst of this craziness, which angered parents and students alike, Dickinson realized we needed to do something – almost anything – to fill that newly created gap of time. Thus the "J" term was born in January 1974. It turned out to be a fresh start.

First, some background. As a sophomore in high school, my English teacher gave me the opportunity to make movies as a special project. The prospect sounded very appealing and certainly more entertaining to a budding media junkie. Borrowing my uncle's 16 mm camera, I proceeded to make short films and loved every minute of the process. I believed I had the touch and promise, certainly the interest and passion, and my teacher and others were encouraging that confidence. For reasons I can't explain, nor recall, I didn't immediately pursue this passion and packed up for Carlisle, Pennsylvania.

As a person who enjoys the pace and vibrancy of cities, the combination of attending a rural liberal arts school, with first year coursework that was largely a repeat of high school, was a bump in the road. That first semester seemed endless, academically. The overall college experience certainly supplied the nutrition of enjoyment, but by the end of that semester it was clear I had made a mistake. It was also clear that I missed making movies, further exploring the world of media, and wished I were attending college back in my hometown of Boston. The first seeds of considering a transfer were thus planted. President Ford's plan led me directly to a new plan and a 37-year (and counting) career in television.

With the newly crowned J term looming, I needed a proposal that Dickinson would accept for credit. Considering the haste with which Ford had implemented his energy plan and the college's acquiescence in enacting it, nearly any proposal would be considered. Having long held an interest in attending an Outward Bound program, a pretty good test of endurance, physical and mental strength, it seemed the perfect opportunity. The centerpiece of "surviving" Outward Bound was the "solo." Three days alone with nothing but a gallon of water and peanuts (for emergency use only). Those days turned out to be most pivotal and productive ones of my life.

On the Outward Bound course list in the winter of '74 was a winter survival training camp down in the Big Bend region of Texas, bordering Mexico on the Rio Grande River. As winter survival camps go, this one sounded attractive to me – 60s and 70s during the day and 30s to 40s at night. I could handle those conditions!

After some modest success as a high school athlete, I had "de-conditioned" a bit, a victim of the "Freshman 15." Other than your payment, the main requirement for acceptance to Outward Bound was their demand that you arrive in very good to excellent physical condition. A specific set of fitness milestones needed to be achieved and personally certified with the application. Lying was not an alternative. It guaranteed you would not enjoy the experience, as one of our group quickly discovered. Outward Bound was as rigorous as anything I've ever done. And it was exactly what I needed.

Two weeks after Christmas, I flew to Dallas and began the eight-hour bus ride across Texas to Midland in the heart of the Permian basin. *Friday Night Lights* territory. The ride was long, straight and relatively fast – other than the bus stops in small towns, which came right out of central casting for the movie *The Last Picture Show*. The tumbleweed rolled across the roads on cue. It was all very new and thus exciting, despite the look of desolation over much of central Texas.

Following a quick visit with family friends in Midland and another long ride to Big Bend, camp began immediately with a long hike designed to further exhaust the travel weary. Outward Bound promised each participant they would be tested, over and over again. In essence, campers would "discover themselves." It sounded too "touchy feely" ('70s jargon) to me, but they certainly delivered on that promise. My experiences over the next month would prove critical in charting a new course and providing that fresh start.

After a week of climbing mountains, rappelling back down them, sleeping in suspended hammocks to avoid rattlesnakes, sleeping less as a result, being woken up at midnight to hike along the side of the mountain on safety lines (simply because we could under a full moon), eating largely pre-packaged food, running 10 miles to a fresh water tinaja for the first shower in five days, building camaraderie and trust with fellow campers who were equally responsible for your safety – these experiences and so much more set the table for the solo.

Outward Bound solos are legendary, the most difficult of personal challenges and centerpiece of their leadership program. Although it has evolved over the years, in 1974 your time alone was just that. Positioned on a cliff, my new "home" for the next three days overlooked a barren stretch of Mexico just across the Rio Grande River. The leader's command was "drink as little water each day as you can; eat only in case of emergency; and do not speak to anyone on the off chance you actually see another human." In the absence of any companionship, my immediate thought was, "These three days are going to be the longest of my life."

After spending an hour or two flicking a bug away from me, only to have it come right back every time, I decided it was best to start documenting my trip in a notebook. With no disturbances, especially in a pre-digital era, I became a very prolific writer. Again, I am not one of those types prone to self-reflection. But when darkness set in, I was left with the biggest star filled sky ever and a lot of time to ponder my future.

By day two, I was as determined as that bug. I kept coming back to the need, the desire, to hit a new start button. For the balance of my solo, I documented, in great detail, everything I was going to do for the next three to four years of my life. The decision to transfer was key but not until finishing my liberal arts electives at Dickinson before transferring to Boston University's School of Public Communication. They had the best film school on the east coast, second only to USC's fabled program in LA. I was extremely excited to put that "plan" down on paper. It was a "done deal," other than needing to let BU know of my intent and actually gaining acceptance. Details!

I chose to take a semester off, work for nine months and make up all the coursework in one summer at BU. I figured out how much money I would need to buy a new car (VW bug with a sunroof), and my own 16 mm camera and to save for a 35 mm as a graduation gift for grad school. This was also a "done deal" in my new plot, although USC, where I was accepted, didn't know it yet. After securing my master's, LA would be my new home and I would begin a life in the film industry.

My parents were great, never once questioning my new plan, although I know the thought of my leaving college for a while created concern. But in my heart, I knew what the future had in store. During those three days of seclusion, my thinking had never been clearer; my goals never better defined; and due to the non-stop physical challenges (before and after the solo) I was never in better shape. Thanks to President Ford, the wheels were set in motion – leading me to a lifelong career in television, a vocation for which my passion has never dampened. (The story of how I moved from budding filmmaker to a graduate of the nation's first broadcast journalism program at BU is an additional story for another day.)

When you depart from your Outward Bound course, they promise, "You will return home a little tired and dirty but having gained the knowledge that you are capable of more than you ever thought possible."

    I can personally attest to the veracity of that claim and the fresh start it afforded me. This experience is documented in the journal I have saved to this day and ingrained in my memory forever!

THE CALL THAT CHANGED MY LIFE
by Michael J. Hayes

It felt like most any other day in March of 1992. Plenty of sun, the winter chills beginning to lift and the sense of nature's impending change to spring hanging in the air.

When the phone rang at a little past three in the afternoon, I had no idea it wasn't only the weather destined to leave a lifetime of yesterdays behind in favor of countless tomorrows down a road never before contemplated.

Unlike most of my friends, classmates, and contemporaries at 27, the vision I had for my life was clear. I was going to be the next Bob Costas.

Indeed, the idea was just as absurd as it sounds. Bob Costas was only 40 at the time and about to host his first Olympics for NBC; he clearly did not need a successor only 13 years his junior. Yet, to me, this seemed very real and possible.

I grew up with big dreams in small town Indiana. The love for sports was rampant in my house as my father was my high school football coach. Our town had a population of around 1,000 people. As kids, we didn't have much to do so we were constantly competing, at everything. I played football, basketball and baseball in high school and, ironically, also got the opportunity to get to know media. During the winter my Dad was a basketball play-by-play man for a small radio station. I happily went riding along, keeping score, helping set up equipment; by the time I was in my teens the broadcasting bug had bitten me.

My passion for a career in television overtook my marginal ability as an athlete, and I passed on some scholarships at smaller schools, deciding to attend Indiana University and study telecommunications. A solid degree from a prestigious school with experience from my youth was a combination I had determined would take me right to the network.

My preparation was diligent, and my effort was significant. However, upon graduation I could not find a job as a television sports guy, and so I headed back to small town radio. With a staff of only seven full-time employees, everyone did what was necessary to get through the day. In addition to sports, I hosted a morning show, and I learned to sell for the first time. A year later, my big break arrived; I parlayed this odd combination into a job in television as a weekend sports anchor and a weekday sales person in Peoria, Illinois. It was a small market, but it was a start. Now I was on my way.

Through my three years there I worked hard to develop my on air skills, but I never got another offer to anchor. Meanwhile, sales had become very natural to me. I worked hard at sales, but it wasn't my passion. However, the longer I did it, the better I got, and the more money I made.

Then the phone rang. A client was on the line and suggested I consider talking to a station in St. Louis about an opening in their sales department. She worked with me through the years and also bought time from them. In her estimation we would be a good match.

This wasn't the first time someone encouraged me to use my talents selling and leave the anchor work behind, but it *was* the first time I ever stopped to consider the suggestion. Was there something to it? Maybe I should just listen.

While I loved working on camera, the truth was, I was just adequate at it. Deep down, I knew that. Concurrently, my success in sales was significant, and I hadn't really invested in myself to develop professionally in business beyond just my natural ability to listen and relate to customers. A couple of days passed – the more I considered the idea, the more I could see my long-term potential on the business side of television. My wife agreed that I should take the interview.

It went very well, as did the second interview with the station's general manager and general sales manager. Just 10 days after answering a simple phone call, I found myself unintentionally at life's crossroads.

As I began to reflect on the choice in front of me, my heart told me to press on, continuing to follow my dream as a television sportscaster. Meanwhile, my head was coming to a different conclusion. Conversely, as I looked at my career path, the notion of selling for the rest of my career was not something I could see myself doing. In my view, my unique skill set of experience on television and the potential of professional development in sales would make me an ideal candidate for a general manager someday.

Quitting on my dream was difficult. I had never quit anything, ever, under any circumstance. Remember, my Dad was a football coach. Until this very moment my entire focus was developing a career path to become a network anchor.

Nevertheless, the more I considered the entire scope of my skill and ability, selling was the right choice. However, at that very moment I made the biggest professional decision of my life, I also made a commitment to myself. I wasn't leaving television sports behind to become a sales person. While this is what most would see, to me, I was leaving anchoring behind to become a general manager in training. Working full-time on the business side of the industry would allow me perspective to understand how programming, sales and marketing all worked. In my years on the air I had already developed an appreciation for the news and technical side. Mentally, I traded in my network ambition for a new goal to be a general manager of a local television station by the time I turned 35.

The next day, I accepted the job and two years later was promoted to local sales manager, then general sales manager 18 months later. Indeed, I became a general manager for 10 years before moving to New York to oversee a portfolio of stations as a group head for Hearst Television.

In the end, I missed my original goal of becoming a general manager before I was 35. I was 38, but the goal drove me to take the chance to look at my career differently and made walking away from anchoring understandable in my own mind.

What made everything possible was a simple moment of pause. An instant to step back and consider a new idea, how it might fit relative to the plan in place, and whether or not my skills were honestly able to take me where my dreams envisioned my life. This hiatus forced me to take a personal inventory and consider a "fresh start" on my career in television. Being open to a new and fresh opportunity changed my life and the life of our family. In truth, had I forged ahead, I would have made an adequate television anchor but not outstanding. I traded something I knew I was good at for a chance to be great at something else.

To me, dreams are meant to ignite the mind's curiosity for what might be possible. In the end, Bob Costas is secure in his post as America's preeminent sports personality, and I remain profoundly blessed to have a hand in shaping local television for the world's best media company.

I think it worked out well for both of us.

LEADING BY EXAMPLE
by Christopher T. Mardany

Shortly after my engagement to be married in 1997 I lost both my parents when they were in their 60s. They passed suddenly within three months of each other due to brief illnesses. Experiencing this loss at such a young age showed me that life can be too short.

Getting married without my parents physically here reminded me there are no guarantees in life. From that day, their passing got me to look forward in life and not backwards. We miss Mom and Dad every day, but hopefully by my actions and the way we are raising our family together, my wife, Elizabeth, and I are making them proud.

Coming off a wonderful experience at the Hearst Management Institute (HMI), I wanted to expand my education in strategic leadership. As a CPA, I felt that continuing towards an MBA was only backfilling talents I already processed. I wanted to continue to learn topics and areas of study from HMI, and as a result, found the Master's of Strategic Leadership (MSL) program at my undergraduate college.

I began the program at St. Bonaventure University in the fall of 2013 at the age of 48. My anticipated graduation will be the summer of 2015. For me, returning to school is an opportunity to lead by example and to show my colleagues, and especially my children, that it is never to late to improve oneself and make your parents proud.

P.S. My dear sister Maureen, whom I share a birthday with though we are not twins, recently passed at the age of 50 from ovarian cancer. Another reminder that life can be short, validating my decision to expand my education.

OMAHA'S PRIDE
by Ariel D. Roblin

In 2011 the President of Hearst Television promoted me to General Manager and President of KETV. This was a tremendous "fresh start moment" for me. Now, I had the opportunity to affect and witness the great work accomplished every day from every department. One of my first responsibilities was to find a new home for KETV.

I began a thoughtful analysis of what core qualities made KETV the dominant television station in Omaha. It didn't take long to conclude that the core of our strength was our people. I realized that the only way a building could add to that strength would be if the building, itself, served as a physical example of our devotion to the First Amendment and our community.

We started to look at several properties. From fields to warehouses, they all seemed to have an equal number of pros and cons, but ultimately amounted to just another building. Not a difference maker. Then, Hearst Television's Senior Vice President of Finance asked our brokers a question that would ultimately change the course of our future home, "Can you show me something you think we would think is crazy?"

Big ideas are born by giving permission to propose the absurd. That's all it took to get The Burlington on our list.

It was in the single digits the day we went to see it for the first time. Snow was falling on the outside and inside of the building. The 65-foot high ceilings in the Grand Hall housed hundreds of pigeons and the mosaic tile floor was covered in six inches of feathers. The last train had left the station in

1974, and it had been abandoned for nearly 40 years. The burden of vacancy bore the scars of the most recent residents. Graffiti called out to a fairer and more just world, while the faded brick walls teased of the opulent history adorned with elaborate hand painted plaster ceilings. It was impressive, grand, haunting and lonely all in one moment. Yet, something didn't feel right. It felt too grand for us. "No," I thought, "this would not do."

Then, we found an old staircase that led to a dark area below. We all pulled out our cell phones and carefully made our way down to track level. It was dark, damp, and quiet. When we reached the track level, the light from our phones lit up the corners of a vaulted ceiling and a rusted door with the words "Telegraph Room." A room that once housed the highest point of technology, now held on to the past by a few rusty nails. It was empty, but there was no echo, as if the substance of the building's history captured every move we made.

We made our way to an opening in the center of the floor below the grand hall. That is when it happened. White subway tile walls curved around a circular opening in the center of the room. Three vaulted openings, now boarded up, led to the trains. This is where the stories where born; where men left their families for war; where loved ones waited for them to return home; where children held their mother's dresses as they ran as fast as they could into their soldier's arms. This was the first impression of Omaha for thousands of immigrants who built this city. For thousands, this ground, this building, meant "home."

None of us had ever done a project like this, so we set out on a 20-month road to discover the feasibility of it all, while continuing to research other properties that might be less complicated. We discovered that "The Burlington" was built for the Trans Mississippi World Fair. It had opened in

1898 on July 4th to welcome and impress 2.6 million people seeing Omaha for the first time. The more we learned about the building, the more we invested in our due diligence.

Converting a century old building into a state-of-the-art television station would not be easy, but ultimately, under the guidance and support of Hearst Television, we decided it was the right thing to do for KETV, The Burlington and Omaha.

The news rattled the foundation of our city. It became front-page news in the *Omaha World Herald.* Senators, congressmen, mayors, and business leaders wanted tours to witness this great work. National trade publications began taking interest in the build. Yet, that was not why we did it.

The television industry is demanding. It requires a passion and drive to serve your city. There are no warnings when breaking news hits – you must always be ready. When tornados hit, hurricanes move in, or a marathon ends in a bombing, most people head home to wrap their arms around their loved ones and wait until someone tells them it's safe to come out. The women and men at KETV make a phone call home and get to work. They have families too – selfless and brave families. Nevertheless, they do this because they understand that local broadcasters have a responsibility to keep their viewers safe and informed. It's the KETV employees that have dedicated their life's work to Omaha that are the true inspiration for our new home. It's not about KETV – it's about Omaha.

I have a deep respect and pride in the people that make up this industry. They see the worst and best of mankind every day, and day after day, night after night they bring these stories home to Omaha. I can think of no better home for them than the Burlington Station, a station built to equal Omaha's Pride.

EMBRACING CHANGE
by Gregory J. Turner

In December 2007, I had lived all my life in one state: 40 years, never leaving Oklahoma. But that month, I was presented with the opportunity to take a job someplace very different. The position would be my first as a department head – and one that would require rebuilding a television station and staff that had endured and survived the devastation of Hurricane Katrina. The idea that seemed most profound to me was this: It would be the first time I would ever live in a place where I knew no one, and more importantly, I would no longer be near the five living generations of my immediate family.

I remember looking out the window of the airplane when I flew down for my interview. I saw homes and traffic moving on the interstate and boats in the gulf (something I didn't expect after watching news coverage that showed nothing but devastation and ruin). This was my first time ever in New Orleans; I had no point of reference.

Upon arrival, I discovered a city that was almost completely starting over. I found myself becoming intimately involved in the local process and far removed from the images that I'd seen so much of on the national news broadcasts.

Instead of a city full of people who felt sorry for themselves and were looking for a handout, what I saw was a largely indigenous group of people dedicated to proving to themselves and the world that they would recover and rebuild. These visions calmed any nervousness and erased the uneasy feelings that followed me from the plains to the coast.

I remember telling myself, "If they can withstand losing everything and respond with such resolve, then nothing that I experience in my new existence – in this new city and career – will prevent me from rebuilding and succeeding."

I walked into the station for my first day of work and was immediately ushered to the upstairs conference room. I wasn't even given time to find my office or to put my briefcase down. What I walked into was a room filled with my corporate engineering management team and vendors from around the country, all enlisted to repair or replace every piece of equipment at the transmitter facility (which had sustained a 13-foot storm surge and thus taken the transmitter off the air). Everyone in the room was eager to rebuild and launch the transmitter that would return our broadcast signal to full power.

Later that day, I had the opportunity to meet with my new staff. To say that they inspired me was an understatement. After I had introduced myself, I opened the floor to each of them to make any statement about themselves or the station – personally or professionally. I wanted them to know that not only was I here to manage the department, but I was also here to get to know them collectively, and more importantly, individually. I wanted them to know that it was my intention to be part of their recovery, as well as part of the engineering team.

As time went on, I learned a couple of things about myself and the "fresh start" I was living. I realized that change sometimes makes us feel uncertain or unsure about our abilities. Watching the true and humbling humanity of others helps us realize that there is no need to doubt ourselves. We would all benefit by becoming aware of our own humanity; remaining grounded and humble; and never being afraid to try new experiences.

There will always be change. Every day we are blessed to be on this Earth is an opportunity for a fresh start.

FAITH MOMENT
by Maureen McKee

I have learned, over the years, to put more and more of my faith in God and realize my "fresh start" moments are orchestrated by Him. I just pray that I recognize them (and slow down enough to notice!) and place my trust in Jesus that through His Holy Spirit I'll wind up in a better place than I could have dreamed of.

When I moved to Colorado from NYC, I never doubted that it was the right move. Everything fell into place. I was the last immediate family member to leave New York. Had it been different, perhaps I would have stayed, but I always knew that my life path had to be my own and not to follow others. Was it tough to see my Dad and Mom off to Florida, followed by my sister, her husband, then my brother, etc.? Absolutely, but I had to do what was right for me, which is different than what is right for others.

I think it takes courage to venture into the unknown, but there's so much excitement when you know it's of God. If you know, that you know, that you know – there's no doubting. I prayed for it to be so, and it was and still is. 18 years later, relocating was a great decision.

I believe God influences our lives and with Him, life can be just as challenging but much more fulfilling!

COURAGE
by Tara Butler Floch

The tagline for my business is "Courageously Leaping in-to Entrepreneurship." For 14 years I have been helping entrepreneurs build businesses doing what they love and prospering because of it. Courage has always been my unofficial mascot. Part of why I chose it to represent my company was because it has always been the necessary ingredient in my life to feel truly fulfilled.

I say that Courage is not the absence of Fear; it is having the Fear and doing what you are called to do because it is simply more important than the Fear. Those who have called me fearless because of the big courageous leaps I've taken in my life have just been dead wrong. Sometimes the fear is so palpable that I feel the adrenaline coursing through my body with every huge thump of my beating heart. But instead of being paralyzed by my fear, I channel it into excitement. Then, I focus on "the prize" and slowly the fear takes a back-seat to my desired outcome.

Courage has been a tool for my success – but having courage has never guaranteed my success. Although I take calculated risks, I move quickly and sometimes land squarely on my butt. Rather than choosing to look at these as fail-ures, I try to focus on what I learned from the butt landing and use that to inspire a better approach that will bring me a better outcome next time. How quickly I recover is key to the better outcome, and I am proud to say that although I still fall, I spend less time licking my wounds than I used to. I recover more quickly and move on faster. I falter often, but it has yet to stop me from moving forward toward a bigger and brighter future.

Like anyone, there are periods in my life where I mustered little courage and it showed. I am talking about times when I got comfy on my merry-go-round ride and stopped trying to grab the brass ring. A ride that was once magical would become predictable and mundane but never quite bad enough to jump off the ride. As Jim Collins has said, "Good is the enemy of Great," and that merry-go-round was the Good that has been known to keep me from courageously leaping into Great.

When I was younger, the Good sometimes snuck up on me and seemed to replace the Great without my noticing. When I was an executive at Getty Images, my job was pretty great for a long time. I felt I was on purpose and making a big difference in the lives of my employees and our clients. When it started to shift, I failed to recognize it for what it was. I thought we were just in a "rough spot," and that I'd work through it like I had for the last six years. Then, one day when I said to my Mom, "Things will shift back to normal soon," she pointed out that I had been saying that in every conversation we had for at least two years and it was clear that my job was no longer fun or enriching and that I was on the road to burnout.

I was a bit stunned by this because, like a frog in a pot of water that slowly boils, I was really unaware of how bad it had gotten. The water was heating up at a rate that would kill me, and I failed to even recognize it, let alone jump out of the pot.

Soon thereafter, I went to my 10-year high school reunion and everyone was oo-ing and ahh-ing that I was a VP of a publicly traded company. I remember thinking to myself, "I would trade places with you in a second," because in truth, although I was successful on the surface, I didn't feel successful. I began to realize that Great had not only slid into Good, but that I was downright unhappy.

That moment was pivotal for me. I knew something had to shift. So I went on a weekend personal development retreat and took a month sabbatical in Italy, hell bent on showing up at work in a different way upon my return. I had spent my whole sabbatical masterminding how to shift things at work to return to that magical feeling where I was making a difference and enjoying the ride. I was convinced I would make it happen.

Upon my return, however, I was slapped with a project to manage: A reduction in force (AKA layoff) of 350 people in our division. All that hope, optimism and desire got sucked out of me in less than 10 days, as I started to meet with my fellow VP's to scope out how to cut 20 percent of their staff (knowing that I had to let three of them go in a matter of weeks, to boot). I told my boss that I would see this commitment through, but that I was leaving, myself, in three months, once the project was complete and the dust had settled.

To Getty's credit, they jumped through hoops to try to keep me, including offering me what looked on paper like my dream job (VP of Organizational Development), but after looking at the role through the filter of my top Values, I knew that this job wasn't a Great opportunity for me and that leaving was still the right choice.

I didn't want to make the mistake of choosing Good when I knew Great was out there for me. I also knew that I had lost touch with my passion and fire (I am an Aries, after all!) and that I had to take a courageous leap across the abyss, trusting and believing I would land on the other side of this huge crevice that had formed between where I was and where I wanted to be.

The trouble was, I didn't know where I wanted to be. I was a 29-year-old woman who hadn't been on a date in two years, who had gained 60 pounds and whose whole world revolved around her work. I had to re-invent myself and re-acquaint myself with who I was without the identity of my job.

I made a commitment that I would not decide what I would "do" for work for at least four months and headed on a personal development journey. This journey had me do some deep soul searching to face my inner saboteurs, head on. It took more courage than all of my courageous leaps put together.

I learned how to fully step into my authenticity and worry less about what others thought of me and more about what I wanted. I redesigned my relationship with myself, my higher power and my friends and family.

It was a journey full of peaks and valleys. I was no longer on a merry-go-round but on a rollercoaster, and what I discovered was I really was a rollercoaster type of girl at heart. I loved the beauty, possibility and joy of the highs, and the realness and aliveness of the lows. The contrast fostered a deep appreciation for the blessings I have in my life and how resourceful and resilient I am. Knowing both has made me a far better and more empathetic coach, friend and wife. Through this amazing personal transformation, I transformed my career, as well. I took the courageous leap of starting my own business, becoming a certified coach, and I now help other entrepreneurs do the same thing.

I know that every step of my journey has led me to where I am, and it all mattered – great, good, hard, painful. I now recognize, when I start to slip into Good from Great that I have tools and strategies to help me stay on track and push out of my comfort zone. Leaving Getty was not only a "fresh start" moment; it helped me create a fresh start life.

I have had dozens of fresh start moments since that pivotal time, including moving from Seattle to a little town in California wine country, without knowing a soul. If I hadn't done that, I would have never met my husband, who is the love of my life. I had to make that courageous fresh start to find him. Now we are hoping to start a family, which definitely brings me back to those adrenaline surges coursing through my body. It is yet another example of how Courage is not the absence of Fear but having the fear and doing it anyway – because what's on the other side of the fear is precious beyond words.

This latest fresh start will most certainly not be my last, but I plan on savoring every moment of this experience, now and forever. And if I fall on my butt, I know that I can stand-up, dust myself off and begin again.

Courageously leap onward!

LISTENING
by Elaine Harris, ESQ

My earliest school days in Long Branch, New Jersey, inspired me to become a teacher. I loved school and loved my teachers and was always happiest in a classroom environment where I excelled. It never occurred to me that I should even consider another career. Besides, in my adolescent years, there were few career options for women. Most of my contemporaries became teachers, nurses, secretaries or housewives, the latter of which, quite frankly, was the most sought after status.

And so it was that I became an English teacher at Red Bank High School. I remember opening my first bank account with my first paycheck in what I called the Long Branch branch of the Red Bank bank. I financed a burgundy Pontiac Tempest convertible, and soon after I found my first home away from home in a garden apartment complex in Matawan. I had a keen eye for bargains at local thrift and antique shops, and my new home was furnished quite charmingly, or so I thought. With my newfound income, I also started building a wardrobe of my favorite fashion statements, all of which were very easy to wear with my 22-year-old slim figure.

To supplement my income in my first year teaching, I accepted a position as the after school debate coach. One of the student debaters was a very intelligent young man who was a senior. After graduation, he went on to college at Rutgers University, but from time to time he kept in touch with a card or phone call.

As the years passed, a droning effect descended in the classroom. With each new school year I had a new group of fresh faces, but they started to look alike. Repeating the same curriculum became very monotonous for me, and trying to keep myself interested became a challenge.

My department chair started a new program called the "Multi-Media" approach to teaching language. It was hoped it would inspire more students by stimulating them through other media such as music, film art, dance, live theatre and visual arts. Essentially, other forms of media were supplementing reading books. Unfortunately, that change brought with it some external problems from parents who did not support this creative idea.

All in all, it was not easy at that time to be innovative and to push the envelope in education.

One spring evening, I received an unexpected telephone call from the young man from my debate team who had just finished his college education at Rutgers. He was very happy and joyfully told me his plans to buy a car and "bum around" for a year or so before entering law school. He wanted to see the country and travel by car to all the states. I pounced on his plans like a feral cat after a mouse. "Oh no," I said, "no you don't. First you go to law school, get that out of the way, and then you can bum around all you want." After that conversation, I had successfully managed to change his plans and he went directly to law school.

What happened next was most surprising. I became depressed. I realized that I was always giving good advice to others but not to myself. I had never considered listening to my inner voice. It was a new conversation and a new learning tool. Hear yourself. Stop talking and start listening.

And so it was that very moment after the phone call, I told myself that I was going to law school, too. The idea had never before occurred to me. I had no idea if I would be accepted or if my grades or scores would enable me to be admitted. But I most definitely recall thinking that I would apply to every law school in the country if I had to until I got in.

As it happened, I applied to Seton Hall School of Law in Newark, and by chance, it was the first year that they were seeking to admit women. I was one of a "huge" class of 18 women who started law school at night the following fall. By going to law school at night, I was able to continue teaching during the day. That way I could pay my tuition.

It is hard to believe as I write this, that was almost 45 years ago and I have been practicing law all these years. For me, that conversation with myself all those many years ago was a "fresh start." Had I remained in teaching, I would have been retired long ago and with a nice pension.

Maybe I would be tending a garden somewhere in an adult community. Who knows? But my career as a lawyer has been priceless. While I may have inspired many students as their teacher, or so I hope, I believe that I have helped exponentially more people along the way in my second career as a lawyer. That conversation with myself was a turning point in my life, and I shall never forget it.

My advice to you is to do the same thing I did. Listen to yourself, and you will learn what you really want, what you need and who you are. No one else can do this for you.

TRIUMPH
by Leah Miles

It was in 2002, my first year of teaching at Collins Middle School in Salem, Massachusetts, that I had an overwhelming feeling of gratitude for my job: I was a music and drama teacher, and I loved it! I got to go to work everyday and make music and theater with some amazing collaborators: My students. Each year got better, and I got more confident in my teaching and wanted to share everything with them. The work we did was hard, but we had so much fun together and learned a lot from each other. It was sometime in the middle of my third year that I thought, "I want to be a student again."

Now, I hadn't been a student since 1994 when I graduated from Salem State University. Those four years were amazing. For the whole four years, I felt like anything was possible. The opportunities I was afforded by the Music and Theater departments and the professors I had all shaped the kind of educator I had become. I was grateful for what I learned there. Leaving SSU, I felt proud of what I'd accomplished as a young artist.

As graduation day approached, the reality of trying to earn a living making music and performing theater started to seem too risky. I considered continuing in my major field of study, which was psychology. And I almost did. But I was strongly encouraged by one of my professors to follow my heart and my passion, which was in the performing arts, and not to settle for the "safe path."

I was not ready back then. It took me nearly 15 years to figure out what I wanted to be when I "grew up." If I had to go back and do it all again, I wouldn't change a thing.

It was my students who inspired me to want to be a student again. It was their artistic courage and risk-taking that made me realize that I was ready to run toward the thing that scared me the most – taking my dreams to New York City and becoming a writer for the theater.

It took me two years of applying to graduate schools for the right program to come along. In 2008 I was accepted into the Graduate Musical Theater Writing Program at NYU Tisch School of the Arts. It was the only program of its kind in the country, making it highly selective and very competitive. I'll never forget the moment when I opened the email with the message that I had been accepted. Everything I had ever done, lived through, fought for, struggled and succeeded with pointed me in this direction and to my "fresh start moment." I was ready for this new chapter. And there wasn't one moment of doubt that making this move and taking this risk was the right thing to do.

Now, nearly six years later, I have eight completed works to stand on proudly and multitudes of projects just waiting for their moment in the spotlight. I have a new "family" in New York City, who are here to hold me up in those moments of doubt and celebrate loudly in my moments of triumph.

It took patience and perseverance coupled with an open heart and mind for me to be where I am today. If I can keep remembering that, my next fresh start moment will find its way to me.

PASSION IN ACTION
by Ronnie Newman

My two passions are spirituality and science. Since adolescence, I have known that my purpose on Earth is to show people the value of spirituality through the language of modern medical science.

When I began meditating and experienced its enormous transformative potential, the benefits were largely unknown and frequently met with skepticism. I felt my life would be well spent by scientifically documenting these benefits for the Western mind and bringing this knowledge to as many people as possible.

I was fortunate to have received my scientific training at Harvard. As a research scientist, my primary focus has been on holistic, mind-body medicine.

When I began to speak publicly about the field, as well as about my findings, I discovered how deeply I touched people. That was affirming and helped build my confidence to move in this direction.

I was drawn to speak in places where my message could have a large impact. Yet, when those opportunities arose, I would get tied up in knots preparing my talk. I was so afraid of failing that it made it almost impossible to move forward in what I knew was my calling.

In 1999, my mentor looked over at me in a meeting and said, "You should speak at the United Nations."

My first thought was, "This is exactly what I am here to do." I felt validated. Until panic set in and I froze. *How could little me speak at the big United Nations?*

Soon, the opportunity to speak there presented itself, and determination rose up in me. I decided I would either die of a heart attack on the podium, or break through the paralysis and take my service to a higher level.

Preparing the talk was somewhat torturous, because I kept anguishing over whether I would be able to convey what I knew inside. Would people be interested in what I had to say? Would I be able to do justice to the knowledge that needed to get out there? Would I be able to take advantage of this golden opportunity to fulfill my destiny?

When I arrived at the United Nations, I was ushered into the Delegates dining hall as a special guest. During the meal, I could hardly pay attention to the conversation or the food; I kept reviewing my talk in my head.

Afterwards, I proceeded to the lecture hall where I was introduced to the other two panelists. One was the renowned Dr. Mehmet Oz; the other, a highly respected Ayurvedic physician. I was so nervous I went to the ladies room to secretly practice some breathing techniques in an attempt to calm myself down.

Dr. Oz was the first speaker; I was to follow. As he spoke, my heart pounded so hard in my chest that I looked to see if anyone could see my blouse moving up and down.

Sitting there, waiting my turn, I could not remember the subtle points of my talk. I could not even remember the main points! I knew I was there for a reason, but at that moment I doubted my ability to give anything that remotely resembled a cogent presentation.

Then the moderator introduced me. In the 20 seconds it took to walk to that impressive, mammoth podium with the imposing United Nations symbol, a miracle happened. I became incredibly clear and relaxed and went on to give an engaging, funny, thought-provoking, successful presentation.

It was so well received that in the Q & A the vast majority of questions were directed to me regarding the material I had presented. People were so interested in what I had been able to convey that they didn't want to leave, despite United Nations security asking them to clear the room. When the meeting ended, they flocked around me like a rock star.

This experience has given me the courage to say, "Yes," every time I am invited to speak. Since then, I've had the honor of returning to the United Nations to address the U. N. NGO Mental Health Committee, as well as speaking at the World Bank and multiple medical schools and universities.

On reflection, my commitment to being the best vessel of change I could possibly be (by sharing this essential knowledge) was greater than my fear.

HOLDING YOUR HEAD HIGH
by Tobie Skolnick Newman

I am a first-generation American. In 1939 at the age of 16, I began my college studies with the intention of becoming a cancer researcher. My father had passed away from prostate cancer, and I was committed to helping find a cure.

I majored in biology, which I loved and excelled at. During my junior year, I was paired with a less than enthusiastic lab partner. I had a strong work ethic and didn't mind doing most of the lab work myself, even though both our names went on our papers.

Before taking an exam one day, she said, "Tobie, do not cover your paper." I replied that I wouldn't help her cheat, but I would not turn her in either.

When the graded exams were returned, my lab partner received an A, while I received a C. I asked her if I could read her exam to compare it with mine. When I did, I saw that my own exam was more thorough than hers. So, I scheduled an appointment with the professor to discuss my grade.

Rather than discussing the exam, my teacher asked about my background. "Where were your parents born? What is your mother's maiden name?"

Questions of this nature were commonly asked in the 1930s and '40s to identify people of the Jewish faith. Anti-Semitism was a reality in America then. Signs like: "No Dogs or Jews Allowed" could be found posted in restaurants, hotels and country clubs.

After this line of questioning, the professor said, "You will never get ahead in this field."

I realized then that the professor, the department chair, had the power to keep me from becoming a biologist. Summoning all the courage of a 19-year-old student, I stood up, looked him directly in the eye and said boldly, "You are a vicious anti-Semite."

My love of science moved me to switch my major to chemistry. I graduated at the top of my class at the ripe old age of 20. At the time, many of my classmates were being recruited to join a top-secret Defense Department project. I interviewed for a position on this project too, but I did not hear back, despite the fact that many students who weren't as qualified as me were being hired.

Anti-Semitism was again showing its head, and I knew I would have to take things into my own hands. So, I told a white lie. I called the interviewer's office and said, "You told me to call you by Thursday if I had not heard back from you by then." The person answering the phone said, "Oh, okay, come in today and you'll be screened with the rest of the new scientists." That is how I got the job.

The Defense Department project I was hired to work on was the Manhattan Project, the secret development of the atom bomb during World War II. One of the missing pieces of the puzzle was isolating the uranium isotope U-238. For some unknown reason, the results from the experimentation were inconsistent. Oppenheimer and the other leading scientists needed to understand why the formula was not working.

Like the other researchers who were assigned to this particular part of the project, I got inconsistent results each time I ran the experiment. Then one day I realized that when it was rainy or humid, or cold or hot, my results were even more erratic. I then began to plot the outcomes of my experiments on a graph, which included the atmospheric pressure and temperature at the time the experiment was being conducted.

With this, I discovered the reason for the inconsistent outcomes when we attempted to isolate U-238.

I prepared my report, put my stamp on it and gave it to my supervisor, who realized that I might have found the solution. Wanting to share the credit, he placed his stamp above mine and sent it on to his supervisor. His supervisor also wanted to share the credit and put his stamp on top of the previous one. And so it went – all the way up to the highest levels of the project. The stamps kept getting larger and larger until the graph itself could not be clearly read.

When the report reached the lead supervisor, he asked the previous supervisor to explain his findings; he was unable to do so. Down, down, down the line it went. Each successive supervisor who was asked to explain his findings referred the inquiry to his underling.

One day, three official looking men entered my laboratory and asked me to explain my work regarding U-238. I said, "I'm sorry. I cannot talk about it. It is a military secret." This was the instruction all scientists working on the Manhattan Project had been given. Not even my mother or future husband knew what I was doing.

My supervisor explained that these three men were top officials from the Army, the Navy and the Marines, who were in charge of the Manhattan Project for their branch of the military. They wore civilian clothing so they wouldn't be noticed on the streets of Manhattan. He said it was okay to speak with them and answer any questions they had.

I then explained how I had reached my conclusion. Some time later, I received a letter of commendation from President Harry S. Truman.

My colleagues and I believed that less death and suffering would ensue by dropping the atom bomb and ending the war, than by allowing the war to continue. When the bomb was dropped and the human suffering revealed, we formed a committee to delve deeply into how science could be used for the greater good of humankind and how to avoid its abuse.

In the 1940s, being a young female scientist in a field predominated by men was challenging. Being Jewish and a child of immigrants compounded it. Thinking back, I am proud I had the audacity to pursue my love of science and dream of making a difference in this world. In spite of the obstacles I faced, I created my own "fresh start" in chemistry when the door to biology closed.

FAITH AND PERSEVERANCE
by Ed Primoff

I have been blessed to be successful at a number of enterprises, but things did not start out that way. From early on, I had difficulty reading and was told repeatedly I was never going to amount to anything. I remember one of my high school teachers asking me what I was going to do when I graduated.

"I'm going to go to college," I said.

She and several of the students laughed. "You can't even read," she said. "How do you expect to go to college or even make a living? I'll tell you what you are going to do. You're going to be a burden on society. You're probably going to be on welfare or in jail. One way or another, your classmates are going to have to support you."

My response practically got me thrown out of school, but my bravado was a cover-up. Failing academically put a big dent in my self-esteem, something I struggled with for years.

I made up for poor grades with tenacity in my life outside of school. I was accustomed to hard work and had been working part-time since I was about 11 years old. I bagged groceries for Jumbo Food Stores, a local supermarket and delivered newspapers for what was then called the *Times Herald of Washington, D.C.* In the winter when it snowed, I shoveled sidewalks and driveways and would accept whatever people would pay me. Sometimes I would get as much as 50¢. In the summer, I cut lawns on a regular basis. I always had money in my pocket. That gave me a sense of security I didn't find anywhere else.

I probably had every low-paying job you can think of, including picking up and delivering diapers. That was memorable. But I never stopped trying to get ahead. I made a firm decision that I would work twice as hard and do whatever it took to prove myself.

My "fresh start" was probably my first job in real estate. I had no experience, no qualifications and a family to support. With nothing but raw determination, I talked a guy into giving me the job by convincing him I would become his top salesman. In return, he agreed to pay me $70 a week.

It wasn't easy. I had to keep pushing, often working seven days a week, 12-15 hours a day. The way to succeed in real estate was to get listings. So without telling anyone, I went door-to-door from 8 a.m. to 8 p.m. "Do you know anyone who wants to sell a house? Do you know anyone who wants to sell a house?" Over and over and over until someone finally said, "Yes, my uncle wants to sell his house."

That was my first listing. I sold the uncle's house and then sold the uncle another house. In a matter of years, I went from salesman to manager to broker. Then, I started my own real estate company.

After that, I had many fresh start moments with my adventurous wife. We began a gemology company and traveled extensively; worked with the FBI and helped capture criminals; got involved in politics; and owned and operated a farm. I even overcame my fear of flying and became a pilot.

I share these diverse experiences to bring home the point that a lack of confidence and low self-esteem is no longer a barrier – once you commit to yourself. Others told me that I would not succeed; I told myself I would. That is how the magic happens.

All these years later, I still have scholastic challenges, but I don't let them define me. Since writing isn't my strong point,

I used voice recognition software and dictated an entire book into my computer. *Driven Beyond Success* was published in 2014 and is one of my proudest fresh start moments.

I admit, I do get a kick out of being called an author, but my real gratification comes from the feedback I receive from readers. It seems that sharing my own challenges has given others the courage to take risks in their own lives. It doesn't get much better than that.

MY AUDACIOUS MOVE
by Gil Eagles

A couple of years after arriving in America, lacking the formal education to secure any meaningful employment, my father and I did what any self-respecting people who can't get a job do – we went into business.

Fortuitously, we ventured into the pizza business. After several years of working 14-hour days, seven days a week, we owned three pizza stores and were doing quite well.

I, however, felt unfulfilled and yearned for more. As a teenager I became fascinated with magic and enjoyed entertaining customers in the pizza store with the few tricks I had learned. During those long days working, a gnawing thought kept creeping into my mind: Could I make it in show business with my few magic tricks?

I finally built up the courage to tell my father that I was leaving the pizza business and going into show business – which was clearly as foreign to us as one can possibly imagine. Neither I, nor anyone in my family, had ever been in show business or had any inkling of the business other than what we saw on television.

My father couldn't believe what he was hearing from someone he thought, up until then, was a sane son. After much badgering and haranguing as to how absolutely foolish I was for entertaining such a ridiculous idea, I was, nonetheless, determined not to stay in the pizza store any longer than I needed to. I promised my father that I would help him out whenever he needed my help and headed for the mysterious and enigmatic world of show business.

I worked incessantly, learning as much as I could while putting an act together. After six months, I secured my first paid engagement, where I earned $25 for the entire weekend at the Café Wha? in Greenwich Village.

The first few years were indeed difficult and lean. Nevertheless, from that first engagement, I have never looked back, and for the past 40 years I've enjoyed a most magnificent and blessed career doing what I love.

I have traveled the world entertaining and speaking and making a handsome living to boot. Had I not had the audacity to dream of possibilities and follow my aspirations, I might still be wearing an apron, standing behind a counter tossing dough into the air.

SMALL BEGINNINGS
by Pam Foss

I can say that I am an artist now after exploring the many avenues my craft has taken me. In the beginning, I was busy having a family and sketching out little pictures for my children. I was surprised when friends and family started asking to buy them.

"I'm not an artist," I would say and gave them my work. I always thought you had to go to college for a degree in Fine Arts to be an artist. My husband would beg to differ, "You are an artist, and you're a natural born artist!" I loved him for saying that. I was not convinced, so I continued giving my work away.

My husband Bob and I became involved with a small racing stable by way of show horses. I had been riding show hunters for a few years, when our friend and trainer, Grover Stephens, convinced us that racing was much more profitable than showing horses, making us believe we had nothing to lose. Surprise, surprise, the profitable part of this scenario never did work out. But we had great fun with the small stable, and my art continued to thrive, drawing horses, trainers and people.

My art career really began at Hialeah Race Track back in the late '70s when Franco Zeffirelli came to town to make the movie *The Champ*, staring Jon Voight, Faye Dunaway and Ricky Schroder. It was very exciting.

The movie studio asked a few racing stables to take part in the movie, and my trainer, Grover Stephens, convinced us to use our horses. We were between race meets, and this would be a good opportunity to make some extra money, so said Grover. I agreed to do it, but only if I could be on set every day to take care of our horses. "Absolutely," said Grover. "It's a done deal."

Watching the big moving vans pull into the stable area and unload the MGM studio equipment was exciting. I have never seen such an operation. The horses were spooked by all the commotion and spun around in their stalls, kicking out at anyone who went near them. They were racehorses after all and weren't used to their barns being invaded by large cameras on long neck cranes. To the horses, they looked like monstrous predators. Their natural instinct to fight or flee went into overdrive.

We asked the studio equipment manager if they could stop unpacking so we could move the horses to barns in the back, out of the fray. The track manager, Frank Tours, was none too pleased with the way the studio took over. He was going to have to teach them Racetrack Protocol.

The horses were bedded down in the back barns to calm down, but it took quite some time till the noise stopped. It was a long but very eventful day.

The next day, the director, Zeffirelli, movie staff and actors arrived to have a meeting with the racetrack employees. Frank the track manager presented the rules and regulations, underscoring the safety of the horses. He said he was to be informed of any changes on the grounds. When they felt conditions on both sides were met, Frank, in true military command announced, "Now let's make a movie!"

The first morning on set was fun. Watching the process gave me great respect for Mr. Zeffirelli. Directing a movie is not easy, and it takes great teamwork. It was like a well-choreographed dance with actors taking their marks and acting their scenes.

Jon Voight asked Grover and me for help in handling the horses, since he had learned everything he knew about horses from cowboy extras, who didn't understand that roughshod handling like you see in the old time Westerns didn't work with high-strung thoroughbreds. After a few days of showing Jon how to brush a horse, put on a saddle and wrap legs, he was off to a good start.

Jon's role in the movie was that of an ex-boxer, now working at the racetrack as a broken down trainer. Grover was a good trainer and knew the role very well from being on the racetrack all his life. So, it was easy for him to offer Jon some insight.

After my morning chores, I would sit off set and do some pen and ink sketches of the scenes unfolding before me. One morning while cleaning out the stalls, Jon walked in before shooting started and said, "Pam, I understand you are an artist."

I looked at him dumbfounded. "What?" I asked.

"I saw you doing some sketches the other day, and I want you to do some sketches of me and Randy Cobb sparring at the gym. Meet us tomorrow at 8:00 a.m.; I'll have a pass at the door for you." Before I could answer to tell him I wasn't an artist, he was out of the stall and gone.

Just then Grover came in the stall with a bale of straw looking at the stunned expression on my face. "What's up? Why's your mouth wide open?"

I blinked and told him how Jon just asked me to do some sketches of him and Randy Cobb sparring at the gym.

"That's great!" said Grover.

"Are you crazy? I'm not an artist. I can't draw them boxing."

"Sure you are, it will be easy for you. But you are not going down to that gym alone. It's a bad area, and you will need protection."

I looked at him and started to laugh. "Listen to yourself, you don't think a Heavy Weight Champion and a World Famous Actor can protect me from some bum in the gym?"

"Yeah, well I'm going anyway. You need me to drive you, Your husband would kill me if anything happened to you."

The 5th St. Gym was famous for boxers like Muhammad Ali, Sugar Ray Robinson and Sonny Liston; it was an honor to be invited to Angelo Dundee's Gym, along with the reporters and a few spectators. I'm not much of a boxing fan and didn't understand the moves, the bobbing and weaving, but it became very clear to me that Jon wanted to prove something to the crowd of spectators there – that he was a boxer in training who could hold his own against Heavy Weight Champ Randall "Tex" Cobb. Randy was hired to teach Jon how to box for the movie, not for the real boxing ring, but Jon had other ideas.

As they sparred, Jon got a little full of himself and started punching Randy really hard, taunting him into a real match. Randy kept telling him that he couldn't fight back because he was a professional and told him to stop fooling around.

I was glued to my sketchbook and sketched as fast as I could to try and capture all the action as it happened. Randy had enough bullying and let Jon have it right to the nose. Jon flew right towards me landing on the ropes with blood pouring out of his nose. My head bounced up and down from sketchbook to Jon's bloody nose, as I sketched a little faster now.

Jon hanging over the ropes looked down at me, "Don't sketch that...."

Randy felt horrible and couldn't apologize enough. "Jon, you told me you could protect yourself. I'm so sorry."

Everybody crowded around asking questions and taking pictures, "Is this going to be in the movie?"

Jon, making the best of a bad situation said, "This was all an act for the photographers and reporters."

The movie set was quiet for the next few days while Jon's nose healed. They shot smaller scenes around the track that didn't need Jon in them. Voight's injury drove Zeffirelli crazy. He snapped at everybody, including the horses that weren't standing still on their marks. It was a crazy couple of weeks.

Jon came back on set and everybody cheered; now it was back to making a movie. I put my sketchbook away and thought it would be bad luck to start sketching again now that Jon was back. Grover and I were busy grooming the horses after their morning exercise, when Jon once again came into the stall. "Pam, I've been thinking, I would like you to do a sculpture of me, Ricky (Ricky Schroder, the child actor) and your horse from the scene in which I'm presenting Ricky his present. What'ya think?"

My mouth dropped open for a second time, and I started to say, "I ... but I...."

Before I could say I never did a sculpture before, Grover reached over with a swift kick to my foot and said, "Pam can do it, she can do anything, can't you Pam?"

"Thanks," said Jon, and he left me in the stall again staring at the barn door.

"What's wrong with YOU?" I shouted at Grover, "I never did a sculpture before, how am I going to do that?"

Grover wasn't very understanding; he only looked at this as a great opportunity to advance my career as an artist. "Just go to the library and get a few books on sculpting, you'll pick it up in no time."

I thought to myself, "This is nuts, I can't sculpt." I called my husband Bob and told him what happened. Just like Grover, he thought that it was great too! I wanted to cry, how am I ever going to get this done?

I went to the library and got every book I could find on sculpting. I studied how to make an armature and went from there. I did everything wrong and pieces started to fall off the clay model, but after a few trial and error sculptures it all worked out in the end. Bob was so proud of me; I was beginning to feel that maybe I was an artist after all.

I delivered the sculpture to Jon and he loved it. He asked me how much I wanted for it. I was shocked; I wasn't going to charge him for it. This was my first sculpture, and I felt honored to have even been asked to do this piece. He insisted that I be paid and asked how much I wanted?

I told him whatever he felt was a fair price, and he gave me $500 and a kiss on top of my head telling me, "You did a great job."

PLANTING SEEDS
by Kira Rosner

It's peaceful working alone in my home office. To my left, there is a wall of windows facing a small lake. A cheerful mix of duck squawks and birdsong filter in through an open window.

One day I hear the words, "Contact the teacher." That same instant, I have a mental image of a writing class I sat in on more than 20 years ago in Marina Del Rey, California.

It was the only writing class I've come close to taking. I remember the teacher. Attractive, insightful, maybe 10 years older than I was. A friend invited me to attend, and I went several times.

The students all wrote at home. In class, everyone sat back and relaxed while each person read his or her story aloud. Afterwards, the other students and the teacher commented. The most memorable part was that the stories were written from real life experiences in first person, present tense. I felt like each writer was speaking into a microphone, narrating their life as it happened. It was personal. Intimate. Engaging.

I don't recall the teacher's name, but I do know the name of a book he wrote: *Writing from Within*. I'll Google it. His name is Bernard Selling. Looks like he's written quite a few books over the years. I'll email him.

"Dear Bernard, I sat in on several of your writing classes many years ago. I am an author myself now and am writing to thank you. Your classes touched me. I offer consulting for writers and have recommended *Writing From Within* to others over the years. Blessings, Kira"

"Hi Kira, Always happy to have had a positive impact. Good to hear that you are now a writer yourself. By the way, I've written three new books (two books, one workbook) – updates of WFW with quite a bit of new material. For an experienced writer like you, I suggest *Writing from Deeper Within*. Thanks for the hello. Bernard"

I call my friend Jacquelina; she's like a sister to me.

"Hi, what's up?" she asks.

"I was working alone when I distinctly heard the words, 'Contact the teacher.'"

"You mean like Kevin Costner in *Field of Dreams?* 'If you build it they will come.'"

"Something like that. There wasn't any sound, but I heard the words distinctly."

"Do you know who the teacher is?"

"Bernard Selling, a writing teacher I met over two decades ago."

"I have been wanting to focus more on my writing," she says.

A day passes. I am sitting at my computer working when I hear, "You've got to teach what he teaches!" This time the words are emphatic. Still silent. An inner voice, like someone is in my head.

Think I will email Bernard again.

"Dear Bernard, Have you ever trained others to teach your technique? My friend Jacquelina and I are both interested. We love to write, and we like the emotional component of creating a safe and nurturing way for people to open up. Your approach weaves those elements together! Kira"

"Hi Kira, Thank you for your interest in teaching my writing method. Yes, I would be happy to mentor you and your friend through the process. Just let me know when you are ready to begin. Bernard"

A month passes. In the last few weeks, a number of my friends express a desire to get serious about their writing. With little effort, I organize a writing class with Bernard and women in three different time zones. We plan to meet every other Sunday. My initial thought is to set it up so we can video chat. No one wants to be on camera, so I set up a conference call instead.

Fast-forward two years. The writing class continues to meet every other week. Some students drop out; others take their place. Jacquelina and I stay with it.

If I use one word to describe our experience, it would be "transformational." That juicy word encompasses so much. There is Bernard Selling's simple yet profound technique that anyone can learn. There is his insistence that giving feedback is about communicating our sensory experience (Do we see the characters, feel their feelings, hear their thoughts?) and not about criticizing. There is the self-reflective nature of this writing approach, which enlivens the potential for writers to heal the past and become more present. There is Bernard's honest feedback and consistent encouragement to let go of old writing habits and write authentically – from the heart. And, there is the strong sense of community within this evolving group of exceptional women, which gives each of us permission to open wider.

I feel privileged to manage this class. Whenever we have a new student, I introduce her to *Writing from Within*. That part is fun. It's like planting a seed, watering it and then watching it grow.

I'll take a break and check my email. Oh, here is one from Bernard. It's addressed to me, Jacquelina and Jody, a close friend and gifted writer who joined our class.

"Hi Kira, Jacquelina and Jody, You have each expressed an interest in teaching my WFW method of writing. I believe you would do well at it. The significant thing from my point of view is that, through your efforts, my work has a chance to live on. That is very important to me. You could teach and eventually train others to teach. Bernard"

It sounds like Bernard is offering to pass the torch to us. I feel humbled by the idea of teaching *Writing from Within* with his guidance. We can teach individually or we can teach together; we can give classes or workshops or webinars; we can teach in the states or overseas; we can train other teachers. So many possibilities!

The phone rings. I know it's Jacquelina before I pick up.

"Did you get the email from Bernard?"

"That is why I am calling," she says.

I hear the smile in her voice and smile back.

MY TROIKA OF FRIENDS
by Bob Danzig

STU, a chemical engineer and seasoned veteran of major corporations, hungered to take the risk and become the owner of a business. He took a year off from work to search for "just the right business" to invest in.

The result was his buying a paper bag printing operation with retail clients throughout the nation. He quickly realized this was a "commodity" business in which any competitor could lower prices and wipe him out.

His answer was to use his engineering skills to create the most cost efficient operation he could create. However, the cloud of commodity hovered all the time.

As he settled into the operation, he noticed some odd shaped molds hanging off the wall. One of the longtime employees/colleagues told him that one of the previous owners, now long gone, had designed those molds to produce plastic garment hangers. Stu learned there were solid patents for each mold. On investigating further, he found a competing plastic manufacturer had stolen the original patents. He dipped deep into his savings, hired a premier patent lawyer and sued.

The lawsuit lasted six years. It was a very tough time in the printed bag business as a recession had set in. However, Stu was committed to doing the right thing and continued to invest in the lawsuit. When it finally came before a patent judge, Stu prevailed and won both a large financial settlement and the exclusive right to use those patented molds.

It was a fresh start moment as Stu shifted his complete operation away from commodity printing to becoming an exclusive manufacturer of the largest business in delivering custom designed plastic hangers.

IRWIN, a pre-med student, was just 18 years old when his father died of a sudden heart attack. He had no choice but to leave college and come home to run his dad's small pest control business to help support his mom and younger brother. Although he had learned the business working summers next to his dad, he never had to interact with customers. Now, he realized why he had resisted connecting with clients. He was shy – very shy.

His solution was to service his father's accounts late at night when there were no people around. Then, early one morning at 2:00 a.m., a bakery shop owner showed up just as he was leaving. Terrified with shyness, he hid behind a concrete pillar in the enclosed parking area.

Standing behind that parking lot pillar, Irwin realized he would never build the business if he were gripped by shyness. That realization was his "fresh start moment." He began working with a professional who guided him to overcome his shyness. Today, Irwin owns one of the largest pest control companies in NYC.

STEVEN, a talented computer engineer, had never let go of his boyhood dream to be a hands-on railroad engineer. One day, his computer based employer offered a buyout package to any employee who wished to pursue another career. Steven leapt at the chance to add a new dimension to his life.

Leaving the company on friendly terms, he signed on to railroad engineering school and was thrilled with every class. He enjoyed learning on a live train and was diligent in his studies.

When he was awarded his conductor's cap, he loved serving the passengers and seeing the country from a railroad car. It was heaven to him every single day.

Then he earned a promotion to the cab as the actual engineer. A dream-come-true. Soon, however, he found it lonely in that engine cab. That was something he had never considered, and he was conflicted.

It set him to reminisce about how satisfying it was working on teams of equal talent in the computer field. Having finally fulfilled his boyhood dream, his fresh start moment was to take a step back and return to his pleasing professional life.

BELIEVE IN YOURSELF
by J. Peter Clifford

Life is a wondrous journey filled with joy, happiness, success and accomplishment; but it also presents its fair share of sadness, failure, disappointment and confusion.

During the so-called good times, it is relatively easy to stay positive and enjoy what life has to offer. However, during the challenging times, it takes more effort to try and get back to those good times.

OK, so we probably all agree that we don't need to really spend too much time when we are in a good place – just sit back and enjoy them while they last.

Life's challenges can come in many forms, death or sickness of a family member or friend, loss of a job, break-up of a relationship, etc. Who hasn't been there at one time or another?

These are the challenges that can weigh heavily on you and put you in a place or state of mind that is a bit darker. These are also the times that can test your character or as the saying goes, "test your mettle."

However, these life challenges are also an opportunity. An opportunity to "turn things around" or get a "fresh start."

I don't doubt that when it comes to life challenges, some are given much more difficult events to overcome than others but with perseverance, determination, a plan – and if available, outside moral support – a fresh or new start can be accomplished.

So here is one of my life challenges. I was 51 and had been working for the same company since graduating college. (I never interviewed, since I had worked with this company for two summers during college.) I was married with three children, two of whom were in college. I completed a three-year tour in the Marine Corps and returned to enter the company's management-training program. During those years, I received several promotions and my family and I were comfortable. I fully expected to eventually retire from this company, as so many previous employees had done.

I haven't mentioned that my wife was trained as a teacher but was riffed after two years, never attaining tenure. We decided that she would stay at home and raise our three children. She had been doing some substitute teaching and was beginning to look for a full-time teaching position.

After 25 years, my company downsized, and my position was eliminated. I could choose between moving my family to Minnesota and taking a package. My youngest child was completing eighth grade, so we weren't going to put him through the difficulty of making new friends while entering high school, so I took the package. Now the challenge began, finding a new job with two in college and my wife not being employed full-time. I took a course in "How to Interview" and began the process of figuring out how to find another job.

Here's what I discovered along the way; perhaps all or some of this will be of some assistance.

• **Set up a Routine:** By this I mean, rise in the morning as if you were still working, and put in as much time as you can searching for a new job. Some days it may be a couple of hours; others may end up being most of the day.

• **Develop a Plan**: Your new mindset is that your "new" job is to find a job.

Fully understand your strengths, as well as your major accomplishments (companies are looking for individuals who can contribute to their success and profitability). In other words, sit down and prepare a "hook" or "pitch" that you can communicate.

Use the Internet to research the company you are interested in. Look for contacts to pursue, information about the company and major competitors. (Companies like the fact that you took the time to get to know their company; this tells them that you are interested and will put in the time).

Don't Wear Blinders: What I mean by this is, don't be so focused on a certain company or job that you don't see an opportunity that's out there.

A personal example: I was in operations for 25 years and was looking for an operations position, but I came across a job opportunity in human resources and realized that I had some background and knowledge in that area. I eventually took the HR position and was very glad that I did.

• **Believe in Yourself:** This is not always easy, because doubt and lack of self-confidence are constantly working against you and trying to creep into your head. Don't allow it. Stay focused on your routine and plan.

• **Stay Busy:** When you are not working on your plan, look for projects at home or opportunities to help someone else to take up the extra time during the day. Idle time is a killer and will put you in a down, lazy or non-productive mood.

Eventually you will be successful and find productive employment.

SALUTE
by Gary Greenfield

In the final analysis, life rewards us on the basis of whether we were ready when opportunity came. To achieve all that we can be, we must invest our time in this life proacting rather than reacting. By proacting, I mean we must constantly strive to get ahead in the game, so that when opportunity appears we can push the start button and pounce with gusto from the depths of our souls.

So, it was with soul-searching gusto that I pounced on my military opportunity when I was 19 years old. In reality, though, I was reacting rather than proacting. As it turned out, the pride I felt at what happened to me during my six months on active duty in the Army reserves is still with me to this day. The experience was the cornerstone to a more confident and assured me. It helped me begin to improve my self-image and confirmed that I could do anything I really made up my mind to do. As a result of my Army reserve experience, I have been more proactive when dealing with my challenges ever since. The story that follows gives some insight into why the aforementioned results occurred.

I don't remember the exact date of my departure from my hometown to report for basic training, but I know it was near the end of July 1963. I do remember exactly how I left, though. It was on an airplane. My first flight! I was exhilarated and frightened at the same time. I knew nothing about traveling by air, and getting from Billings, Montana, to San Francisco, California, was not a direct flight. There was at least one plane change and a long layover between the two cities. As the sun was setting over the Golden Gate Bridge, I finally arrived at San Francisco International Airport.

Next stop, a military transport bus for the ride to Ft. Ord, located just south of Monterey. It was about 100 miles to the fort, and I don't think the bus could go any faster than 45 miles per hour. It was a long ride at the end of a long day in less than economy-class accommodations. I am not sure what the stuffing was in the seats, but I can confirm it wasn't soft. Frankly, I have had better rides on my horse in Montana!

Finally, the bus arrived at what was referred to as Reception Station at the fort. Nice name – not a warm reception! Immediately, life changed from the relative peace of Montana civilian life to a life directed by the cracking commands of an Army drill sergeant. I must say those commands did give one a sense of urgency. Not that I understood how to follow orders like: "Fall in!" "Attention!" "Left face!" "Right face!" "About face!" "Forward, march!" "Detail, halt!" Who knew what they really meant? I had never been in the military before! I didn't understand the language! Immediately, I began to react as best I could and go with the flow, so to speak.

I'll never know how I ever got to my barracks after being herded off the bus that night, but I did. It was the first night of what was to be almost a week of processing into the Army life. I can't say it was a good night for sleep. Besides being cooped up with approximately 40 other guys in the cramped, noisy quarters of a World War II-era barracks, the anxiety of the unknown got my mental wheels spinning. The shock of actually being in the Army hit me in the gut. I was here! There was no turning back! It was an interesting feeling having to be totally committed rather than following the more flexible approach I had taken in my civilian life.

At the time, Ft. Ord was home to more than 50,000 U.S. Army personnel, most of whom were going through their basic training experience. It was a huge installation made up of the main post area that included barracks, motor pool facilities, Post Exchange (PX, for you ex-military types), various administrative facilities and thousands of acres of coastal countryside in which the combat training took place. It was a little overwhelming at first for a kid from Montana who had only been out of his immediate region once.

The next few days were devoted to all that goes into becoming a private in the United States Army. The days began with reveille (and the scream of a drill sergeant) at 5:00 a.m. and it was lights-out at 9:00 p.m. Sound a little early for both ends of a day? Trust me – with what went on between those times each day, 9:00 p.m. couldn't come early enough. And with what was to come, my time in Reception Station was the easy part!

There were a myriad of details attendant to becoming a private in the army. One of the first of those details was being issued all the items of military gear required, from fatigues to weaponry. It was an assembly-line process for each aspect of the issuance of our gear. There was a line of hundreds of recruits moving through the process and exiting the other end of the supply area with what felt like 500 pounds of clothing and equipment.

Even though there was a mass of confused recruits, it seemed that each was receiving individual guidance through the process with the understanding, direction and coaching of a very assertive drill sergeant! The experience could not be compared to being fitted for a full wardrobe in a fine men's clothing boutique.

Then, there was the pleasure of learning how to stow the equipment in one's wall and footlockers. Folding my clothes example, had to be folded so that the owner's name appeared on the front edge of the fatigue shirt. Then, the collection of shirts had to be neatly stacked in absolute alignment inside one's wall locker. Every item had its own required folding format and location for storage. Imperfect folding, alignment and stowage resulted in disciplinary action. And so, the initial lessons of military discipline began to be learned. They weren't easy, but one did learn quickly!

Another big event in Reception Station involved the medical aspects of being indoctrinated into the Army. This was not a kinder, gentler version of a consultation with one's private doctor. Oh no! This was strip-down, get in line with hundreds of other recruits, while trying to grin and bear the poking, prodding and general indignities of the military version of a total medical and dental check-up. It seemed to me, as suggested by the rough manner of the medical personnel involved, that they were under duress and very much annoyed at not living the civilian version of their chosen professions.

Finally, the big day came. All of the processing that was done while in the Reception Station was over. The hundreds of guys I had been with since arriving at Ft. Ord a week earlier were rounded up and given orders for their assignment to a basic training unit. These units would be home for the next eight weeks, otherwise known as the living hell of basic training! On that day, I was assigned to 2nd Platoon, Company A, 5th Battalion, 3rd Brigade. Staff Sergeant Jerry Pyles was the platoon sergeant.

Sergeant Pyles was a stoutly built man of approximately 5 feet 7 inches and probably weighed about 190 pounds. He was powerful. His arms were the size of cannon barrels, and his thighs would rival those of an elephant. He had the physical presence of a pit bull! His face was round and seemed to be constantly flushed with emotion. His eyes were a piercing, dancing, explosive, icy blue. His personality was just as powerful as his physical presence. For me, he had all the attributes of a leader. He was tough, demanding, expectant, unwavering, unapologetic, organized, caring, inspirational and knew how to get the most out of the men in his platoon. It's easy to say, but in the depths of my soul I know if we had ever gone to war together, I would have died for him. Sergeant Pyles became one of my heroes. He also became one of my mentors and helped me push the "restart button" to my life after a very rocky childhood.

The military works as a social structure for a number of reasons, not the least of which is its dedication to the chain of command. It was the existence of that chain of command that allowed me the opportunity for the first serious recognition of my potential leadership qualities.

With each cycle of putting new recruits through basic training, a platoon sergeant is challenged to get his people organized into a cohesive, performing group as quickly as possible. The challenges of basic training can be life-threatening under the best of circumstances, but even more so if discipline is not quickly established and maintained through the chain of command. That means a platoon sergeant needs help managing the 40 to 50 people in his platoon. The help comes in the form of dividing the platoon into four squads, then naming a leader of each, who is directly accountable to the platoon sergeant for the performance of the people in his squad.

Sergeant Pyles chose me as one of his four squad leaders. I remember the event as if it were yesterday.

Within a few days of being assigned to the platoon, I was ordered to Sergeant Pyles' office without any explanation. I had great anxiety about that order. I couldn't imagine what I had done wrong! The rest of the guys in the barracks, who had heard the order for me to report, were brutal with their suggestions of how much trouble I must be in. They took great glee in conjuring up all kinds of horror stories as to what was about to happen to me.

There's an old cliché in the military that states, "Never volunteer for anything." It was better if one could remain figuratively invisible in the Army – just do your job and keep your nose clean and everything would probably work out fine. It was hard to remain invisible when called, individually, to the sergeant's office! It was worse if one didn't respond to a direct order, so off I went to see the sergeant.

There I was, standing at attention in front of the sergeant's desk. He was superbly military-like, sitting behind his desk with his fatigues starched so that even if he wanted to slouch, they would hold him in an erect, military bearing. Both of his elbows were resting on the edge of his desk, and his hands were clasped together in front of him. His explosive blue eyes blew through me like I wasn't even standing there. His few words are etched in the archives of my mind: "Private Greenfield, I have selected you as squad leader of the 1st Squad. Are you up to the challenge?"

Stunned doesn't even begin to express my state of mind in that moment. Through the fog created by his words wafting around in my head, I heard myself say, "Yes, Sergeant!" His next words were, "Congratulations, Corporal Greenfield. Dismissed!"

It was not a time to ponder what had just happened and get into a discussion with the sergeant. I did a crisp about-face and marched out of his office. At least I think I marched out. I was so filled with elation and a sense of pride at having been selected that my feet might have not even touched the floor as I exited. Me – a squad leader! My, my! I couldn't even get elected by my classmates as school hall patrolman when I was a kid.

Interestingly enough, of the four squad leaders Sergeant Pyles chose, I was the only person who did not have a college degree. At 19, I was also the youngest. I guess the sergeant liked my appearance, neatness, discipline, alertness or something. It was never really clear why he chose me but I knew I wanted to be a leader, so I was glad he made the choice. There wasn't time to ponder the reasons because the pressure of the responsibility was immediate.

Besides myself, there were 11 other guys in my squad for whom and to whom I was responsible. It was a tough learning experience for a farm boy from Montana, but learn I did and quickly. I had to – those 11 guys were depending on me to do the right thing by them in carrying out whatever orders we were given. Those orders could include everything from cleaning the latrines to crawling under barbed wire with live machine-gun fire during combat training exercises.

My squad, along with the other three, contributed to the bigger picture of our platoon earning the distinction of being named Honor Platoon for each of the entire eight weeks of basic training. My squad had to contribute its share to that distinction, and they did. The whole platoon was a model of discipline, dedication, competence, team spirit, desire and toughness. The people in the 2nd Platoon, Company A, 5th Battalion, 3rd Brigade were awesome! I still consider it a privilege to have been a part of that group.

However, mine was not a military experience destined to be filled with the glory of being a combat infantryman. All the psychological and academic testing done directed me toward a different Military Occupational Specialty (MOS). For me it would be Personnel Administrative Specialist School following basic infantry training. It was an eight-week course of study covering a myriad of administrative processes, forms and regulations, among other things.

Following the grind and sometimes terror of basic infantry training, studying to be an administrative specialist was an easy "about face" in my military life. Yes, I was still in the military and had to follow the rules and regulations. However, the hardest thing I had to do all day was trying to type 50 words per minute during typing class. While I was filled with pride for having successfully completed the relative misery of the basic training experience, I enjoyed the comforts of being in class all day; sleeping in a barracks every night and out of the weather elements; and the wonder of having three square meals in the mess hall each day.

So, the eight weeks of Personnel Administrative Specialist School flew by, and then came graduation day. It was a day that was supposed to be dedicated to recognition for a job well done and then receiving orders for our next assignment. As it turned out, it was a day the heart of our nation temporarily stopped beating. It was November 22, 1963, and at almost precisely the moment that we were to march from our barracks to the site of the graduation exercise, word came that President John Fitzgerald Kennedy had been assassinated. Everything stopped – all activities for the day were cancelled.

The next day, tens of thousands of troops were gathered on a massive parade ground in a bone-chilling rain. In an hours-long ceremony, the thousands of us went through the various procedures of a solemn parade to honor our dead Commander-in-Chief. For me, I went from the exhilaration of a successful basic infantry training experience, to the comfort and ease of Personnel Administrative Specialist School, to the deep, gut-wrenching sorrow of hearing taps played for my fallen President – what a rollercoaster of emotions.

My active duty experience in the Army would ultimately prove to be a huge cornerstone for the rest of my life. The fact was, I had always known I needed to be a leader; to have people look to me for direction and counsel; to receive the psychic income of leadership; to take control rather than be controlled; to be the one ultimately responsible for the results of the group. I had always known I needed to feel like I was growing, rather than stagnating. All of these needs were met in the active duty military experience that I had.

The experience also confirmed that I had courage. It proved I could organize people to get a job done on a timely and correct basis. The Army proved to me that I could use my ability to take effective instructions and transfer those to other people. It proved that I could earn the respect of older, more educated and more sophisticated people. It proved I had an unusual amount of raw, natural leadership ability that several people recognized.

One of those people was my last active duty commanding officer, who asked me to consider going to Officer Candidate School. I had other plans. My time at Ft. Ord had given me a clearer sense that I was better off proacting rather than reacting. I was honorably discharged from active duty in January 1964.

Chapter Three

Let There Be Light

"Each of us has an essence worthy of sharing. A light deserving an 'ON' switch. Turn yours on every day. Let the world be lit BY YOU!"
– Bob Danzig

The stories in this chapter explore relationships, parenting, aging, health challenges, renewal, transformation and inner strength. All testaments to our innate ability to stay open, embrace change, persevere and push forward to a brighter tomorrow.

They bring to mind the ten most powerful two-letter words, passed on to me by the gifted author and speaker, Og Mandino, "If it is to be, it is up to me."

LIVE IN THE MOMENT
by Hilda Zoldan

A former co-worker and dear man asked me to write something about my new experience of no longer being part
of the work force.

I had been working for 26 years for this great company.
For a number of years, I was in one position, but then there
was a major move in the company, and I ended up working
in a few different departments over the years. I enjoyed what
I did and the people I worked with.

For the past few years though, the work environment had
changed. My job was no longer fun but a grind that I had
to do daily like millions of other people. Even though I was
unhappy, I wasn't ready to throw in the towel. I thought about
it, but it was just too scary for me. What would I do with myself if I left my job? Since I was so close to retirement age,
looking for a new job did not appeal to me. Yet, I also felt I
was wasting my days and my life.

The decision was taken out of my hands. One fine day I
was told that my job was eliminated. I felt many things at that
moment. I felt shock and yes, excitement. But mostly, I felt
that I was given a new lease in life. As a religious woman, I
believed that a higher power was guiding my life and I would
only be there as long as He wanted me to.

I was excited and happy for the first two weeks. No more
getting up at the crack of dawn to the shriek of the alarm clock.
I was free to do whatever I wanted, whenever I wanted. But
then I felt real grief for the people I no longer saw and the set
routine I no longer had. What would I do with all this time?

I refused to follow that route. I found Bible classes I was interested in and forced myself to go for an exercise walk every day. But what I think I am really learning to do is to "live in the moment." When I am taking my walks, I think about how blessed I am to be able to walk and breathe on my own. I look at the beautiful trees and enjoy the movement of my body. When I'm in my classes, I think I am learning and growing as a person, not stagnating and becoming an old person. Heaven forbid!

It is my belief, no matter what faith you are, that everyday you have an opportunity to become more than you were the day before. Now that I am no longer constrained by a 9 to 5 job, I can be or do anything I want.

ADOPTING DAISY, THE YELLOW LAB
by Conna Craig

Each friend represents a world in us, a world not born until they arrive, and it is only by this meeting that a new world is born.
 — Anaïs Nin

Who knew that a yellow lab could change everything? I had never thought of myself as a "dog person." As a child, I had a turtle – and that seemed just right because, like a turtle, I tend to pace myself, slow and steady. For most of my life, I have been happiest in my own shell. When circumstances brought me into a crowd or onto a stage, I craved returning to somewhere peaceful, alone. So many days of my life have been quiet days: working, studying, writing. Being alone was what I knew, and it was pleasant because in that solitude I found my energy and my focus.

I had no idea what I was missing.

If someone had asked me a few years ago if I could see myself in an entirely different way – putting a morning walk with a curious dog at the top of the list of things I treasure – I could not have imagined it.

Then I met Daisy, the yellow lab.

Before Daisy, I had convinced myself that there was never enough time. I felt that time was slipping away, that I should be so much more far along in my life by now, that I would never "catch up" with everything I wanted to accomplish. At the end of each day I felt a bit defeated. Every morning, I awoke with the sense of already being behind.

Now, there is always time. Daisy knows a few things about time; she knows play time, nap time and snack time. She may not understand what is happening on the evening news, but she knows that after the news it's dinner time. There is time to give Daisy a hug or a treat or a tummy rub. There is time to praise her and pet her and find her lost toys. There is time, when it takes her 20 minutes to get into the car, to wait for her.

Letting go of my ideas about time, I am learning patience.

On our walks, Daisy stops to smell *everything,* not just the roses. What most people would step over, she closely examines. If it has a scent, it's fair game. She doesn't seem to be in a hurry to get anywhere because it's the walking she loves – until she decides she has walked enough. Then she lies down, on the grass or the sidewalk or at the farmers' market, just under the "No Dogs Allowed" sign. She's 12 years old now, and sometimes she needs to gather her strength.

I am learning that age is relative.

I never knew Daisy when she was younger, but I have heard stories. For her first few years, she had two speeds – fast and faster. She ran nonstop, chewed on Lego pieces, ate rocks and barely graduated from obedience school. Now, she looks on as other dogs run past us at the dog park. She runs for her ball, but after a few throws she is ready to lie down for a rest. People ask me, "Is she old?" and I say, "She's Daisy, she's happy. She's 12."

Daisy was 11 when I adopted her. My mom worried that it would hurt too much to "lose" Daisy. First, I told Mom that I wasn't planning to misplace my dog. But I know what Mom meant: Daisy is an older dog, and she won't live forever. But then, do any of us know how much time we have? Whether Daisy lives for six more months or six more years, she will be loved.

On our walks, when we turn the corner to the street where she can see the sand and smell the ocean, she becomes a puppy again. Her eyes light up, she smiles the sweetest yellow lab smile and seems to remember how to run like the wind. She jumps into the waves until the water gets too deep … then she looks up at me as if to say, "Can you help me out here?" I can't swim, but I have carried her in my arms from the pull of the ocean.

I remember, before Daisy, many trips to the sea. My dad and I would fish from a pier. I always waited for him to tell me something, to offer up some insights about the world and life. He did not say much. So I watched and took in every moment. Sometimes I'd take notes – even as a child I wanted to capture everything with words.

I am learning that words are not as important as I once believed.

Daisy knows a few words, like "food," "treat" and "good girl." I am not sure whether she understands the words or simply responds to the way I say them. I think her favorite word is "Daisy." Just like each of us, one of the first words she ever heard was her name. It's so important that it is consistently spoken with love.

Daisy moves through the world as if everyone she meets already loves her. She sits still when children ask to pet her – sometimes just one little tap on her head from a child meeting a dog for the first time. On Daisy's birthday we went to her favorite place: the post office. While we were there we met Jacob, who explained that he was waiting for a birthday too; he was 6 ¾ years old. Jacob asked if he could give Daisy a birthday present and then tied his friendship bracelet to her collar.

Not everyone is as friendly. Once, a woman at the beach kicked sand on Daisy and told her, "Go on, get away!"

Daisy just wagged her tail and smiled. I learned something, at that moment, about forgiveness. Sometimes letting go is the best option.

I would like to protect Daisy – from sand-kickers, from whatever it is about big waves that scares her, from pain and mostly from time. I think, though, that being present for her is just as important. As far as she can run into the sea, I will be there, just in case. When she needs extra time to muster the energy to jump into the car, I can wait. For of all the things she has taught me – to be patient, that age is relative, that words are not everything and about the power of forgiveness – the most important is mindfulness. Daisy lives in the moment. To me, that's what mindfulness is about.

One of my favorite authors Thich Nhat Hahn wrote, "When we are mindful, deeply in touch with the present moment, our understanding of what is going on deepens, and we begin to be filled with acceptance, joy, peace and love."

I learned, first-hand, about mindfulness from a dog named Daisy.

Sometimes, people observe her struggling a bit to jump, or run or even to walk. It's not uncommon for someone to ask, "Did you rescue her?"

My answer: "Daisy rescued me."

THE MOMENT I WOKE UP
by Kirsten L. Seymour

I was the ultimate "Party Girl." There wasn't a party I didn't attend, there wasn't a happy hour I didn't partake in and then keep going for many hours more. My house was always full of laughter and friends. My phone was always ringing with invites. I stayed many a weekend out with my faithful hound Chloe; my car was equipped with changes of clothes and a toothbrush (you can't forget about dental hygiene). My outfits weren't always put together sober, and my makeup consisted of Glitter with a capital G. I drank more calories than I ate; I smoked more than I drank; and there are some moments that I can say were not my proudest; some I don't even remember.

I always thought and hoped in the back of my mind that I would find someone to live out my days with, my soulmate, a good friend who I could love more than life itself. I dreamed of having children, but you wouldn't have thought so watching me, nor was I inviting it. I was living for the moment, and the moment better be fun. I was the stereotypical angry teenager with daddy issues, and I had built walls to protect myself that were not easy to penetrate. I was surrounded by people, but my true friends were few. I caused my poor mother more pain than I can ever take back. Luckily, she is still one of my biggest fans, strongest supporters and closest friends.

I think my "fresh start moment" would have to be the day at work that I found out I was pregnant. It was one of the scariest and happiest moments of my life. I rushed home, stick in hand, to tell my best friend. His car was in the driveway, but he was nowhere to be found, and there were about eight Polish men performing various tasks building our new addition. Each one stopped at the sight of the homeowner running around frantically waving a positive pregnancy test. Finally, Jake came home from getting gas for the lawn mower, and together we embarked on our first pregnancy.

Nine months later our Sadie Piper was born. A beautiful, healthy girl. She got a little stuck, and we had to do a C-section, but she was in my arms in no time at all. We had chosen not to find out the sex beforehand. Well, I chose, if I am honest; Jake would have loved to know. I always felt I had a mini me inside, but I was not prepared for how much I would fall head over heels for this precious human. Every wall I had built around me melted as I held her in my arms. Every angry feeling dissipated into thin air, as there was now no point to any of it. I had finally found what I was meant to do. I finally got it.

Sadie Piper taught me every day about love, patience and how to just sit and take in your surroundings. She was very quick to learn to walk and talk. I had this, and I had the love of a wonderful man, and on those days where sleep was non-existent or teeth were making baby cry, he was there to make me laugh, hug me and support me.

When Sadie was 8-months-old, we learned that we were pregnant with another child. This pregnancy had more issues, but all in all I was very lucky to have great pregnancies and my baby boy, Ryker Lewis, came into the world. I delivered him naturally and both my husband and my best friends were in the room with me. It was yet another life changing moment.

Sadie Piper will always be my first, and there is something you just can't quite explain about the sheer wonder of this human life you made, carried around and then delivered. Some day my second child, Ryker Lewis, will tower above me and have to stoop to kiss me. But he will always be my baby, no matter what.

So, as I now prepare to send my little girl off to school in the fall and watch my little boy climb everything and anything in his path, I take a deep breath and feel so very grateful.

Every night I get to go to bed, albeit exhausted, with a man that loves me for who I am and tells me it will be OK when it feels like the worst day ever. I get to sleep under a roof of my very own home with two happy, healthy, beautiful little humans that we made together. I also have my puppy, Buster, growing up in our house full of love.

We dance, we sing, we run and wrestle.... I still enjoy my invites, my parties, my nights out with friends and my nights in with friends. Although they are much less frequent, they are so much more cherished.

I was the ultimate "Party Girl." I had that life, and I did it well. Some may say a little too well, but I have a new life now. I am a Mum. It is the greatest gift in the world to me, and I am hoping a happy Mum makes happy kids. So far it seems to be working.

OLD HANDS
by Judy Allen

I woke up this morning with old hands. I didn't notice them as I straightened the bed or made my coffee and buttered the toast. They didn't call attention to themselves as I put the leash on the dog to go for a walk or rinsed the dishes and put them in the dishwasher. They went all morning doing all the ordinary things, being the same hands I have had all my life.

Then, in the early afternoon, I sat down with a book and a nice cup of tea. When I lifted the cup to my lips for my first sip, my world changed, as my hands brought attention to themselves. I abruptly placed the cup on the table and held my hands up to take a better look. "What's this?" I thought. "What is with the prominent veins and brown spots I can no longer call freckles? What about the thin, wrinkled skin on top while my palms are still soft and smooth, the square nails in need of a manicure? Where did I get these old hands?"

As I studied them in disappointment and horror, for they had changed so much, I began to see that they were my grandmother's hands. They were strong and capable and kind. Her hands bathed me as an infant and caressed my forehead when I was sick with fever. They made me chicken soup and cherry pie. They made dresses from print material, braided my hair with shining white bows and gave me hugs. I loved my grandmother's hands.

I looked some more and saw that they were my mother's hands. They drew me beautiful pictures for my room and tried to teach me the piano – quite unsuccessfully, but I got to watch her lovely hands on the keys. They strummed the guitar, made me paper dolls for my collections, wrote stories to read to me at night and tucked me securely under the soft covers with my tattered teddy bear. They petted animals, loved beauty and brought all this magic into my life. I adored my mother's hands.

As I looked at my own hands, which so recently seemed so old and ugly to me, I saw them through generations of work and giving. I began to smile. Through these generations and the things my own hands have done, which my children may remember with warmth, I see these hands not as old but as well-used and loved, and they make me happy.

PERSPECTIVE
by Dr. Dorothy Martin-Neville

When the last of our children leaves home to begin the next chapter in their lives, whether college, marriage, or even moving into their very own apartment, there can be a wild mix of emotions for everyone involved. Joy that they are now adults and ready to start the next stage in their journey, fear in not knowing if they're ready, and sadness in not knowing if we are ready for them to go, all combined with relief that now we are free. It's a freedom that we have, on occasion, longed for. Yet now that it is here, it can be hard to take in.

For me, it wasn't until after leaving my son at college and driving for six hours home to an empty house that I realized this was now officially my next chapter. I hadn't spent any time thinking of what I would do or where I would go before then. I opened up to whatever would feel right for me, but I had no clue.

Rather than keeping things basically the same with a few minor changes, I decided I needed a brand new way of life. A smaller house or apartment wasn't sufficient; I wanted to live in a new country. After an hour of thinking and planning, I called American Airlines and got a one-way ticket to Anguilla, British West Indies. I called a real estate agent and put my home on the market, and I notified my patients I would be leaving the country in three weeks. After a massive tag sale and donations to charity, I left the USA, and for 10 years I lived on a small island of 6,000 people and more goats than you can count.

I had a school I founded still thriving in Connecticut, so I came back to the states every two months for a week to teach adults integrative health care and to speak whenever requested. Most importantly, I had an opportunity to absolutely have a fresh start to my life in an environment that provided peace, laughter, warmth, water, dancing and a chance to rediscover the woman I once was, yet who had grown to become so much more. By moving so far away I was forced to find a new way of being, a new way of living my life and a new way of looking at how I fit in the world.

In the 10 years I stayed on Anguilla I learned of strengths I never knew I had. I realized I could be dropped anywhere, and I would be OK. I learned I could make friends, no matter where I ended up. I learned that I had an amazing ability to adapt as needed. I also learned that although I love my alone time, I needed people in my life. They challenged me. They called me to grow, and they taught me so much about the true values of life.

Starting fresh, starting over, starting a whole new approach to life meant the start of a new version of me. By taking such an unconventional route to the next stage of my life, I let go of any concept of the "right" way to do things. I realized that I would continue to grow until I return to God. I also clearly saw that everything in life is about perspective. Life is empty or full; it all depends upon perspective. I am rich or poor; it all depends upon perspective. I am old or young; again, it all depends upon perspective.

Finally, I learned without a doubt, that starting over opens up a whole new world and a whole new you with unlimited possibilities except for those that you choose. Because I risked, I have noticed so many others who are risking at this stage of life as well. Girlfriends packed up and moved to Florida with only what fits in their car. I've had friends who have moved across the country simply because they always wanted to. Others have left jobs they could now retire from to work at jobs they have always wanted to try.

Life is the adventure we wanted as kids and now get to live. We raised the kids, now it's our time. What a blessed time of life if you allow yourself to be open to new adventures and especially new beginnings.

A FRESH START ... AT 50?
by Felice M. Dawson Hamilton

"You could never make me happy!" were the words I heard come from my husband's mouth. We had been having a strained relationship for a couple of years and had basically drifted apart. Neither of us had the energy to "try again," but neither of us wanted to be the first to walk away.

By all appearances, we had a good life together. A nice home, empty nest (he had five children, I had one, but we had none together), upper middle class and a good reputation in the community. But we were miserable. I had stopped communicating with him because I did not know how. I had been raised with the words, "If you don't have anything nice to say, don't say anything at all." Most of the time, I did not feel like saying "anything nice." So I suffered in silence.

He said I had changed from the person he married eight years ago. Maybe I had; all I know is I wanted peace and wanted to feel happy again. The more he pushed me to "change back," the more I pulled away.

Finally, after the individual and couples counseling, prayer, advice from friends and others and everything else we could think of, one November morning he posted a "For Sale by Owner" sign in the front yard.

I asked myself so many questions as I left the house for work and saw the sign for the first time. How does a 50-something-year-old person just start again? Was this what I really wanted? What would my family (or his family) say? How would this affect my professional life? Where am I going to live?

I thought about a scripture that said to, "Seek peace and pursue it." For me, that means peace is something to pursue at whatever cost. It's what everyone lives and longs for.

Our home sold before Christmas. Although my husband had been "going to file for divorce" since March, he had not done so. I asked him when he planned to file so I could plan where I would live when we closed on the sale of our home. He got very upset and started ranting about all the things he had to do and that I should do something. So while my husband was still talking, I texted my attorney and asked if he would file the divorce papers. The next day, New Year's Eve, the papers were filed, and I began to process what a "fresh start" would look like.

Three weeks later our divorce was final, our home sold and I was in a brand new home. For the first time in a long time, I understood what peace felt like. It was incredible!

It's not about what you have or don't have. It's about how you feel about your situation. I knew it was time to move on but was afraid of what that meant or how OTHERS would react. I could have focused on the fact that I would be single again, have one income, be socially ostracized and would be alone. Instead, I was excited about being single and making my own choices, having a handle on my finances, going where and when I wanted to and being alone!

My life makes so much sense now. It's not always about pleasing others. It's about being able to make choices I am responsible for. Wrong or right, it's my choice and I have to live with it. Each day I wake up with my finger on the start button and say "Lord, thank you for another opportunity to start again. It's just You and me so let's go!"

I have a joy I've never experienced before. It's a joy learning about who I am each day. It's a joy knowing there is so much more to conquer, and if I choose to go after it, I can.

If I choose not to, that's okay too. I've learned that no matter what I do, as long as I have given it my all, I am happy with the results.

So though it's not perfect, it's my life and I live here!

DARK TO LIGHT
by Charles H. Green

Not all "fresh start moments" look fresh at the moment they start. At least, not all of mine.

It was December 26th, the day after Christmas, when my wife informed me that we were getting a divorce. I was completely shocked.

Yes, she had been complaining that I paid her no attention, that I was neglecting the family, that I drank too much. I had even gotten a phone call from a woman telling me that her husband and my wife were having an affair. But this? Overwhelming. Completely unexpected.

I drove around aimlessly. I left town for a few days to visit an old friend. I called several other friends for advice. In those first few days, I felt like a horror was closing in on me.

Even then, a friend's advice cut through the haze and I was able to hear it. "You won't believe me now," he said, "In fact, you have no reason to. I didn't believe it when it was told to me, either. But I'll tell you anyway. One year from now, your life will be far better. In fact, it will look better than you could have imagined. You will look back on this moment as the time the tide turned, and you may even be grateful for it."

He was right – I didn't believe it. But I did hear it and remember it. And he was right about the big picture. Life did get immeasurably better. When I look back at that moment, I realize it had everything to do with getting better.

I quit drinking. She was right about that. In fact, she was right about pretty much everything. It was just that I couldn't/

wouldn't see it. But it's not about who was right. It's about a moment of choice.

As I see it now, when relationships go wrong you've got three choices. One is, you can choose to continue living miserably, denying that you have a choice at all. That would be the wrong choice. Of course, it's the one I had been choosing all along.

That left the other two choices: Either to leave or accept that everything needs changing. Both of them, fresh starts. In my case, my wife made the decision for me – it was leave (hey, somebody had to make a decision). And for us, it was the right call. Neither of us regrets it, and each of us has done very well.

The thing is, very few of us get up in the morning and say, "You know, what the heck, I think I'll just change everything in my life today." We don't get to that fresh start moment without some travail along the way. Maybe we can't recognize what it looks like without some stale, rotting history to compare it to.

If you are lucky, it may smack you in the head (though if you're like me, you may not recognize it at first). But if you would like to make your own luck, you can. Just remember, the opposite of a fresh start moment is not a bad-ending moment – it's the continued refusal to recognize that things can be better, if only we're willing to choose.

RENEWED UNDERSTANDING
by Gail Field

My husband Marty stood by the window in the living room, shifting his feet and looking at me. His voice came out in low squeaks. "I just can't go around pretending to be something I'm not."

"What do you mean?"

"I don't want to live the heterosexual lifestyle anymore. In fact, I can't do it."

I couldn't comprehend what he was saying. "You have to tell me more than that."

Marty's square jaw set itself, the muscles beneath his beard tightening, his breath shallow. He looked away from me; his eyes glazed over.

"What's happening? What changed?"

He looked back at me. "I met someone."

When our marriage failed, I struggled to find my place in the world. We had been a close-knit couple for five years of marriage. We held dinner parties and discussion groups in our home. Trips to the Grand Canyon, to Acapulco, and local parks and playgrounds opened our eyes to new vistas. We welcomed our beautiful newborn son, Glenn, and showed him off to our relatives. I knew who I was with Marty; who was I without him?

I had always thought love was the answer – that with love everything would turn out all right. I loved Marty and he loved me. That didn't change his decision.

I needed to rethink everything. For as long as I could remember, I had been a "people pleaser," always trying to be accommodating – putting other people's needs before my own – wanting approval wherever I went. If I didn't succeed, I was filled with anxiety, which was now compounded by the shock I was feeling. I couldn't think clearly. I was distracted and filled with tears and regret.

My husband took our son to live with him. He said he and his new partner would take care of Glenn so I could get a job, and Glenn could come to my house on weekends. I felt powerless and was too scared to protest. I thought that eventually I would make enough money to support myself without having to rely on Marty, so I agreed. We split the proceeds from the sale of our house, so I had a cushion, but I needed a steady income.

Weekends with Glenn brought great happiness to my otherwise stressful situation. He and I were soul mates—he at age 5 and me at age 30. We went to the local library together, built model ships, took weekend trips to the zoo and visited museums in town.

During the week I focused on my work, trying to find a career. My first job at a department store, wrapping Christmas gifts, held me over until I could find permanent work. At the end of the Christmas season that same store hired me as a personnel clerk. I discovered I liked the corporate environment, finding solutions to problems and meeting business challenges. I developed professionally and grew into responsible positions in human resources, but something was missing.

I was good at dealing with people, but there was a lot of politicking among my bosses. I wasn't savvy or assertive enough to know how to handle it. I couldn't reconcile my admiration for my employer with the scorn with which she treated me. Whatever I did was not enough. My people-pleasing self was stressed to the limit, and I began to sense that the problem might be mine.

One day I saw a notice in the local newspaper for a class: Love Shuts Out Fear. I attended the meetings at the local church and started to connect to deeper parts of myself. In doing so, I realized I had been blaming others for my own failures. I came to understand that we each have a spark of the Divine within us. That recognition helped me develop a more loving relationship with myself. With this growing awareness, I began to feel more confident and needed less approval from others. I learned to trust that Divine spark and could sense what was right for me. My life became more peaceful.

I went on to have a successful career consulting with intelligent clients at high levels of a large organization. My relationship with my son was loving and mutually rewarding, and I appreciated heartfelt connections with friends from all walks of life.

With renewed understanding, I finally found what had been missing. A life partner – a man who made my heart sing and with whom I could share my spiritual life as well as my everyday life. Together we celebrate a love that is constant and enriching.

In spite of the initial turmoil, my husband Marty and I remained close friends. When he passed away just a few years ago, I was present at his bedside. As the priest performed the last rites, he said, "We thank God for this life and for the blessings of love."

The greatest gift of all is to know a Presence greater than our individual lives, to know that we are indeed loved and that we have a great capacity to love others if we only tap into it. This all-encompassing love allows life to be joyful, no matter what.

Love really is the answer.

A GIFT BETWEEN THE LINES
by Leslie Ryan

My late husband, Mark, has been a gift to me both in life and in death. He was a brilliant, insightful and wonderful man. I was blessed beyond measure to have had him as my best friend, my husband and the father of our two amazing sons. He was loving, kind and compassionate. No matter your transgression, he would forgive you immediately.

Because Mark was so bright, doing any single thing required a much smaller portion of his attention. Therefore, he would often do many things at once. It was his habit to doodle, write intriguing questions, make lists, and copy his favorite prayer and quote while he watched TV.

Lord, make me an instrument of Your peace. Where there is hatred, let me sow love; where there is injury, pardon; where there is doubt, faith; where there is despair, hope; where there is darkness, light; where there is sadness, joy.

O, Divine Master, grant that I may not so much seek to be consoled as to console; to be understood as to understand; to be loved as to love. For it is in giving that we receive; it is in pardoning that we are pardoned; it is in dying that we are born again to eternal life. – Saint Francis of Assisi

When you visualized a man or a woman carefully, you could always begin to feel pity ... that was a quality God's image carried with it ... when you saw the lines at the corners of the eyes, the shape of the mouth, how the hair grew, it was impossible to hate. Hate was just a failure of imagination. – Graham Greene

Mark told me that of all the prayers and all the books that he had ever read, these two pieces of writing had made the strongest impressions on him. It did not surprise me that he had chosen the prayer of Saint Francis of Assisi. It was my favorite prayer as well, but his selection of the Graham Greene quote mystified me. Being an avid reader, he had read every classic literary work in existence. Surely, I thought, he could have found a more poetic and profound passage with which to be enamored.

Somehow he knew that one day I would recognize its importance in my own evolution. Whenever I forgot about the quote, I would find yet another copy of it that he had left for our family.

It has been 10 years since he graced this world with his presence. Since then, my journey of healing, revelation and self-discovery has dramatically changed my world view. My experience has motivated me to find ways to expedite the grieving process for others, and to this end, I have been collecting insights that I believe will prove helpful.

I knew that there was something missing from my own healing process, so I asked God to give me a definitive sign about whether or not Graham Greene's quote had anything to do with this missing piece. I picked up a novel that I had not yet begun to read. I opened it up to a random page, and there, under my thumb, was the very same Graham Greene quote from *The Power and the Glory* that Mark had left for us.

I had never seen that passage cited in any other book that I had read up until that point. The chances of my opening to a page that contained that specific quotation were infinitesimal. Clearly, there was a message in it for me, but it took me a while to decipher its meaning.

Following Mark's death, I cared for my father for a few years until his passing. Though I did not regret this choice,

I was nonetheless disappointed that I had not yet embarked on a new career. My perspective and beliefs had changed so dramatically over the last few years that I wasn't sure where I belonged. Though I was eager to put my keen new insights to work, I was unsure how best to do so. I had always been very proactive before Mark's death, but losing him marked a turning point for me in a myriad of ways. Since that time, I have been constantly castigating myself for not getting back into my former proactive modus operandi.

Prior to losing my husband, like most people, I had been so busy taking care of my family and working that I had spent little time on self-reflection. After reflecting, my standards for how I wanted to spend my remaining time were raised along with my consciousness.

This made the prospect of finding an appropriate career more daunting, especially since I had been out of the workforce for so long. I was angry with myself for wanting more in a career, precisely when my position dictated that my expectations should be dramatically lower, not higher. Once again, I chastised myself for not being more pragmatic and for not doing everything sooner.

One night, I asked God to help me understand why Mark had chosen to leave these specific words of wisdom as his literary legacy. That night, I dreamt that Mark came to pick me up. As we drove off, it was clear that there was a rift between us. Although I had no idea what had caused it, his demeanor indicated that it was probably my fault. I was not the least bit worried, however, because I knew whatever it was – we would forgive one another. I'd kiss him, and all would be right with the world again. I had absolute confidence that there was nothing that could break our bond. His sweetness always made forgiving him easy, and I was certain that he would forgive me instantly, even if I were unable to forgive myself.

The dream reminded me that I have always found it easier to forgive others than to forgive myself, and that it has never been easy for me to accept my own shortcomings. Mark had no trouble forgiving anyone, including himself. Unlike me, he understood that our inadequacies and failures provide us with obstacles and challenges that focus our efforts, strengthen our characters and offer us the greatest opportunities for personal growth. He knew that our weaknesses are gifts just as surely as our strengths are. They open our hearts to compassion and empathy, and they are the source of our humility and understanding. They are what make us human, and without them, we would find it impossible to love one another. Like Narcissus, we would believe that no other could compare to our own divine perfection. Then it hit me – both the prayer and the quote are about duality – about humanity and divinity – and ultimately, about the divinity *in* humanity.

Accepting this wisdom at all my levels of consciousness has been a giant step forward for me. Embracing both my talents *and* my deficiencies as divine gifts has enabled me to forgive and love myself in my totality. I am now able to love myself, not *in spite* of my imperfections but *because* of them.

This was the gift that Mark had tried to impart in life and succeeded in relaying in death. It is indeed ironic that our own imperfections, which make it possible for us to love and forgive others, often prevent us from loving and forgiving ourselves.

SOME FINALS BECOME STARTS – A GIFT FROM MOM
by Eileen McDargh

Sometimes, a "fresh start moment" is not obvious until it has passed – until the reflective memory becomes potent with meaning. Such was the gift Mother gave to me in January 2012.

At the age of almost 96 and on hospice, Mom moved up and down like a rollercoaster. We called her Yo-Yo Ma, one of our ways of staying sane when our hearts were so heavy. That yo-yo behavior prompted my sister and me to agree that I could go on my annual New Year's retreat at a center about three hours away.

That morning she would not open her eyes or acknowledge I was there. But in the afternoon, when I returned to see her before heading out of town, her little blue eyes were bright and she said, "I'm hungry. Let's go eat. I'll buy!"

"Wow, Mom. Okay, what would you like?"

"Food. To get out of here."

"Okay Mom. I am on it."

I asked our care manager to get the print menu from the assisted living dining room. Mom was totally paralyzed on her left side, and unless I had a van with a wheelchair lift, Mom was going nowhere. The benefit of Alzheimer's was that she couldn't remember any of this.

"So, Mom, while we are waiting for a menu, let me tell you about where I am going."

She snuggled down, closed her eyes and listened as I described The Center for Spiritual Renewal in Santa Barbara and the old house where I would go on retreat for a few days.

She then blurted out, "Okay, I'll go with you. Let's be daring. Let's have an adventure."

I blinked hard to keep tears from spilling down my face. Indeed, this is the legacy that Mom always intended to leave us: to have an adventure, to be daring. It's what called her to med school when there were only three other women attending. It's what called her to hop in a plane and fly with the Women's Air Force Service Pilots during WW II. It's the same daring that could turn the howling wind of a hurricane into an adventure as we gathered in the center of the house, far away from the picture windows and told stories by candlelight. It's the same daring that helped her pick up the remnants of her life and re-enter the job market in her mid-50s. And it's the same spirit that propelled us to drive her across Ireland, taking back roads and having no destination other than where the wind blew.

"Do you know where the restaurant is?" she asked.

"I do, Mom. Let's get some clothes on you and get you into your chair. We'll head out to the Bistro."

When we went through the locked doors, it didn't register to Mom that we had not left the building but rather gone over to an alcove with three tables and a little bar-type setting.

"Great," said Mom, "We're at the bar."

She looked around and marveled that there were no people in the "restaurant." She didn't hesitate or question the two teaspoons she ate of Bill's soup or the tiny bite of peanut butter and strawberry jelly on a sliver of toast.

"Mom, thanks for taking me to lunch. Shall we split some ice cream for dessert? Susan will be along shortly and join us."

Our wonderful care manager made vanilla ice cream appear as if by magic, and Mom ate a few spoons with relish.

My sister Susan was coming to take my place so I could leave. I had called and given her a heads up that we were "dining out."

Susan appeared as if on cue, and I reached down to hug Mom.

"Do you have my wallet?" asked Mom.

"Indeed, I do, Mom. I will pay the hostess when I go out. Thanks again for lunch, Mom. It was great!"

I left with her happily looking at my sister, as Mom used her one good hand to offer Susan ice cream. It was great. It was grand. For Mom, getting out of bed and eating was daring, even if she didn't know it.

Two days later, I raced back. With my twin brother, John, and my sister Susan, we kept vigil, praying and letting go.

The pain of loss and grief held me tight for months – until one night I dreamt of our last full conversation. Mom had indeed given me the green light, waved the flag for my departure, demanding a fresh start. "Let's be daring. Let's have an adventure."

"Got it Mom. I'm on it."

AUTOBIOGRAPHY OF MY SPIRIT
by Colleen McKenney Lehr

As a child, I longed to be an artist. Finally, I earned a fine arts degree. Then the universe threw me a curve ball in the guise of breast cancer, while offering me a different career option. My spirit offered me a path that has been about the willingness to hold hope, hearts and hands in this journey we are all on. My journey has been about reaching out to others in times of turmoil and trouble and reaching back when offered help in my personal times of trial. My spirit has taught me the importance of reciprocation.

One gift of age is that of understanding the importance of balance. I have been offered the gift of acting as a catalyst in the lives of many, a rich and meaning-filled spiritual experience that has fed my soul.

Yet, in recent months my spirit has been sorely tried. The death of my husband and then of my teenaged grandson have challenged my equilibrium. Added to this is the helplessness of being unable to change the suffering of my family. The emotional weight has been daunting. This is a time of challenge. How to get through each day became the initial focus. Emotions swirled, and when it all seemed too much, angels appeared.

They looked like people, but they were most definitely angels shining a light that was so sorely needed. Family, friends, neighbors, ministers, even strangers reached out so that my family and I were not isolated. They called from afar. They came in groups and alone and stayed to offer hearts and hands. They came with food, drink, a prayer shawl, hugs and caring. They were emotionally present and willing to sit with the pain. Generosity of spirit surrounded my family and sustained us.

As time passes, precious relationships formed through the years have been a stabilizing force. There have been acts of kindness that I did not know were needed. There were so many unexpected lights in that darkest time of life. There is a miracle in the love and caring offered without reservation. These friends, these angels, these lights, gave and continue to give more than I will ever deserve, and I receive the gifts of caring with deep gratitude.

I am slowly adjusting to a new normal, in a new place and surrounded by angels who reach out and offer hope, like a bright light in the darkness. For now, each day I take time to focus on and record in my journal the goodness and kindness that is integrated into my life. Change is a constant, and leaning into the change is beginning to move me in a new direction.

Gratitude and grace are present all around, and love is the gift I carry from those who have gone sooner than I would have chosen. Pain is the price of love and attachment, and it is a price worth paying. Living in this day and this moment is a gift. The power of caring cannot be measured; yet it is the magic ingredient that makes all the difference. I could not have made it through the darkest days alone. The lesson in all of our stories is that we need each other.

The stories I carry in my own heart have become a beacon of hope for the future. Living beyond tragedy is a skill others have demonstrated, and those are the stories from which my spirit is gathering strength. As I move toward life's next lessons and ride the swelling waves of change, the road to healing is being woven under my feet.

A LIFE TRANSFORMED
by Norma Locker, Msc.D.

Sometimes it takes a flash of insight spawned by a frightening event to effect a miraculous transformation in a
tormented life. Prior to 1965 I was a hopeless, mean-spirited,
neurotic hypochondriac with myriad medical complaints.
I had never thought to seek the solace of prayer because
although I was born a Jew, my upbringing was more secular
than observant. The only God I knew of was the one who
would punish me if I was a bad girl.

In 1964 my husband, Charlie, and I purchased a large,
old, two-family house in which the ground floor flat was
already rented. We decided to modernize and renovate the
two upstairs spaces for our living quarters, after which there
was a series of calamities that ensued as a result of contractor
corruption. It's a very long story that is detailed in my book,
*The Miracle Years: What I Learned about God, Miracles, Life,
the Paranormal and Why We Are Here.* However, the outcome
was that Charlie, my "Rock of Gibraltar," became completely
overwhelmed by business pressures, all of the unforeseen ca-
tastrophes, and my meticulous demands for detail, relentless
nagging and complaining. This capable, energetic man for
whom no challenge was ever too great – a perfectionist who
took pride in his incredible skills, just gave up and retreated
to our bed, refusing help of any kind.

Each night as he turned his back on me with recrimina-
tion in his heart, I cried myself to a fitful sleep, praying to
God for the first time in my life from the depths of my soul
to bring this man back to the living. Soon after, he arose and

inspected his disheveled image in the mirror. Sobbing un-
controllably, he asked, "What am I doing to myself and you
and the kids?" I held him close and convinced him to see our
family doctor, who prescribed a mild antidepressant, which
was successful within a few days.

Meanwhile, something profound and mystical had happened to me. I realized that I could pray and prayers were
answered by an invisible force known as God, which had the
power to implement the solution. In spite of all that had trans-
pired, I was filled with a joy, an inner exhilaration that I had
never before experienced. Wherever I moved, a light seemed
to follow me. It was more visible when I walked through our
long, dark foyer. Later I learned that I had become aware of
my own aura.

With my newfound enlightenment, I had finally gained
insight into my own shortcomings. I thought, "If I could ask
for help for someone else and that was provided, why can't I
do the same for myself?" So I naively asked God to help me
become a positive thinker, not quite certain what that was.

The following Friday evening we attended services at
our temple and at the Oneg Shabbat (collation after services), I overheard a woman who was chatting with the rabbi
mention the word "metaphysical." That was an unfamiliar
new word, but something stirred within me. My curiosity
was piqued, so I lingered around until she moved on, then
I intercepted her. I introduced myself and explained my
ignorance about the word. She then introduced me to her
husband who towered over me. He appeared to be in his
70s, and he claimed to have been a Science of Mind practitioner for 40 years. While he explained what that was, I
became so absorbed in his erudite discourse it seemed we had
risen above the din of the crowded room and were alone in
oblivion. I listened wide-eyed and tingly all over. This was

the answer to my prayer. I felt it in every fiber of my being. He insisted that there was no need for anyone to be unhappy or to suffer in any way, as he related how Science of Mind had changed his life. "We are the cause of all of our problems," he asserted confidently.

Charlie interrupted to remind me that everyone was leaving, and I snapped back to earth, reluctantly yielding to obligation. Dave hastily asked me what my problems were. I began to enumerate all of my ailments, which obviously seemed endless to him for he winced and smiled patiently.

"Whoa! Let's take one at a time," he advised. "Which one do you want to be rid of first?" That wasn't a difficult choice. I had been suffering painful, ineffective treatments for a severe urinary tract infection for almost a year. More than anything, I wished to be rid of it forever. I felt I had no control over the intolerable symptoms. He swiftly scribbled a "mental treatment" on a scrap of paper, explaining what I should do. "I'll send you healing, and you do your part, and I guarantee you'll be fine in short order," he promised as we parted. "Keep in touch with me as to your progress."

Two weeks later I was healed. I had learned to treat the cause, realizing that all of my ailments were psychosomatic. It wasn't long before doctors, pharmacists and hospitals became strangers to me. It was such a revelation that I began to study with this man, and from then on I expanded my metaphysical studies, while continuing to heal myself mentally, emotionally, physically and spiritually with the techniques I learned. All I had to do was express the desire to learn more, and another teacher miraculously appeared. I felt as though I was living a charmed life. I knew that God was in my corner guiding and spurring me on to higher consciousness.

In 1967 I founded "The New Life Concept," based on "Science of Mind" and psychic development. I also offered programs in my field and subsequently earned my Master's and Doctorate degrees in Metaphysical Science. I am still teaching classes with holistic and metaphysical themes in Century Village, Deerfield Beach, Florida, and have been faithfully meditating every day since 1965. In 2011, at age 86, I published my book – but my life actually began at age 40!

CONNECTING TO THE HEART OF LIFE
by Ariel D. Roblin

By three o'clock in the afternoon, my eyes would be fighting to stay awake. "Home is just a few hours away," I'd tell myself. "This isn't you, Ariel – get it together and perform – be passionate – listen – inspire – motivate! It's on you – so DON'T FALL ASLEEP!"

Hours seemed to last an eternity until that glorious moment when I could leave work, go home and lock my door. I would fight to stay awake the entire two and one fifth mile drive, sometimes holding my eyes open at a stop light. I would enter my house, hug my kids and my husband and be asleep by 6:30 p.m. The worst part was how active my brain would be throughout the whole experience. I wanted to read my kids a story, to play with them and be a mom again. My body would not allow it.

This went on for four months. Every day seemed to get worse. Every test found nothing but suggested a scarier test that needed to be done to "rule it out." Then, a wonderful doctor came into my life. She ran some blood tests and determined I had chronic Epstein-Barr, also known as chronic fatigue syndrome. I felt an immediate sense of relief. We had found out what it was. Now we can get on to fixing it, right?

That is when I learned the definition of "chronic." I must live with it. She told me she sees it in many women in high stress jobs, often with kids as well. Some refer to it as "The Executive's Disease" because it is brought on by a lifestyle that tries to do way too much all the time. In other words, I made myself sick.

Not accepting my reality, I asked her for a way to "cure" myself. She explained that there is no cure, but she had seen cases that appeared to heal themselves through a healthy plan.

My orders were as follows:
1. Don't drink more than two cups of coffee a day
2. Don't have any sugar
3. Don't eat meat
4. Don't have any preservatives
5. Don't sleep more than seven hours
6. Exercise every day

When I got home, I drew a bath. I was angry for pushing myself so hard that I almost lost the very thing I love the most, my family. My self-pity quickly transformed into the realization that I needed to tell people about this. I needed to warn them how important it is to find balance in their lives and discover just how much they can actually handle.

I know! I should write a book about the truly incurable disease brought on by an incurable host! I'll call it, *I Can't Walk a Mile in My Own Shoes,* and the cover will have high heels all over, and I'll design a health plan and find other women to contribute … then, I realized what I was doing and burst into laughter. I laughed so hard I cried.

That was my "fresh start" moment. It began the minute I stepped out of the tub.

I committed to healing myself. That night I didn't sleep more than seven hours; I only had two cups of coffee; I stopped consuming sugar, meat and preservatives; and I began exercising every day. Two weeks later I had more energy than I had ever had. My doctor told me it could always come back, so consistency was paramount. Knowing the alternative, it was an easy decision to stay on my healthy routine. I had no idea how this would serve me in the next year.

A few months later, my beautiful 5-year-old niece died in a horseback riding accident during a lesson. I was visiting my sister for her 35th birthday, so I was able to be with her and her family throughout the entire tragic event. My health and focus on balance allowed me to truly serve in any capacity that would be helpful. Health gave me the opportunity to provide strength and support to my family at a time when we relied on each other to get to our next breath.

Prior to my illness, my career was developing into something I had only dreamed about. In 2007, I had the good fortune of meeting with the President and CEO of Hearst Television about possible work opportunities. It was a meeting that left me grateful and inspired. Had it come at another time in my life, it would have been another fresh start moment. But all things happen for a reason, and not moving at that point allowed me to care for my family in a way I could not have done if I had.

I continued to work in a small town in northern California, just a few hours from my sister. I stopped looking for a job for two years and spent many weekends with my sister to bring all the cousins together. I surrendered to it. I was grateful for my job, grateful for my friends who gave so much support, and grateful for my husband's strength and much needed humor. The pause on my career trajectory was a welcome gift. As we began to heal, we tried to help the children make sense of their new reality without their sister or cousin and grew even stronger as a family. We had been through our worst nightmare and survived.

Through my niece's death and my illness, I learned just how important our health is for connecting to the heart of life. It allows us to live fully every day, to care deeply, to connect more genuinely to all that matters and to provide an environment that makes the right thing to do the easy choice.

Because in the thick of it, it will always be those moments that will bring us the peace we need to get to our next breath.

Hearst, a company I admired and wanted to be a part of since my meeting in 2007, came up again about a year-and-a-half later. It was time to take another fresh start. This time I would do it with newfound physical strength and an open heart ready to love and live more fully.

HEALTH LAUNCH
by Jacqueline Whitmore

At an intellectual level, we all know that our bodies function better when we take good care of ourselves, but it's easy to take our health for granted, especially when we work a lot and take care of others. In my case, it took a major health scare for me to learn this all-important lesson.

In 1998, I got laid off from my job at The Breakers Hotel in Palm Beach. It was then that I decided to start my own business. I was so consumed with the responsibilities and stress of starting a new business that I neglected to go to the doctor to get my annual well-woman exam. Four years breezed by before I decided it was time to go and get a checkup. Two weeks after I got my Pap smear, my doctor called to tell me the bad news – I had cervical adenocarcinoma in situ. I was diagnosed with the early stages of cervical cancer.

How could this be? I didn't have any symptoms or warning signs. Fortunately, the doctor caught it early enough, and I am cancer free. Both my husband and I went through many months of stress and emotional duress that could have easily been avoided if I had taken better care of myself. But with every cloud in life there is a silver lining. I was one of the lucky ones who were given a "fresh start."

My cancer experience taught me to take my job less seriously, to live in the moment, spend more time doing what I love to do and appreciate the little things in life. But mostly, my brush with cancer made me stronger, wiser and more compassionate toward others who may be going through a similar situation.

It is so easy to put work ahead of others and especially yourself, but it's also detrimental to your health. If you don't have your health, you can't go to work. And if you can't go to work, you can't take care of your financial responsibilities. And if you can't take care of your financial responsibilities, you go bankrupt.

Now I listen to my body, and I am careful not to allow myself to go mentally, physically or emotionally bankrupt. Whenever I feel stressed out at work, I ask myself, *Is this really worth putting my health at risk?* I've learned to delegate, ask others for help from time to time and take breaks (and naps) when I need to. When I'm healthy and happy instead of sick and tired, I'm a better wife, sister and friend.

LOVE HEALS
by Jody Draznin

I'll never forget the call I received from the internist at the University of Iowa. "You need to come in right away. We've found something in your pancreas."

"You must be looking at the wrong records," I said in disbelief. The voice on the phone insisted I come in.

In early 2006, I was diagnosed with a rare form of pancreatic cancer, called a neuroendocrine tumor. According to the specialist, the slow growing tumor may have been growing in my body for 10 years. In addition, I had cancer cells in my ileum, part of my colon, and a non-malignant tumor on my thyroid.

I was told I needed to have Whipple surgery as soon as possible – an extensive and complicated procedure most surgeons are not skilled at. I realized that finding the right surgeon was a matter of life and death.

First, I had to go home to Los Angeles to break the news to my family. My mother was about to go through a mastectomy at Cedar's Sinai. I waited until I saw her safely through her surgery.

My family gathered in my parent's living room, California sunshine streaming through the window. I told them what was going on, and we all began to cry.

I had my surgery on Thanksgiving, and it went well. Each day, friends and family came to sit vigil near my bed. A week later, something happened. I don't remember much, but this is what I was told. I started writhing in pain and screaming. The doctors rushed in and grabbed me, wheeled me down a narrow hallway and into an operating room. All I recall is the long, cold hallway and the sound of concerned voices and bright lights. I remember them lifting me off of the gurney onto a cold, metal surface. Then my lights went out.

Apparently, I had a rare blood disorder and had almost bled to death. After re-opening my surgical sites and cleaning things up, I was put into an induced coma to give my body time to rest.

I'd like to say I had beautiful visions of angels, celestial communications and the wonderful things some people claim to experience, but I was dead to the world. When they tried to bring me out of the induced coma, I did not respond.

On the seventh day, a significant memory occurred. While in my slumber, I had a very clear thought, "I'm tired of struggling. Tired of my life. Tired of all the challenges. Worn out. I'm ready to go." Immediately after that thought, I remember thinking about my parents, my family, my friends, my pets and all of my loved ones. The thought flashed through my awareness, "It would kill my parents if I left now. I need to be here to take care of them."

In an instant, I was out of the coma. Nurses and doctors gathered around the bed in hushed tones, checking my vitals. I recall opening my eyes to bright lights. Seeing a nurse, then my mom and dad, my brothers, my sister-in-law, my boy-friend, Paul, and my best friend Sue … all coming into my limited line of vision. "Was I in an accident?" I asked. I had no memory of my surgery or the reason for it, or any of the tough complications.

It took me months to recover. I had to force myself to go on walks and push myself to eat when I had no appetite. When I first got out of the hospital I weighed 92 pounds. The first time I put on my old jeans, they fell down around my ankles.

My parents wanted me to stay with them so they could take care of me. Instead, I stayed with them for over a year and took care of them.

My father and mother were both in their 80s with failing health. It was hard to see them in the throes of aging and illness. My maternal instincts kicked in, and I discovered I was stronger than I ever thought I could be. With the generous help of close family and a cast of caregivers, we brought them through some rocky times and they each lived several more years.

My "fresh start moment" was when I decided to live. I am grateful for having that epiphany while in a coma (a rare talent indeed). I am grateful for surviving against dangerous odds; the medical care I received; my present ability to function and the renewed appreciation I have for life; my sense of humor, which helped me get through so many difficult times; all my caring friends and family and the support they've given me over the years; and the opportunity to share this story and perhaps remind others how resilient we are, even when faced with adversity.

NO SUCH WORD AS "CAN'T"
by Hank Price

I was born in 1947 in Jackson, Mississippi, and at age 2 was one of the last kids to contract polio before introduction of the Salk vaccine.

My case was severe, particularly on the right side, and complicated by a second strain. As a result, I ended up in an iron lung at a facility in Vicksburg, MS, that warehoused patients dying of polio. At first, my parents were told there was no hope. After a number of months they were told I would survive, but never fully recover, perhaps never leave the iron lung.

My mother was a strong willed woman who had already survived a tough life, and she refused to accept the diagnosis. My earliest memories are of her forcing me to exercise and drink orange juice.

At age 6, my father died of a heart attack, leaving my mother, sister and me not quite penniless, but close to it. We moved to Gulfport to be near family, and my mother went to work in a dress shop for $35 a week.

I grew up an angry child. Angry that my father had died, angry that we lived close to poverty, angry that I was different. School was a challenge. Today I would likely be diagnosed as having a learning disability and anti-social personality. I got in trouble a lot.

My mother, with her unshakable determination and faith, did everything within her power to help me. She took me to a psychiatrist. She bullied my seventh grade teacher into passing me even though I had failed. She refused to let me use the word "can't," saying, "There is no such word as can't."

During this time, my mother was also searching for ways to help me physically. She heard about a free service called The Crippled Children's Clinic, run by an orthopedic surgeon named Dr. Griffin Bland. The Crippled Children's Clinic was the place people went when they had no money and no other options.

Month after month, year after year, we would go and sit in line waiting to see Dr. Bland. Most of the kids were in far worse shape than I was. I will never forget an older couple, farmers from in the country, whose son had almost no control over his body. When their time came to see the doctor, the farmer would lift his son up in front of him, put his son's feet on his boots and "walk" his son in to see the doctor. That image will be with me always. I've often wondered if the son outlived his parents, and if so, what happened to him.

Over the years Dr. Bland operated on me seven times. He slowed down the growth of my left leg to lessen my limp. He fused my right foot. He gave me the ability to walk without braces.

While all of this was going on, something else was also happening. A sense that I was never alone, that everything that was happening was just a phase of my life, that the future would be different.

People talk about finding God. I didn't find God. He found me.

I am a Christian not by my choosing but because I had no other choice. The problem with being a Christian is you cannot live your life the way you want. I didn't want to give up my anger, my jealousy and my overwhelming sense of mistreatment. I was forced to because the alternative would have been misery for the rest of my life. I didn't figure this out, I just knew.

When I was in high school, some kind of academic light came on. I still wasn't a great student but managed to get through. I doubt any other members of Gulfport High School's Class of 1965 would remember me. My only achievement was a pin for serving three years as an assistant librarian.

A second light came on during graduation. I had somehow gained admission to The University of Southern Mississippi. No one there knew me or knew anything about me. Sure, I had a limp, but I also had an opportunity for a new start. After all, there is no such word as "can't."

WILLING TO FALL
by Catherine Dewar Paul, RN, MPH

Sam Bridgman defines determination. For his regular work-out, he points the wheels of his chair towards the top of the hill. He secures his ankles with straps to keep his lower legs in place. Dressed in athletic gear, he faces the summit, where a sign reads, "13-15% Grade 1,000 Ft. Long." His gloved hands grab the top of the wheels and force them forward. His long, sinewy arms propel him closer and closer to the sign. Halfway up, each thrust is accompanied with a grunt. The front wheels pop up and the chair careens backwards. Sam pivots to the right, stabilizes the chair and then continues. After 15 minutes, sweating and breathing hard, he reaches the top. Sam confesses, "Sometimes my mom hikes behind me. If she helps, I stop, turn around and head towards the bottom. When she walks away, I turn around and start back up."

Sam says this with a grin, his trademark smile. He knows someday the hill will be too great a challenge. The condition that altered his boyhood dream of becoming a professional athlete will eventually end this daily workout. But Sam focuses on what he can do to stay strong mentally and physically and to help others do the same. For now, Sam lets his mom know he can do this climb on his own. He doesn't need help. He is willing to fall, knowing he'll figure out a way to get back up and continue to climb the hill.

Sam grew up in Seattle, active in many sports, but in love with baseball. "I think I liked baseball even before I started playing it. Just something about having the ball in your hand," he says. He was the talented kid that pulled the rim of his well-molded baseball cap down over his eyes before sending a pitch. When he missed fielding a play or pitched a bad game, he peppered the coach with questions, asking what he needed to do different next time. Practice sessions with his dad, his younger brother Max or friends often lasted hours, repeating drills, striving for perfection, dreaming of one day playing Major League Baseball.

Sometime in middle school Sam noticed friends on his baseball team getting better while he grew progressively worse. "I was catching my toes on the ground," Sam says. "I didn't know why. I thought I needed to work harder."

March of his freshman year, Sam tried out for the high school baseball team. Years of practice, passion and playing in All Star games should have led to a position on the team. Sam expected it. Keith Bosley, the high school baseball coach, remembers Sam at the plate. "He had a left handed swing that was quick and natural and a good arm. But his lateral movement and reaction time had started to slip. When he ran, it was as if he had 25-pound weights on each foot."

At the end of the third day, Coach Bosley called a group of boys to the pitcher's mound to tell them they didn't make the team. As they started to pack up their bags, one of them approached the coach. "What do I need to do to be on the team next year?" asked Sam.

Since he first started tripping and loosing balance, his parents suspected something wasn't right. They took him to different medical professionals. After he didn't make the freshman baseball team, they tried an integration specialist. He discovered Sam had no sensation in his toes. That was when his parents decided something was definitely wrong and took Sam to a neurologist. Sam remembers, "The neurologist was one of those guys that talked really slow. I just wanted to leave. I didn't really care what he was saying. I just wanted to go home, to go back and practice." After what seemed an eternity, he got the news. Friedreich's ataxia, a rare inherited neurological condition that causes gradual degeneration of the spinal cord and peripheral nerves, was the reason for his awkward, unsteady movements and impaired sensory functions. He learned that FA progresses differently for each individual. Many develop heart complications and diabetes. It can be life shortening. And, despite promising research on preventive and palliative therapies, FA has no treatment or cure.

The diagnosis explained why his body wouldn't do what his mind was telling it to. "But," Sam said, "there is a difference between knowing and accepting. I was going to be the first Major League Baseball player with FA."

Sam kept his diagnosis a secret. No one knew but close family connections, relatives and teachers. He didn't want pity, and he didn't want to stop being an athlete. He continued to play baseball and other sports he had always excelled at. But diminishing coordination and agility often left him frustrated and angry.

While skiing, Sam, his dad and a friend headed down a narrow steep slope with Sam in the lead. A group of young skiers stood in the middle of the path. Sam veered to the side of the path to avoid a collision, and hit a slight upward slope just enough to slow down, lose balance and fall. Lying in the snow with legs that would no longer slalom over moguls, he pummeled the snow and cursed his fall. The skiers were too close not to hear his rant. "You shouldn't say that," one of them yelled. Sam dug his poles into the snow, righted the rest of his body with his upper arms, and pointing his skis downward, landed close enough to the group to return just two words as sharp and clear as a line drive into center field.

Over the next three years, the symptoms grew worse and Sam's focus shifted. Unable to play for his high school baseball team, he worked as manager, practiced alongside his teammates, took the bus to away games and encouraged the other players. When pre-season temperatures plummeted below 35 degrees, Sam showed up for practice, always in uniform, always a part of the team.

In the fall of 2009 he entered the business program at the University of Portland, a flat campus with a Division I baseball team and a coach interested in Sam's knowledge of the game. He began helping with recruitment of new players and videotaping, but switched to less physical jobs as the FA progressed. Sam used an adapted tricycle to go between classes. By the end of his freshman year, he resorted to a wheelchair part-time.

Sam recalls, "There were times when I was really sad. But I don't think there was ever a time when I truly wanted to give up. I remember at UP, breaking down crying to friends because things were getting bad, and I had no idea what to do. It was probably harder for them to watch. Because they couldn't do anything either."

But friends did help, opting for less physically challenging activities, giving piggyback rides down stairs, offering physical activity during off hours, or just telling him they would always be there for him no matter what. Most important for Sam, friends treated him no differently than others.

A teammate of Sam's from UP remembers Sam sitting in his wheelchair in the indoor hitting facility watching players work on their swings, taking notes, offering encouragement. Sam picked up a bat. One of the players asked him, "How good a hitter were you?"

With a big smile Sam said, "I could probably still hit."

"Let's see what you got," one of them said.

A friend helped him up out of the chair and over to the plate. Sam, who throws right handed, made his way to the left side of the plate. With wobbly legs and bat in hand, on the first toss swung and hit a line drive towards left-center in the cage. The momentum threw him on to his back. The others stood silent. But his smile told all. Helping him up, they broke into a cheer as loud as if Sam had hit a home run.

Sam wasn't a kid who needed to figure out what he wanted to do – he had to figure out what he could do. In the spring of his senior year, Sam's parents signed up the family: Mom, Dad, younger brother Max and Sam for Ride Ataxia, a 13-day bike ride, a fundraiser for FA organized by Kyle Bryant, a 33-year-old athlete diagnosed with FA at age 17.

He rode the trip alongside Kyle, both on recumbent tricycles. After miles of flat desert, the highway climbed towards Las Vegas. At the summit, the road plunged towards the city. Sam hit the hill at what he remembers to be about 35 mph, dodging debris and lumber, avoiding semi trucks barreling down the highway. Again, he was Sam the athlete who could do anything. Over the years, Sam, through Kyle, started to envision the kind of life he could have.

Sports for Sam always meant team. A childhood friend recalled, "My mom called him the general of the basketball court, calling fouls, telling other kids how to play, acting as referee. He was fiery but also incredibly positive."

As Sam's limbs weakened, his focus on helping others grew. In high school he attempted to replace the rocky, pocked field his team had for practice and home games through Make-a-Wish Foundation. After months of failed negotiations with the city, Sam settled on his second option, a day with the Seattle Mariners. The day included the opportunity to throw out the first pitch for the night's game and tickets for family friends and teammates.

At the University of Portland, Sam along with another UP baseball player, initiated a wheelchair basketball competition between the UP men's and women's basketball team and the Portland Wheel Blazers, a member of the National Wheelchair Basketball Association. They named it SamJam. At half time Sam spoke to the crowd of over 500 about his personal experience with Friedreich's ataxia. The event raised $7,000 for FA research.

Sam stayed in Portland after graduating. He lives with his brother Max and lives life to the fullest. He has worked at the Nike World Headquarters, raised over $80,000 for Friedreich's ataxia research through his involvement with the Friedreich's Ataxia Research Alliance (FARA), assists coordinating activities for FA families and volunteers for an organization that builds accessible playgrounds.

At his graduation from the University of Portland, his name was called, and Sam pulled himself up out of the wheelchair. With friends on either side and legs that could just barely support him, he walked the distance to the podium and accepted his diploma, a Bachelor's Degree in Business and Finance. The crowd, 5,000 strong, stood, applauded and cheered.

In December of 2013 on an early Saturday morning his high school Sports Boosters drew a full crowd to celebrate Sam as their honorary hero. Athletes, their families, friends and coaches gathered to celebrate their alumnus. They gifted Sam with the honor of again throwing out the first pitch at a Mariners baseball game.

Accepting the gift, Sam spoke to the group. Those in the back craned their necks to see him over the crowd, all on their feet, applauding. Sam said, "Champions are not made on an individual basis. You need a family base to win a championship. Great teams treat each other as a complete family."

The following spring, game day, Sam published a condensed version of his story in the *Seattle Times*. A local television station along with ESPN covered the event. Old friends, mothers of athletes, parents of children dealing with chronic conditions and individuals with their own challenges wrote in to thank Sam for his message of perseverance.

That night, Sam Bridgman held the baseball in his hand ready to throw towards home plate. After wheeling his lithe, athletic, 22-year-old body to the pitcher's mound, he prepared his pitch. Seattle's cold windy weather didn't bother him. The wheelchair didn't inhibit his wind up. Sam looked intently at the Seattle Mariner crouched down at home plate and lobbed a perfect throw directly into the glove. All stood applauding, the crowd, the players. And Sam smiled his infectious smile.

After the game, Sam returned home to Portland, back to daily life and back to his afternoon regimen. He parks his accessible van just south of the University of Portland, works his way into his chair and wheels himself to the hill. He straps his legs to his wheelchair and climbs, sometimes pivoting backwards to the point of falling, but always persevering until he reaches the top.

NEVER GIVE UP
by Dr. Dale Kennedy

On a cool, clear early Monday morning at 7:30 a.m. on September 21, 1996, I reported to the office of my surgeon friend for a biopsy report, following a mole removal two weeks prior. My friend stated he had some bad news and said, "Dale, you have malignant melanoma. How well do you know your Lord?" After I laughed with denial, he convinced me when he said, "This is a Clark's level 3.5 aggressive bug that has penetrated 1.75 cm into your abdomen with likely regional organ involvement and a survival prognosis of normally six months."

What do you do with that? Missing the graduation from high school and college of my three adorable children. Not seeing them happily married. Losing the joy of walking my sweet daughter down the aisle. How could I miss growing old in the rocker on my back porch with my loving wife? This just was not going to work for me.

Time to negotiate a new life plan with my Higher Power. After falling to my knees in prayer to calm my fears, dealing with the anger of how I had let this happen and finally accepting the reality of terminal cancer, a plan to fight was developed. I had all my lymph nodes removed from my left shoulder (22 total), reported for seven months of melanoma immunotherapy at Duke University and changed my diet and lifestyle.

With faith to assure me, family who loves me and friends to support me, my cancer has been dormant for over 18 years. As time passed and the cancer threat decreased, what did not get better was the chronic pain following shoulder surgery. In the early years, I was a three-sport athlete and continue to be an avid slalom water skier and passionate snow skier, so I am no stranger to injuries and pain.

This was different. This was chronic pain that would not go away.

From March 1997, the shoulder surgery date, until August 2000, I searched for answers to ease this pain that often kept me awake at night. I was examined by four physicians, including back and shoulder specialists, had MRI's and CT scans, endured physical therapy during this entire period, and the only answer was to increase the dosage and amount of narcotic pain medication.

Over time I began to need more and more Hydrocodone to find relief. At the point when Hydrocodone proved ineffective, I was given Oxycodone. As that need for Oxycodone increased, I was referred to a pain clinic, where I was diagnosed with left shoulder fibromyalgia and switched to Oxycontin, while asked to continue the Oxycodone for break-through pain. When all this was still not enough, I knew I was in trouble. I was at risk of losing my practice and the family I worked so hard to stay alive for, by falling victim to an increasing need for narcotics.

Practicing on patients or driving under the influence was not a good option. Risk or injury to my patients, my family or myself could have meant "Game Over." I grew up on a farm with adversities, survived a stint in the Army, worked hard for a dental education and then met the challenges of building a successful dental practice. None of that compared to this struggle with chronic pain and narcotics.

After sharing my concern of losing hope, my pain-control physician suggested that I contact the Dental Wellness Committee and seek advice. I was directed to an Atlanta treatment center for evaluation and treatment. What I found in treatment was a much-needed sabbatical, a safe program to free me from the grip of a narcotic and an evaluation that led me to a referral for deep massage therapy, performed weekly to this day. Deep massage therapy eases the muscular pain of lactic acid buildup caused by my true problem, lymphedema, with the loss of lymph nodes in my left shoulder.

I also gained a new awareness and understanding of dealing with the terminal diseases of malignant melanoma and substance dependence. I now realize how, when faced with terminal disease, many people lose hope and give up. The path I chose was to fight, seek answers and do whatever it took to LIVE. Asking for help was difficult, accepting help was even harder, but learning to trust others more than my foolish pride was liberating. I was ready for a new beginning.

Following a life changing path of a healthier lifestyle, armed with the spiritual tools of faith, hope and love, life just keeps getting better. Every minute of every day is a precious gift I plan to enjoy.

THE SUN ALWAYS RISES
by Sheridan Cyr

Every night that the sun sets, the Earth darkens and be-comes a very different place. It can be frightening for those who are sleepless, and often the mind wanders to places so dark that the hope of the sun rising is nothing but a flicker. But despite the blackness that leaves us itching and squirming under our covers, the sun always rises again.

In seventh grade, I developed a darkness within me that I swore I'd never be able to shake. My childhood, happy-go-lucky aura seemed miles away, and I allowed myself to fall deep into a world surrounded by negativity built on anger, loneliness and uncertainty. I began to injure myself whenever I felt worthless, which grew from a few times a week to once every hour. My skin remains traced with the scars represent-ing the path of my dark journey. In high school, I felt that my being was so utterly worthless that I was undeserving of food. For a year, I lied and hid and pushed away all that was good and loving. I became so sick and frail that I was sent away against my will. I had lost it all and sheltered myself even further.

The time that I'd spent in the residential mental hospital near Boston, Massachusetts, was the darkest, coldest, most lonely time of my life. Nothing was worthwhile, especially not me.

I was quartered in the only three-person bedroom in the tiny, off-white-everything building from September until December, released only by request of my parents, who felt I should not miss my 16th birthday, as well as Christmas.

I had already missed half of my junior year of high school, Halloween, Thanksgiving and much more. Upon release, I was not better but some things did change.

As I watched every bit of fall go by from the white wicker chair in the main entrance of the hospital, I realized something that I've never forgotten: "There is nothing that I can do to change the fact that, right now, I am here. But the thing is, no matter how long it takes, I WILL get out. I cannot possibly be here forever." It did seem like forever, but a month later, I was brought home.

Today, I still continue to struggle with these demons, but my perspective on life has altered immensely. People know me as the happy-go-lucky character I used to be. They come to me for advice and compassionate understanding. I wake up every day with the sun and leave the darkness behind, feeling enriched, blessed, empowered and alive. While I am still greatly burdened by a natural tendency to be attracted to negativity, I have learned to fight it and remind myself with each passing day that no feeling of darkness can last forever. The sun always rises again.

YOU HAVE TO HIT BOTTOM BEFORE
YOU CAN SCALE THE HEIGHTS
by Anonymous

Sunlight slowly invaded my eyeballs. Pain shot through my soggy brain cells. I pulled myself upright. The pounding in my head was non-stop, and my stomach was unpredictable. After a few minutes, the room stopped spinning. I realized I was at home, hung over and haunted. I had no memory of the night before. It was like so many mornings for over 20 years. I knew some "friend" would call and tell me of my latest stupidity, my latest drunken embarrassment. I cried out in anguish, "I can't live like this anymore!"

Twelve Step programs call this insight *hitting bottom* and Buddhists call it *right view*. It's when the veils of denial and delusion are lifted for a *moment*. I saw clearly what a mess I had made of my life and the damage I was doing to everyone I loved, especially my young daughter.

I made a phone call and started getting the help I needed.

Life is full of inflection points, where I can choose a path that will take me upward to more positive results or a path that will spiral downward to more destruction. Throughout my former life, I usually chose the easier, negative path, consistently squandering my gifts and opportunities. As soon as I succeeded, as soon as people recognized my accomplishments, as soon as I had an opportunity for something new and wonderful, I had a *compulsion* to destroy it all. And I did.

That bright May morning over three decades ago, for some reason I do not pretend to understand, I decided to stop making the wrong choice. The new path I chose was not easy. It was a steep climb with many stumbles, setbacks and suffering. Every painful step was worth it.

Yes, that decision meant that I could gain professional and economic success. But those were not the true rewards for taking the *right path*. I slowly developed human relationships, the most valuable manifestation of learning to live a life that "requires rigorous honesty."

Today I am free to use my gifts productively in service to others, to enjoy the beauty of the world and my family, and meet wonderful people. I enjoy finding a lovely little snail on my morning walk, seeing a friend find her own *right path*, or watching the waves roll in on Omaha Beach at a D-Day celebration.

I took a very big leap 30-some years ago at that turning point. Now, finding *the right view* and taking the right path seems natural, if not easy. Each time I make the choice, I find joy in the new hard work and uncertainty. Fear dissipates with each step forward and each new service for another person.

Chapter Four

Spreading Light

*"Most champions are individuals whose strength
is their kindness and compassion
for the well-being of others."*
– Bob Danzig

Each of us has the potential to positively impact the lives of those around us. While we can't change the past, we can change the future.

These stories are sparked by the impulse to support, guide, uplift and inspire "fresh starts" for others – often in the face of adversity. Here we witness the human heart overflowing.

OPPORTUNITY TO LAUNCH
by Cindy J. Arenberg Seltzer

My first memory of a "fresh start" moment occurred just prior to my 14th birthday, when my parents told me we would be moving to West Germany (as it was known at that time). Although I was the youngest of five, I would be the only one of the children who would be leaving our cozy home in Long Island, New York, as my siblings were 8, 9, 12 & 13 years older and had begun their adult journeys. I was fairly traumatized at the prospect of leaving family, friends and all that was familiar for a faraway place filled with people who had killed much of my extended family.

I should mention here that I am a first generation American. My father emigrated from Lithuania at age 9 in 1936, and my mother emigrated from Vienna at age 10 in 1939. But, being an obedient child (with no real choice), off I went.

We lived in a small village in the Taunus Mountains outside of Frankfurt, and I attended the Frankfurt International School (FIS). FIS had 1,000 students. The student body was 50 percent American, 35 percent German and 15 percent from the rest of the world.

When we were at the airport preparing to leave all that was familiar, I told my parents through my tears, "I am sure I will appreciate this someday, but right now I don't want to go."

Truer words were never spoken. Once we got there, my finger never left the start button. My eyes were opened to the vastness of the world. I gained a fascination and appreciation for the beauty of different cultures and languages. I tried every school activity from yearbook, to volleyball, to starring in the school's first three musical theater shows: *Annie Get Your Gun, Guys & Dolls* and *You're a Good Man, Charlie Brown*. Even today, 35 years later, those memories bring a smile to my face. I also learned to adapt to new places, people and things, which has stood me in good stead during my peripatetic life.

With my ties to Long Island severed, I had no hesitation leaving my parents in Germany and heading to Southern California to attend college at the University of California, Irvine. When I graduated, I once again crossed the country to head to Washington, D.C., to learn about our federal government and eventually go to Georgetown University Law Center in the evenings.

Upon graduating from law school, I pulled up stakes again and built a life outside Hartford, Connecticut. When I found that the law didn't suit my temperament after all, I pushed the start button again and transitioned into public policy work.

Another move, to Harvard's Kennedy School of Government, was a huge start button. It began the path to my current home in South Florida, where I have had the opportunity to launch and grow the Children's Services Council of Broward County (CSC) under the guidance of committed council members and supported by the best staff any CEO could wish. CSC, created by the voters of Broward County through a referendum passed in September 2000, is devoted to improving the lives of the children of Broward County. Over the intervening years, we have helped hundreds of thousands of children and their families. That is a terrific story for another day – all made possible by pressing many start and restart buttons.

THE CHOICES WE MAKE IN LIFE
by Barry Miller

Life is full of choices and crossroads. Do I take the road to the left or the right? Do I go straight ahead and do nothing at all and hope for the best? No one can predict the future, so life choices are always a matter of taking a chance, weighing and balancing your options and determining what seems to be the best choice for you at the time.

I've made many choices in my life, from family life (marriage, divorce, second marriage), to education, to jobs and much more. Each path has led me to the life I lead today; the friends I have made, the women I have married, the child I have raised, the career I have chosen.

I was not one of the fortunate ones who knew at age 10 or even at age 20 what I wanted to do with the rest of my life. In college, I knew I wanted a career that had to do with children and family life but nothing more specific. I explored physical therapy, public health administration and family counseling to name a few. I went to college and received a Bachelor's Degree in Sociology from the University of Maryland. Once I graduated, after exploring my options, I determined that the only thing one could do with a degree in sociology was to continue on to graduate school.

After much deliberation and applications to different graduate schools, I decided to pursue a Master's Degree in Child Development at West Virginia University. My educational path gave me the opportunity to meet and be influenced by some wonderful teachers including nationally known figures such as Polly Greenberg, Wanda Franz, and Julie Vargas, the daughter of B.F. Skinner.

After graduation, I ended up with a career I "fell" into. Never anticipating I would stay in West Virginia once I graduated school, a job became available at a nearby settlement house. I started my career as a childcare teacher and eventually a childcare center director. Working in a settlement house outside a university town gave me the opportunity to work with and come to know a very diverse population, which included doctors, lawyers, college professors, college students, coal miners and others.

My "fresh start" moment came after seven years in West Virginia. The economy was slow, and there was not much opportunity for career advancement. Did I want to go back to the safety and security of the Washington, D.C., area, where my parents lived and where I had spent my high school and undergraduate years? Did I want to move 60 miles north to Pittsburgh, a beautiful city in its own right with multiple job opportunities and where I had spent many weekends while living in West Virginia? Or did I dare take a big chance and move to South Florida where my wife had some relatives?

The deciding moment came when we came back to West Virginia to 20-degree weather and a snowstorm. It wasn't long before we sold our house, packed our belongings and moved to South Florida. With a wife and no job, was this the right decision or one I would later regret?

For the first year I held a variety of different jobs, somewhat related to my field, including a childcare bus driver, childcare teacher and a childcare center director. Continually seeking other job opportunities, I noticed an ad in the newspaper (for younger people reading this, newspapers used to have an entire section with hundreds of Help Wanted ads). I applied for this position and did all the right things; prepared for the interview, researched the company, etc. Several weeks after the interview I was told that I did not get the job.

Though disappointed, I continued looking and applying for other positions. A second job opened at this same company and again I applied and was granted an interview. This time, I was sure I would get the job. How could I not? After several weeks of waiting for a response, I received a letter (never a good sign) that again, I did not get the job.

Still working in related jobs, a third position opened at the same company. Either through sheer perseverance, or more likely naiveté, I again applied and interviewed for the position. They say the third time is a charm. I finally got the call I was waiting for and was offered the position. I have been with this company now (Family Central) for over 25 years.

Though it is rare to be with a company for this long, rare to maintain the same career your entire adult life, and even rarer to be a male in this field, my choices have led to many great opportunities in my life. They have led to a great son, two wonderful stepchildren, an amazing new wife, a beautiful grandchild, delightful friends and a great family.

The job I have held for over 25 years has given me the opportunity to work with state-wide organizations, present at national conferences and oversee many different programs – everything from foster care, to childcare administration, food programs and hundreds of others.

Through my years, I have learned that life is a journey with many different pathways. Whatever pathway you decide to take, leads you to your life today. I am happy with the choices I have made at the many crossroads I have come to.

AGE-OUT ANGELS – "WHO IS THERE FOR ME?"
by Greg Rapport

Adopting a child is a traumatic experience. It does not begin with the adoption process, as most people think. It begins with the first sign that what is supposed to occur naturally … won't.

My wife and I waited longer than most to have children. We were in our mid-30s when the urge to parent became insurmountable. That's when the nightmare began. With every miscarriage, every medical test, the tension built. And it never let up. Doctors, specialists, injections, procedure after procedure, all designed to allow science to take the reins from nature, creating a cocktail of stress. The feelings of failure, guilt and inadequacy rose to a fever pitch.

Finally, we accepted the fact that we weren't going to have a baby naturally and began the adoption process. Talk about having your privacy invaded. A parade of social workers was assigned to judge our potential as parents. The irony was palpable. A drug addict could trade their child for dope, but we, a pair of upwardly mobile Manhattanites, with nothing but love in our hearts, had to grovel for a child.

Emotion clouded our judgment, and we became easy prey for thieves. We gave $2,000 to one agency that promised us a child from Romania. One "lawyer" wanted $15,000, and we were just lucky he got arrested before we wrote the check.

The process was all consuming. It is all we talked about and all we did for over two years. Then one day, magic happened. The phone rang, and we were told to go to the hospital and pick up a two-day-old baby. The nightmare was over. We were a family.

This experience left me with a strong desire to help other potential adoptive parents. I figured I'd either start an adoption agency, or at the very least, write a book containing information that might ease their pain.

That's when the responsibilities of being an actual parent kicked in. I couldn't quit my job to start an adoption agency. I had a child to consider. Sure, I could write a book in what little spare time I had. But who would actually read it? How would I market it? After a few years, we started the adoption process again and were blessed with our second child.

The idea of helping others remained simmering in the back of my mind. Last fall, when my youngest went to college and we became empty nesters, I began to research what it would take to start an adoption agency. It turned out to be bad timing. In fact, if we were trying to adopt today, the process would be much more difficult that it was in the '90s. Today, adoption agencies are reducing staff, and there are stories about couples waiting for seven years without adoption success.

What did keep popping up on my research radar was the foster care system. I couldn't quite make sense of the math. Apparently, there are thousands of children who need a home and thousands of couples looking to adopt. Somehow, these two groups manage not to find each other.

Turns out it's more complicated than that. The foster care system is not a giant adoption agency. Its first responsibility is to the welfare of the child, and its second responsibility is to make an effort to reunite the child with their biological family. It's easy to sit outside the system and judge it, but I doubt anyone could find a simple fix. It's too complicated.

For example, there are parents who have the best intentions, but life-circumstances intervene, and they end up in a situation where they can't care for their child, temporarily.

Consider the plight of a single parent, who lives paycheck to paycheck and suddenly gets sick. The downward spiral begins. They lose time from work, get fired, can't pay the rent, barely have money for food, get evicted, can't collect welfare because they don't have a permanent address and can't care for their children. That parent can get back on their feet and reunite with their children.

There is also another kind of parent with whom the foster care system must contend. These parents are probably damaged in the first place. They inflict physical and sexual abuse on their children. They push the children into drug dealing and prostitution to support their own addictions. They have untreated psychological problems and make their children live in a torturous world. I just can't imagine what horrors some parents inflict on a child.

BUT … in both these scenarios, children (generally speaking) seem to have this incredible loyalty to their parents, even the abusive ones. It boggles my mind how a child with scars from being purposely burned with a cigarette by an abusive parent remains loyal to that parent and longs for the day when they can be a family again.

See what I mean? It's complicated.

I began to learn more about what happens to children in foster care. How some children respond positively and others don't. How many children are placed in multiple foster homes over a number of years. How children frequently bring the scars of emotional and physical abuse to their foster care settings, and how some deal with issues of abandonment for the rest of their lives.

I was trying to establish a foothold from which I could function within the foster care system and offer some form of help, when I chanced upon a book called *On Their Own* by Martha Shirk and Gary Stangler. This book follows the lives of young adults after they aged-out of the foster care system. Some were success stories; many were not. The very first profile is about three male siblings. One became middle class, one ended up in jail and one ended up dead. The subjects of the book called out to me. It seemed as though the support that is already in place for children in foster care all but disappears when they age-out. As the book says, they are truly on their own, but many don't have life skills.

One theme that seems common to the children in foster care (that heightened as they aged out of the system) is, "Who is there for me?" It's an expression that represents the support most of us take for granted because we got it naturally from our parents. Think of the blessings that most of us enjoyed growing up. When we played on a sports team, graduated high school or played in the school band, someone was always there for us. Someone was there to make sure we did our homework and drove us to play dates and scout meetings. As we grew older, we were taught how to drive, got dating advice, were offered career coaching and fell in love. I know it's not as perfect as the picture I paint but when you think your family is dysfunctional, remember you had a family. Foster kids don't.

No one is there for foster kids. Some foster parents are better than others. Some are just in it for the money. But generally speaking, foster children grow up seriously devoid of life skills and human connections. As they age-out, there are services available to them, but they don't always access them, and no one is there to make sure they do.

That's how I got the idea for Age-Out Angels. I learned about two existing agencies. One is called the Jim Casey Youth Opportunities Initiative that supports age-outs in approximately 12 pockets around the country, and the other is CASA, which supports children in the foster care system.

I decided to emulate the CASA model of assigning a one-on-one volunteer to support an individual child. CASA provides one person to serve as an advocate for the child in legal proceedings serving as Guardian Ad Litem. In Age-Out Angels, the one-on-one relationship would be less legal and have more to do with providing emotional and tangible support to an individual age-out.

Specifically, I've identified nine key areas where age-outs need support: living accommodations, food and clothing, healthcare, education, employment, transportation, psychological counseling, legal services and emotional support.

It's beautiful how our society has structures in place that already provide many of these services to age-outs. They just need help to access them. For example, many age-outs qualify for financial assistance, but they have to get transportation to the office to apply and need help with the paperwork or they won't get it. The disconnect is not in the availability, it's in the access. Age-Out Angels will enlist an army of volunteers to help age-outs make those connections, stay on course and move their lives forward.

The stakes are high for us as a society. The cost of an individual who is a burden on our social welfare system, versus the savings resulting from converting that person into a tax-paying citizen, are astronomical. And that's just to please the number crunchers.

In the broader sense, we need to unshackle a population containing potentially great thinkers, innovators and contributors to our society. Helping them find their best possible future makes the future brighter for all of us.

My plan for the next 20 years is to develop an army of volunteers to enact a one-on-one relationship with each and every young adult who ages out of the foster care system. One day, I would like to see some of those young people grow up to be volunteers and extend the program for generation after generation.

For the moment, Age-Out Angels wants age-out youths to know that when they ask the question, "Who is there for me?" they hear an answer come back, "We are in your corner."

SCHOOL READINESS
by David Lawrence Jr.

I thought I would work all my life in newspapers. Loved newspapers so much that I never missed a day of work (minus vacations and some weekends) in 35 years at seven newspapers as reporter, editor or publisher.

Where else could I work with such good people? Idealistic and optimistic people like myself. Be part of something new every single day of the year. Work as a trained "skeptic," but never be a "cynic." Interview the President of the United States on Air Force One and the dictator of Cuba in Havana for five-and-one-half hours and, yes, have dinner with the Queen of England. Participate in the sort of journalism that makes a difference in people's lives.

I started working in the back shop of a now-defunct daily in Sarasota, Florida, when I was 15 years old. Finished my shift in the afternoon, and then scooted over to the newsroom to beg the city editor to give me news releases to rewrite. Became editor of my high school newspaper in nearby Bradenton. Became editor of my college newspaper at the University of Florida. Interned during the summers at the *St. Petersburg Times*. Graduated and was married the same day in December 1963. A week later, I was into journalism full-time. Managing editor of *The Palm Beach Post* by the time I was 27. (Yes, too young to know any better.)

Then back in 1996, the then governor of Florida, Lawton Chiles – an especially good and caring public servant – asked me and 54 other Floridians to serve on his Commission on Education. Its mission: Look into the state of Florida's education and make recommendations for the coming millennium. I continued as publisher of the *Miami Herald* and its Spanish-language sister *El Nuevo Herald*, but took this on, too, as a two-year civic "assignment."

There were six task forces. One of them was "School Readiness," which I was asked to chair. I am the father of five but had never heard of the principles of high-quality, early childhood development, care and education. (I was to discover that my children were raised according to those principles.)

I came to learn that 85 percent of brain development occurs by the age of three. And I came to learn that up to a third of all children enter formal school way behind. Then, most of those children get further behind and come to be tracked and triaged. I also came to discover that research tells us that if 100 children leave first grade not really knowing how to read, then 88 of those are in much the same shape at the end of fourth grade.

And then I came to know that if we spend a dollar wisely up front in children's lives, we would save perhaps seven dollars in money we wouldn't need to spend on police and prosecution and prison – and remediation. Finally, I came to believe that the very future of our beloved country is at stake – that we are seriously slipping in education and falling behind many countries in the world.

What I learned led me to decide to "retire" in 1999 to devote my full-time energies to matters of "school readiness."

As a reader of history, I believe strongly that real movement toward "school readiness" cannot be achieved unless we do so for *everyone's* child. All children need the quality early care and education that my own children and grandchildren received. One can never build a real movement based on *those* children (whoever they are). In the words of the author

James Baldwin: "For these are all our children... We will all profit by, or pay for, whatever they become."

Believing in *all* children, we help all of us. It simply makes sense – practical, economic and moral – to be mindful of how *everyone* is doing. If we want safe and secure neighborhoods, if we want less crime, if we want more people to grow up to own homes and cars, and more people to share the basic costs of societal well-being, then we simply must know of the quite extraordinary evidence of the power of early investment and the power to grow children who dream and have a real chance to achieve those dreams.

From that vision has come:

•The passage of a constitutional amendment for free pre-K for all 4-year-olds in Florida, one of only three states where the family of every 4-year-old is entitled to free pre-kindergarten.

•In my own community of Miami-Dade – larger than 16 states and on the cutting edge of American pluralism – the passage of a property tax for high-quality early intervention and prevention. That's $100 million extra a year to invest in the future of children.

•The building of The Children's Movement of Florida, with more than 100,000 followers pushing to make *all* children the No. 1 priority for investment.

We are nowhere near the "promised land" for children anywhere in America. The mission of "school readiness" will not be completed in my lifetime. But I do have the now life-long blessing of being able to devote my full-time energies to these crucial matters. I am not saving my energy for the next world. There will be time to rest when I get there.

"Retirement" seems to me a perilous state. The novelist Edith Wharton reminded us a century ago: "In spite of illness, in spite even of the archenemy sorrow, one can remain alive long past the usual date of disintegration if one is unafraid of change, insatiable in intellectual curiously, interested in big things and happy in small ways."

And I should also share the words of the educator Horace Mann, who told the graduating class of Antioch College just before the dawn of the Civil War: "Be ashamed to die before you have won some battle for humanity."

BECOMING A CATALYST
by Danny Andrews

When you've done something you've loved for 39 years, the idea of "changing jobs" is a bit unsettling.

In the spring of 2006, I was comfortable as the longest-tenured editor in the Hearst newspaper chain with 28 years in that role at the *Plainview* (Texas) *Daily Herald*, probably ranking in the top three in longevity among daily newspaper editors in Texas as well.

Life was good – I was a "big fish in a small pond" – and figured I'd probably drop dead at my desk some day as retirement was still a good 10 years off, best I could reckon.

But the same person who introduced me to my wife in what we called "dummy's geometry class" as a junior at Plainview High School 40 years earlier, suggested I apply for the vacant alumni director's job at hometown Wayland Baptist University.

Although the job was appealing, journalism was the only profession I had ever really known – aspiring in high school to be "a sportswriter in the worst way." And some waggish friends later attested, "You certainly succeeded in that."

But the more I pondered the possibility, certainly not without some anxiety, I came to the conclusion: "If I'm ever going to make a job change, now is the time to do it because the desirable opportunities aren't likely to come along often at my age (57)."

The job not only included friend-raising, no problem since I can talk to fence posts and fire hydrants, but also fund raising, something at which I didn't have much experience.

However, within about a year, an appeal to Plainview native Jimmy Dean, a genial country music entertainer-turned-sausage entrepreneur, for a $25,000 endowed scholarship in honor of his beloved mother eventually resulted in a gift of $1 million – the largest single donation from an individual that Wayland has ever received. Subsequently, his widow, singer-songwriter Donna Meade Dean Stevens, gave Wayland another $5 million to erect an addition to the existing museum on campus to honor Jimmy's considerable and diverse legacy.

God has allowed me to be a catalyst in several other significant gifts and projects for Wayland including about$100,000 toward the university becoming an all-Steinway piano school, one of less than 150 in the nation – major remodeling of our men's and women's basketball dressing rooms – several endowed scholarships and the establishment of some neat new traditions for our students.

Oh, yeah, as a bonus, I also get to do some writing, including a column for our alumni magazine published three times a year.

Even after almost eight years, someone occasionally will ask, "Danny, how are you liking your 'new' job?" Although I still miss writing – including a twice-weekly column – I can truthfully answer, "I left the *Herald* happy and I am very happy at Wayland."

You can't beat a deal like that!

GO WEST
by Douglas Cohen

I was called to move west, for the second time in my life, from New Jersey, based on a love story that started as more than a small surprise.

Meaning comes in such a rich array of discoveries of what is unseen and yet right around the corner. This is a layered story of a "fresh start" that bridges three cities, three time zones and reunited three people after many years of separation. We had started out in the same New Jersey locale in the 1950s and were spread across the entire U.S. continent until "life happened" and everything changed.

In 2009, I was sitting in a New York City restaurant in lower Manhattan waiting for a lunch meeting with a close friend. Rick was the founder of a personal growth & development group in NYC called the Life Purpose Forum. Together with our colleagues, we co-facilitated the program meetings, which brought forth the life stories and aspirations of people from New York and those who had traveled to live there from throughout the world.

I got to the restaurant early and had email going on my laptop and was shocked into a "past meets present" moment by an email from a "girl" I once knew. Cynthia and I had dated briefly at the end of high school in Oradell/River Edge, New Jersey. She was the "girl next door" to my best friend John from junior high through high school and throughout our lives. Cyn and I went out and hung out in the summer before I went off to college. At that youthful time, we had not yet progressed to a serious relationship, so I went off to college, and as with many aspects of my hometown life, moved on and "didn't look back" for many years. Then came this email. I was in a state of disbelief hearing from Cynthia again after 34 years.

To deal with my shock, I immediately called her childhood next door neighbor, my lifetime friend John in California and told him about the email in my inbox. He confirmed that he'd been in touch with her online and encouraged her to look up all the activity I was engaged in, educating youth on leadership and citizenship as a board member of a national "Education for Sustainability" campaign. I had been chairing the youth arm of this U.S. based non-profit in collaboration with the United Nations. Upon hearing the news that confirmed we were all in the same story, I was all kinds of excited and ready to respond to Cynthia.

So I wrote back to her that moment and said, "Call me, Call me, Call me, Call me." A number of hours slowly passed. Then she called me that night. (Let the games continue....)

We started talking and quickly were talking regularly. Soon, it was several times a day. Four months later I visited her in New Mexico. On the first day of that visit she took me to Madrid, a former mining town in the high desert mountains outside of Albuquerque filled with art, history, motorcycles and aging hippies. I immediately felt like I'd found a possible new home base. So I visited over the next two years and began staying longer and longer, until I moved to New Mexico permanently in 2011.

Setting the Stage for the Bookends to Complete the Fresh Start

This dramatic life stage change tale began when I was living in the greater New York–New Jersey area and was deep in a career path as a societal educator (teaching "between the sectors"). I was consulting and training leaders in a number of social and business arenas. For years, I'd had positions in consulting firms training senior level managers around the world in leadership and change management. At this point, in a sector shift, I had been advising in child welfare and foster care management improvement for nine years. The companies I was associated with had multi-year contracts with New York and California agencies and governments.

As you have seen, after the lunch with Rick and the call from Cynthia that night in 2009, the hand of fate that shaped that day had spoken. Several years later, it spoke even louder.

Gradually and then permanently moving to New Mexico brought with it the love story with Cynthia and also falling for the spectacular landscapes and cultural richness of the Land of Enchantment. My experience became a blend of going deep into a "culture of two" as a couple, while doing outreach and networking for career opportunities in the sun drenched high desert of the Southwest.

Workwise, I had been fortunate to have had a four-year run of consulting in Oregon. In between trips, I pursued both pro bono and freelance consulting in New Mexico, while I began to re-focus on "localizing my life" in the greater Albu-querque area. I joined the leadership team for the New Mexico Outdoors Coalition and a regular meet-up group affiliated with the Institute of Noetic Sciences. Once the Oregon con-tracts ended, it was time to pursue full-time employment.

As the son of a mother who became a manager in the NJ State Child Welfare Agency, I am a member of a sibling group, all of whom went into some version of the helping professions. Based on my years of work in foster care and child welfare leadership, lightning struck in Albuquerque.

In December 2013 a job posting appeared with New Mexico State University for a senior position in training and development with the state child welfare agency. The match with my background in leadership training and organization development was uncanny and spot on. I wrote a summary of my accomplishments in the field and was hired two days after my interview. I joined a team helping to weave a stronger social safety net for children and families across New Mexico.

Got the girl, got the job, got the re-location, and the key to it all is the later stage in life "lifestyle." We live right next to the Rio Grande River in the "Bosque," the forested section of greater Albuquerque nestled in the high desert. We have Cooper's hawks, wild turkeys, coyotes, and for four months of the year, a cluster of migrating Sandhill cranes in our yard. We get to live in a place of beauty and grandeur under the 10,000-foot Sandia Mountains of the Rockies.

As of this writing, we just hosted my 23-year-old son in New Mexico, who was here for a conference on the Evolution of Human Consciousness. Cynthia and I were recently back east with my son and 17-year-old daughter for a family wedding celebration in Maine earlier in the summer. We travel to places of natural wonder and camping at music festivals. And have a revolving door of visitors to our guest room including both sets of our children, as people are continuously traveling through or to New Mexico for its many treasures.

Given my work in training and workforce development, each day is an opportunity to learn and teach and shape a healthier organization in the service of well-being for communities in the Southwest. And in our relationship journey, each day is also an opportunity to learn about love and to live into tales of giving and receiving.

REBUILDING NEIGHBORS
by Chuck Malkus

Sometimes in life we witness a crisis close to home and find ourselves with choices to make or a desire to help others.

The first major crisis that hit my life was when Hurricane Andrew hit South Florida and the East Coast on August 24, 1992. Tragically, there were 40 deaths and over 1,000 homes destroyed in Miami alone. Over 50 percent of Miami was without phone service, and about half the houses in South Miami were without electricity.

One working phone line happened to be at my home. On the following day, August 25th, my phone rang with a call from the CBS television station. Since my house was in Fort Lauderdale, CBS was calling to find a temporary building where they could help launch a relief and rebuilding effort.

I set up a meeting between CBS Television and the Jaycees. During the meeting, it was determined that someone was needed to head up the relief effort, and I was nominated to be chairman.

In less than 24 hours, Rebuilding Neighbors Helping Neighbors was born out of the devastation of Hurricane Andrew. We set up a 15-line phone bank, where people could call and volunteer to help. As chairman, I coordinated more than 4,000 volunteers within the first month, who put up plywood and delivered food and clothing.

This choice led to much more than I could have ever dreamed. I would learn how to adapt to situations I had never thought about facing, while at the same time helping tens of thousands of people in dire straits.

On the second day of this effort, I organized a caravan with two buses and three pick-up trucks loaded with food, supplies and clothing. When we reached Homestead High School, we found a makeshift shelter overwhelmed with families who had been left with almost nothing. It looked like a war zone with tents and people walking around without any purpose.

I'll never forget the first person I met when I stepped off the bus. An African-American woman named Yolanda was standing with her two children, a three-year-old son and a two-year-old daughter. I introduced myself and then went back to the bus and got two teddy bears for the young children.

Yolanda looked up to me and said, "Thank God for giving my children hope."

This experience provided me with additional motivation for organizing teams of neighborhood volunteers to construct roofs on homes; put up tents as temporary housing; read books to young children and lend a hand in the cleanup of entire neighborhoods.

In the wake of Hurricane Andrew, since we had a partnership with the CBS television station, we were able to organize individuals who called our phone bank offering help. And following this life event, Rebuilding Neighbors Helping Neighbors has activated hundreds of volunteers over the years to assist with Hurricane Katrina, with relief for Haiti and countless other natural disasters.

I learned about the power of partnerships, in this case the Jaycees and WFOR television, which resulted in making a difference in hundreds of thousands of lives – as well as in our own.

Today, Neighbors is still performing this type of work. Although the scope changes from time to time, the goal is the same, connecting those in need with individuals wishing to provide a helping a hand.

During its first two decades, over five million calls have been logged in at our phone bank. Over $11 million in donations of cash, food and supplies have gone to those in need. More than 300 local service organizations have received direct support.

I'll admit to you today something about the first choices in August 1992. When we started Neighbors, we thought this was going to be some type of relief effort for four to eight weeks. That was what I and a dozen other people thought. It was believed it would take no more than two months to take care of the needs after Hurricane Andrew.

The reason for sharing this life event and choice is that whether you have a Category 5 crisis or a smaller disaster (perhaps an electrical fire hits your building), there could come a time when you find yourself making choices under the most difficult circumstances. And, if you would like to be prepared for dealing with the unexpected, you could make important choices in advance of a storm, a crisis and a dark cloud. There are choices you may wish to consider for involvement with your community and for your family.

This experience not only helped me to become a stronger person, it allowed me to take on additional challenges in the years that followed. By being a volunteer for Neighbors, I've been able to reach new heights personally and professionally.

Choosing to become a volunteer can help you when it comes to making difficult choices. The road ahead may be navigated more safely when you have already experienced the unexpected.

SPUNKY OLD BROAD
by Dr. Gayle Carson, CSP, CMC, SOB

My husband passed away six years ago. It was the first time in 10 years that I had real free time for myself. We had a wonderful 45-year marriage, but it was hard to concentrate. Every time I focused on my business, there was another doctor call, or we had an appointment to go to, or my husband came in with some type of issue.

To complicate matters, during this time I had my third case of breast cancer and my 12th to 16th surgeries. I don't mean any of this as doom and gloom – just a reality check for people who think they are living a charmed life with no problems.

Life doesn't give you anything you can't handle, and I have come through with flying colors, while my husband is now at peace and watching all of us from above.

All of this spurred me on, however, to begin my Spunky Old Broad movement in earnest. Officially I'm known as Dr. Gayle, S.O.B. or Spunky Old Broad, and I am creating Spunky Old Broad Clubs around the country.

Why? Because there are many women over 50 who believe life is over. I believe it's just begun. Rather than believing the best years of your life are over, it's important to believe that all the experiences you've had are leading to the most important adventures of your being.

We are forming a community of women who want to be anything they desire. It is compassionate, empowering, fun, educational, life enriching and best of all, supportive. This is so exciting to me because I have wanted to leave a legacy, and I truly believe this is it.

So many people have asked me why I am always so happy. It's because I believe in the nine secrets to living regret free and a formula I call ENERGY: E=Enthusiasm N=No Nonsense E=Exercise R=Re-Invention G=Goals and Y=You.

This is a fresh start for me and hopefully in the process, for a lot of other women. We have raised children, started businesses, worked in minimum wage jobs, volunteered in our communities, taken care of households and had a major impact on the world around us.

Here's to all the S.O.B.'s.

THE MEMORY LESSON
by Judy Allen

Dressed in bib overalls, my brown braids hanging down my sides, I sit on an ottoman at my grandfather's feet holding an old, well-worn book. It's faded red and embossed in gold – *The Big Quiz Book.*

I read questions from the book, haltingly at times because I am very young. Some of the words are hard to pronounce, and I don't understand them all. I look at my grandfather after each question and wait patiently for him to respond. Sometimes he asks me to read the question again. He may even explain a word to me in a stumbling fashion.

My grandfather sits in his old leather, overstuffed chair and thinks about each question. He answers them slowly and with great care. Sometimes he has to stop and start over. He never shows signs of frustration, nor great triumph when he answers these questions, because they are very elementary for him and he is a highly intelligent man.

The reason for his hesitation would become obvious if you observed the drawn side of his face, the eye that doesn't open quite right and the mouth that doesn't do what he wants without tremendous effort. This is only the latest in a series of strokes that have attacked his body and mind over the years.

The routine is always the same. He comes home from the hospital, recovers somewhat physically and regains some strength. Then our memory lesson begins. I ask every question in the book. My grandfather answers every question in the book, and we go over and over again.

As time goes by the book is no longer needed and things return to normal. My grandfather begins his farm chores again, and I return to my animals and play. Memories have been regained, and new memories have been made. Lessons in patience, perseverance, love of learning and a little bit of reading have been learned. *The Big Quiz Book* is put on the shelf until the next time.

EVOLUTION OF A COACH
by Evelyn Chau

The seed of my "fresh start" was sown more than a quarter of a century ago. I was working at Mother Corp (Canadian Broadcasting Corporation) and things were busy. The Radio Current Affairs unit had about a dozen seasoned journalists all working on tight deadlines. They were among the country's best and not to be trifled with. Stakes were always high – the program won a lot of awards, and the tradition had to be upheld.

They consumed a lot of coffee, chain-smoked and worked feverishly. At the beginning of the week they chased stories. When they brought back tapes of colorful interviews they would edit for hours, shaping the story into something engaging, informative and illuminating.

My job? I was the production assistant and responsible for all logistics and filling in gaps, such as holding of hands when interviewees got the jitters. I also did some editing and when the program went on air at 8 a.m. Sunday and everyone had gone home to sleep, I might have to take out an offensive word or two from the master tape during a five minute news break. That was nerve-racking to say the least.

One day I came across an ad for something called the Relaxation Response. It was taught by a pleasant man with a Buddha-like serenity. Later I would find out that he was one of the pioneers in stress-reduction teachings. I signed up. Classes started with breathing exercises because slow, deep breaths work wonders for lowering stress. That was my first exposure to this all-important tool and Eli Bay's mind-body techniques.

Next, we did mind exercises while in this relaxed state. Eli led us through mental journeys that were designed to uplift, inspire and heal. We typically lay on the floor in rows, all blissful and immune to the world's chaos. I benefited during the six weekly sessions and even bought tapes to remind myself. Those, however, sat on the shelf for years.

Another propitious day happened, much later. I noticed the tapes while moving things, opened the plastic cases and revisited the course. I invited friends and neighbors to be my subjects.

To a person, they loved it. They reported instant calm, a deep sense of purpose, peace and well-being. Practice and more practice later, I found something powerful to work with in my small sphere of influence.

While getting treatment from a chiropractor, I was introduced to a pair of young figure skaters who trained at the prestigious Granite Club of Toronto. Nitin, my chiropractor, was concerned that the boys weren't getting any mental training. They were promising skaters with good skills, strong stamina and motivation, but when they fell during a performance their confidence plummeted and recovery was difficult. I agreed to work with them, and one of their mothers would bring them to my place after their daily training sessions.

Jonathan and Serge (the boys' names have been changed) were attentive and had wide-open minds. Before the third session, their visualizations were bearing fruit. They were able to execute the jumps and axels they mentally practiced under my guidance. Their coach noticed.

A lunch took place at the Granite Club. I introduced my techniques to the boys' coach and the sports director. Shortly after, I did a sample session with a group of high-performance skaters, whose ages ranged from 8 - 14, including Jonathan and Serge. The brightest-eyed, keenest of the group was a boy named Patrick Chan, who was to become three-time world champion and seven-time Canadian champion.

My coaching career should have taken off and flourished but didn't. Even though I was very confident in my techniques, I was stumped by my lack of marketing savvy and felt unschooled in the art of networking. As it happened, I got a job offer that I couldn't refuse. I became a staff interpreter at the Ontario Provincial Courts, working with the accused, their witnesses and lawyers in a colorful but stressful setting.

During those days, I kept up with exploring mind-body techniques and reading books by great teachers and gurus. While standing in the spotlight next to people who were to be found guilty of various crimes and misdemeanors, I relaxed my mind with healing thoughts and positive energy. I visualized a strong voice coming from my tired vocal cords.

At the same time, I organized my life so that coaching became an integral part. I worked with boys in a group home. They were about the same age as the young figure skaters at the Granite Club. Their circumstances were the polar opposites of the wealth and privilege enjoyed by my athletic clients. I guided them to visualize a bright future around the interests and preoccupations they showed. Most of them became more animated, hopeful and opened up considerably after a short time.

I enjoyed the challenges of simultaneous and consecutive interpreting, as well as the camaraderie of court interpreters. However, after 10 years of court work, I was ready to make the leap. One fine, cold winter day in the middle of January 2012, I left my job. There was no safety net, no secure 9 to 5 job waiting for me. Just a feeling that I would make it. A fresh start.

Since then, I've had the pleasure of working with high performance athletes and professionals, who are motivated to push past real or imagined barriers to grow. I have worked with a variety of highly motivated athletes, including swimmers, half-marathoners and a number of squash players, one of whom won the National Championship as well as the gold at the PanAm Games in Brazil.

This summer, I began working with corporate and legal professionals, using the same techniques that propelled athletes towards success. I also got my Practitioner's accreditation with NLP Canada, adding Neurolinguistic Programming to my EFT (Emotional Freedom Technique) and guided visualization. These tools are not only powerful for my clients – they help me with the tasks I used to find challenging. I'm much more conversant with marketing and networking than 10 years ago. I feel good helping people shake off limitations and change their mindsets to stride forward.

The fresh starts within the fresh start are unexpected bonuses. I am thankful to Bob Danzig for bringing my attention to them.

CONNECTING THE DOTS
by Jill Mindlin

My "fresh start" moment occurred in the early '90s. It began with just a few red dots on my knee. I told my husband I needed to get to the emergency room immediately. He looked at me like I was crazy. He tried to tell me that people do not go to an emergency room for what looked like a minor rash. He suggested I go to sleep and call a dermatologist in the morning. Something kept me from listening to him. I kept repeating the phrase, "No, something is wrong. Something is horribly wrong." I felt like the world was about to end.

Despite the fact that he thought I was crazy, he finally agreed. By the time we entered the emergency room (only two blocks away), I was suffering from what I later learned was anaphylaxis (a severe, life-threatening, allergic reaction). By then, I was covered in hives, swollen from head to toe, had difficulty breathing and my blood pressure dropped so low that I lost consciousness. Being in a major metropolitan hospital, they knew what was happening, administered epinephrine (which is adrenaline, the first line drug for anaphylaxis) and saved my life.

I later learned that overwhelming feeling I had – fear of impending doom – was a symptom of anaphylaxis. It is like the body's early warning system. It tells you that what may seem like a minor problem (like a slight rash) is, in fact, life threatening and can cause death if you do not seek medical attention right away.

Fast forward to 2001. My 9-month-old had her first spoonful of yogurt and began breaking out in (what I now knew to be) hives. Her demeanor changed dramatically. While she did not have the language skills to verbalize a "fear of impending doom," I could tell something was drastically wrong. I called the doctor right away and told him I believed she was suffering from an allergic reaction. Based on my description, he recognized the signs and directed us to get the help she needed. This saved my daughter's life.

Unfortunately, that was only the first of several anaphylactic reactions my daughter experienced. She was later diagnosed with a severe allergy to dairy products, eggs, peanuts, tree nuts and sesame seeds. She suffered anaphylactic reactions over a half dozen times and nearly lost her life twice.

Each reaction begins in the same way. She gets a few hives and then that "fear of impending doom" sets in. Experience has enabled me to recognize the gravity of the situation and administer the emergency medicine without delay.

Parenting a child with food allergies has many challenges, not the least of which is feeling helpless when you don't have control over the situation. I chose to take control in the only way I know how – by helping others.

For the past 13 years, I've used my legal background to advocate for the rights of individuals living with food allergies; as well as educating and training others on how to provide the proper care. I have worked with local, state and federal legislators to pass legislation that increased education about and access to epinephrine.

In that time, I've been fortunate enough to work with the Center for Disease Control on producing their *Voluntary Guidelines for Managing Food Allergies in Schools and Early Care and Education Programs*, which is available on their website and distributed to schools nationwide. This document is the leading resource for educators to understand the best practices for caring for children with food allergies.

It was also due in large part to my persistence that "fear of impending doom" became a recognized symptom of anaphylaxis on the emergency action form produced by the leading not-for-profit in the food allergy community: Food Allergy Research and Education (FARE). Parents, teachers and medical professionals everywhere use this document (available on their website) to educate caregivers on how to quickly recognize and treat anaphylaxis.

My fresh start moment recently culminated in a concrete way. I was invited to participate in a summit on food allergies and anaphylaxis held in Chicago for leaders in the emergency medicine and EMT community. Apparently, since the field of food allergies is relatively new, there is a big learning curve, even for medical professionals.

Those of us at the summit worked for days to impart a better understanding of how to recognize and treat an anaphylactic reaction. I stressed the importance of recognizing this "fear of impending doom," which many of the participants had never heard of before.

As a result of the knowledge shared that weekend, this task force has embarked on a five-year plan to educate emergency room physicians and EMTs to better recognize and quickly treat anaphylaxis. This will definitely help save countless lives.

I am so grateful my fresh start moment enabled me to "connect the dots" in order to help others.

AN INSPIRED CHOICE
by Pat Grimley Williams

During the first semester of my sophomore year in college, I was concerned about my major. I had thought that I would major in French and, eventually, become a translator with the Foreign Service. Not a very practical choice for a student from a lower-middle-class family. I knew that I needed to be totally self-supporting from the minute I graduated.

I was attending a state university and could not afford to study abroad, even for a semester. (Back in the very early '60s not many students studied abroad anyway.) Also, due to the method of teaching foreign languages in the public schools at the time, I did not have much oral proficiency and was finding that although I read and wrote French extremely well, I really couldn't speak it very well, and I did not seem to be making any progress in conversing in French despite six years of study.

During a trip home to Worcester, Massachusetts, my two-year-old brother was hospitalized for several days, and I was impressed with the medical and nursing staff I observed while visiting him. Meanwhile, I befriended several nursing students at the university I was attending and was also impressed with what they had to say about the nursing program. At the time, I was taking a course in zoology that focused on human anatomy and physiology. It was fascinating, and I was getting an "A."

Within days after visiting my brother in the hospital, it hit me, "I'll change my major to nursing." It would be a "win-win" situation. A major that leads to a job (nurses will always be needed). Helping people appealed to me. The subject matter was to my liking. I could live just about anywhere. I could get married or be single, etc.

After a conversation with my folks, I switched my major to nursing. It wasn't quite as simple as expected because I needed an additional (fifth) year and a summer of required science courses. The Pell grants and the National Student Loan programs were just emerging and helped to fund the extra costs.

I completed the five undergraduate years in June 1964, successfully passed the grueling three days of licensing exams (now it's a one-day computerized test) and was hired for my first nursing job. I worked in clinical nursing services for the next 13 years.

In 1977, with a great husband and three growing children, I completed the requirements for teacher certification (receiving my Master's degree several years later), and I spent almost 25 years as the Director of Health Education, Health Services and Safety in a local public school department. It was a great career that allowed me to be involved in school administration, grant writing, classroom teaching, school medical and nursing services, child abuse prevention, liaising between parents and the community, social services agencies, fire and police departments and much more.

All because of those visits to my 2-year-old brother in the hospital.

P.S. That 2-year old brother became a grandparent for the first time on November 16, 2014.

BY GOD'S GRACE
by Brenda Carney, MS, RN, FNP-C

Shortly after my birth, my mother decided to "give me up" and place me in a foster home. The compelling decision was not an easy one, even to a rather stoic family such as mine. Their lack of resources and support made this move the only reasonable one. As fate has a way of unfolding, I returned to my birth home and into the single household my father abandoned periodically for long lengths of time.

I was 7 years old when I first felt the emotion of "pride." My mother had worked diligently for months through a then governmental program called Manpower, which was aimed at helping poor families receive educational training in the nursing field. I tried heartily to pronounce the "big words" and help her study. To see her in a crisp white uniform in many years to come was nothing short of fulfilling.

My grandmother suffered a stroke leaving her paralyzed at the young age of 55. Her left side was paralyzed, and it took time for her to learn to walk with a cane and functionally manage her activities of daily living. Cooking and cleaning, dressing and eating were all new again. So was her mood. My grandma had become funnier, light hearted and loving. She hugged more, she giggled more. Since I spent my weekends and most of my summers there, I became quite skilled in cooking, cleaning and assisting another human being with the simple things we take for granted, like cleaning dentures or glasses.

At 16, I got involved with a "boy-man" who was seven years my senior and ultimately ended up pregnant. I was entering

11th grade. We married by Christmas. I doubled up my junior and senior years of high school. Within the next four years, by the age of 20, I produced one son and three daughters.

Life as a grown-up was lonely and persistent. I worked part-time in a nursing home and again was in awe of the nurses and their roles – how much they cared for and helped others, keeping the direction focused for the whole team.

When my youngest entered Head Start, I decided to go back to what I loved, caring for people. By fall, I was enrolled in a nursing program. In two years I received an associate degree in nursing science and was on my way to empowerment as a parent, and fulfillment as a person.

Over the next 10 years I studied dutifully and got my Bachelor's degree. My role in the local hospital took me into the fields of oncology, intensive care, orthopedics and neurology. I landed in the midst of the Emergency department and found an exciting, never-ending demand on my energies.

One thing I took away from nursing was the desire to better advocate for patients. People do not realize the demands on healthcare professionals. In the blink of an eye, everything can change. It's magical and mysterious, more than rewarding and nothing less than frightening. I was in many positions of authority, was asked to be a supervisor and manager, but my true role was as a patient advocate.

In the year 2000, my grandson was born by C-section after experiencing fetal distress. It was a nightmare and he suffered severe brain damage, living a short 13 months. This event enveloped my young family like an igloo. We helped and cared for each other, but the walls outside were cold.

My children were just young adults, and this was a traumatic life changer. To this day, I am proud of the way they persevered and helped care for Jaden Zechariah, my sweet forever baby grandson.

At 45, I decided to use my retirement money to go back to school to become a nurse practitioner, a role that has only been around for 47 years.

Nurse practitioners are not physicians. We are nurses who exemplify the highest ideals of nursing science to provide safe effective care to our patients.

In New York State, I can legally be someone's primary care provider. What does this mean to me? Whoopee! I can advocate to the fullest extent of my license for my patient. You see, as a nurse, we suggest and offer our bird's-eye view to the provider, many times a doctor. We express our observations and occasionally make suggestions to increase comfort or improve function. The provider's written order is a hit or miss. Sometimes they remember to write an order we may have suggested, sometimes not. My role no longer depends on that chance, because I am now an advocate and can write any needed orders myself.

Working as an NP took me back to the Emergency department and then on to the inner city to open a federally qualified health center focused on caring for refugees from all over the world. In our little city of 60,000, there are 41 different cultures and 39 languages. I was happy to be a part of something so needed in our city.

I have been vice president and president of our local nurse practitioner association. What's our goal? To inform the public about nurse practitioners, what we are, what we do! And learn, learn, learn!

The smartest person I know admits to knowing very little, and I love being in the company of someone like that! Oh, it is not a real person, it's the element any person along your way possesses. I follow this element everywhere, and I bring my commitment and the desire to do the best I can for others right along with me.

Today I work as a primary care provider and oversee about 1,500 patients in the rural community. My next stop? I've been offered a hospital position in North Carolina in a Level 1 hospital.

Weeeeee! I'm going to learn, learn, learn!

WE'VE ALL GOT THEM
by Patty M. Kearns

Your "start button" is on when the Spirit is moving you. As a writer, I pay the utmost attention to my Muse. When the angel enters the room, I drop everything else and begin taking dictation. There's no communication without listening, so I listen closely. It very well may be that I am being called to something, something I wouldn't want to have missed on my daily to-do-list, or bigger – a goal for the next chapter of my life's purpose.

In search of direction, I learned all this early on and I'm the wiser for it. I've lost hold of a good paragraph or two in my day simply because I did not, with undivided attentiveness, put it in writing.

If you catch yourself in this misfortunate moment, go respectfully to stillness. Their words are carved in gold, and most times your angel will not repeat the same ones twice. Pivoting from one side of a sentence to another, you may need to extrapolate and get creative about making something fit until the thought comes back to you. But you could in a nanosecond forget a spectacular new idea, a whole concept, the cause for the inspiration, the reasons you are still with someone, the precise context that illuminates the message, or worse – the entire direction in which you were being sent in the first place. I know better, so I bend over backwards to avoid those missed-message traps that are the true time wasters.

The start button, I learned, is for beginnings along new pathways. You just press it when you are derailed from your former tracks and, if you've paid attention, your detour zooms you safely away from a horrific major crisis.

I caught on suddenly. I had this precious 1-month-old baby girl and had to find somewhere to live. With no money, no job, no car, no husband and no education, I smiled and told my beautiful baby, "Jillian, you and Mommy are going to go to college."

She absolutely ate it up. What I recall most about her first thoughts on life was how compassionate she was. She administered a message of uncanny relief: "Don't worry, Mama. Everything always works out."

Great words for getting you out of your own way, she still employs them as necessary. She has a powerful start button and keeps it in the "On" position. Angels always say, "Fear Not." She gave me step one of my Darwinian program of resilience.

For 16 years I pressed the start button each semester, while I worked a full-time job plus three others. A start button can get you a summa cum laude in communications if you are judicious with it. Jillian, after becoming a Mom of two, earned herself two Master's degrees in Education that advance her classroom work.

We also had something else going for us: the Cookie Jar. You can use the start button as much as you like … but you Don't Touch The Cookie Jar. You wait patiently for years until you know what it's for.

Penny by penny, our cookie jar grew modestly because we went without. You know how kids are. Bubble gum machines in the super markets? "No." Balloons for birthdays? "No. And no pizza on Friday night until the new job starts Monday."

Don't think all this was sad. It was glorious. We had direction. Nevertheless, our college payments for Jillian were like a tsunami. And when my Mom's Alzheimer's got worse and she was sick round-the-clock, I had already forfeited my job to the Great Recession.

It's amazing how anyone lives on no income for more than 10 weeks. Mom and I were homebound, but the start button got me up every morning with or without the sleep. For more than a decade, Mom and I walked together through a darkening tunnel. Then her spirit rose into the Light.

During it all, I had discovered that the darkness makes the joyous moments flicker with cherished, shared understandings. Alzheimer's, I found, stretches our capacity for a divine kind of love. It grows our ability to commune in higher ways.

What about that Cookie Jar? Well, it was for Mom and me. It bought us 10 years of a roof over our heads, a bit of heat, some food and precious togetherness.

The piles of paperwork were daunting, but with a start button, you can move mountains. While caregiving, I had somehow managed to create a meditation CD program and author two books, all of which have helped move mountains for others. Isn't that what our start button is supposed to be doing anyway?

I see now what my struggles were all about. My treasure is in the slow, steady, patient level of kindness—the "Faithful and Constant" of my Dad's Irish coat of arms that has cost me my lifetime to master.

Fortunately, I had grown up with something my Mom's own darling mother told me one night as we said our prayers, "Ask for a sign."

My Grandma's suggestion ultimately helped me polish my intuitive listening skills, critical for recognizing each new start. From all sides, it seems there have been great forces at play. Asking plus listening equals prayer and meditation.

See how the ideas arrive? The connections keep getting stronger, full circle. Sometimes I can't even hit the start button fast enough! But my own two grandchildren can, with all the exhilaration of balloons, pizza and bubblegum.

Every morning our beloved planet keeps spinning, and my start button gets a fresh new chance like none ever before.

MUSIC LIVES IN ME
by Mike Moscovitz

Music was in me from an early age. As a young kid, a boy soprano, I remember singing in a local choir with a great tenor who was older than I was. His name was Jacob Perelmut, and he became the renowned tenor Jan Peerce.

Years later, when I was stationed overseas during World War II, I sang whenever I was off-duty. Sometimes another soldier accompanied me on the piano; other times I sang on my own. Singing was more than a way to pass the time. It was a way to bring "home" a little closer.

Those were tough times for all of us. When London was bombed, entire streets crumbled. I remember helping a little 5-year-old girl out of that rubble. My parents had sent me some Bit-O-Honey candy, which I shared with her.

Like all of the brave soldiers I served with, I saw firsthand the destruction caused when our differences divide us. Maybe that is why music played such an important role in my life. Music connects people in a way that goes beyond differences.

After the war, I sang at the VA every Friday night. I sang other places, too. My "fresh start" began when my friends Sylvia and Phyllis invited me to the Northeast Focal Point Senior Center in Deerfield Beach, Florida, one town from where I lived.

In addition to providing valuable programs for children and seniors, they had an Alzheimer's day care center. I felt inspired and offered to entertain them.

I sang songs from Broadway shows and songs from my youth, like *Take Me Out to the Ballgame*. Depending on their condition, many of the participants knew the words and sang along. I began to perform there every month. I loved them and they loved me.

When Phyllis and I were married in 1964, we went to the Northeast Focal Point Senior Center together. I would sing, and she would put her arms around the patients. Phyllis had her own special way of making people feel good.

I'm in my 90s now and have been singing for Alzheimer's patients for more than 26 years. I might even be singing while you read this.

JOY OF SINGING
by Bea Rosner

I grew up singing. My father, Haskal, had a beautiful voice and sang at synagogues all over New York City. He taught me many Russian and Jewish songs, and we often sang together at home. I just never imagined doing it in public.

During World War II, I felt patriotic and wanted to find some way to contribute to the cause. So, although it meant traveling for hours, I left my bookkeeping position and went to work at the Brooklyn Navy Yard, where they assembled ships for the war. Working there changed my life and seeded my "fresh start" moment.

At lunch, a few of us would get together and entertain. With a little encouragement, I began to sing. It was a large navy yard, and some of the workers would leave their stations to watch us.

One of the men I met there was a tap dancer who worked as a volunteer entertaining for servicemen. He asked me if I would like to join him and his friends. As a result, I became part of a group of young people who put on shows for the armed forces in NYC.

My first performance was singing for troops at a base in Brooklyn. My sister and I took the subway from our home in the Bronx. Then we took a taxi because we didn't know where it was. The taxi driver took us to our destination, two blocks away from where he had picked us up.

I sang *I'll See You Again Whenever Dreams Come True Again.* That was the first time I performed at a public event. It was exhilarating.

The Army would send vans to pick us up and take us to Veteran's Hospitals and different locations throughout the city. I was happy to be giving something back to our soldiers who were sacrificing so much.

The leader of our group found us other places to perform. Once, I sang at a local movie house where they also had vaudeville acts. I wore theatrical pancake makeup, red lipstick and a long gown that I bought on sale for two dollars. I sang *Long Ago and Far Away* and was followed by a dog act, which I enjoyed watching.

Throughout the years, I've sung in different theater productions. My husband, Sam, was also musical. He was British and taught me wonderful English songs that I loved. At home, he would play the harmonica and I would sing. During the summer, we worked at a resort in the Catskill Mountains and performed for the guests.

Today, I am 95 years of age and still love to sing. I belong to a weekly singing group; have parties at my home where my friends and I all sing; and every month I perform with several other volunteers for Alzheimer's patients at the Northeast Focal Point Senior Center in Deerfield Beach, Florida. We sing songs from our youth, and sometimes they remember the lyrics and sing along.

Although my voice has changed over the years, the joy of singing is still with me.

GAINING VISION – RICH RUFFALO
by Bob Danzig

When sports psychologist Dr. Rob Gilbert heard that I was collecting information on leaders for my first book, he suggested I seek out Rich Ruffalo. I had just finished addressing Dr. Gilbert's graduate class at Montclair State, when he told me about this extraordinary teacher, motivational speaker and athlete who had spoken to his class earlier in the semester. I decided to contact him.

The night I went to call on Rich at his home, he opened the door and warmly welcomed me in his sharp, clear voice and said, "First, you must give me a hug."

We had just settled onto his open, airy porch and begun getting to know each another when his 6-year-old daughter, Sara, came bustling in on the scene with her equally enthusiastic mother, Dianne, to make sure Rich and his guest were comfortable. Sara offered to sing a song for me, and, after placing her rosy cheeks close to her father's rugged face, harmonized her perfectly pitched voice with her father's sweet baritone to croon a beautiful duet version of the theme song of the American Teacher Awards, *We Have Come To Teach.*

Indeed, Rich Ruffalo had come to teach. When his vision began to blur in his sophomore year of college, it did not stop him from his dream of becoming a teacher. And, when his sight left him completely as a result of the eye disease retinitis pigmentosa, his principal, Michael Lally, rejected his offer to resign because, "Mr. Ruff," as the students called him, was a superb leader in the classroom. A proctor assistant was hired to correct papers and do the chores that required sight.

Rich concluded that he had been chosen to be a role model to show his students that when adversity strikes, life doesn't stop; it merely changes direction on the pathway to success.

When they finished their song, Rich turned to his daughter and said, "You see Sara, we have come to teach, just like our song says."

Rich, a lifelong jock, is the image of the fit athlete. His movements are as full of grace as they are of power. He told me he had always been a Class-A competitor in high school and college, with a specialty in the javelin. He only began to compete in the shot put and discus when he was totally blind.

The loss of his sight created a huge vacuum in his life. It induced an uncharacteristic despondency in him, until he discovered the United States Association for Blind Athletes. Through them, he was introduced to the Paralympics, which brought together the premier disabled athletes of the world to compete. Newly inspired, Rich went on to win 20 national titles and set 15 national records in track and field. In international competition, he achieved 14 gold medals, including the 1988 Paralympic Javelin record in Seoul, Korea.

Rich's "fresh start moment" was a chance meeting on the athletic field. In his mind, it clarified the reason for his blindness and made him realize that when he lost his sight, he ultimately gained his vision.

On June 9, 1984, while competing in a St. Louis track event, a thread of life was passed to him, the way a runner is passed a baton. It ignited his leader within him. Before that day, all of his competitive, athletic competitions had been focused on the objective of lifting his personal sense of worth and self-esteem. The operative words in his meets were me, myself and I.

As he prepared for his event, he felt a tug on his arm and heard a small voice say, "Mr. Ruffalo, I'm here with the children of the St. Louis School for the Blind. They are hoping you will let them 'see' your arm and feel your strength."

Bewildered at first, Rich knelt down on one knee. One by one, the children came up to him to run their fingers over his well-veined hands, to rub the texture of his muscular arms and shoulders, and finally, to kiss his cheek in gratitude.

On that day in St. Louis, he set a new record in the Javelin throw. Hearing the special roar of excitement from the cluster of blind children, he knew that his loss of sight was a gift to inspire him to lead others to sense their own promise in life.

Since the moment that internal light kindled his life's purpose, Rich has dedicated himself to leading others to an awareness of the gold within themselves. An acknowledged leader, he is most satisfied whenever he has an opportunity to provide insights of hope and possibility, igniting the lives of everyone who crosses his path.

"The mind is a powerful tool."

Chapter Five

My Fresh Start Moments

"The mind is a powerful tool. At any moment,
we have the potential to redefine ourselves."
– Bob Danzig

Encouragement goes a long way. We never know what
our words or actions may mean to someone choosing to
win at their life.

In this chapter, I share personal stories about the many
friends and colleagues who have enriched my journey.
Great is my gratitude.

EIGHT WORDS
by Bob Danzig

This story is about eight words that changed my life and gave me a fresh start. To give you some insight into why they impacted me so deeply, I would like to share a glimpse of my choppy beginnings.

I was abandoned by my alcoholic mother when I was 2 years old. For 15 years, I bounced from one foster home to another and was often taunted, neglected and abused. My earliest memory is when I was around 5-years-old and living in a drafty Victorian house with a red-haired woman and her two aggressive sons. They were older than I was, but I did many of the household chores.

One of my jobs was to go into the dark, cold basement several times a day, fill two heavy buckets with coal and carry them up a rickety flight of stairs. My thin arms trembled at the weight. I was terrified to go into that basement alone, but there was no one there to comfort me. Nor was there anyone to rescue me when the brothers chased me down and attacked me with a belt. I learned early on to be as invisible as I could. Like many foster children, my focus was on survival.

In another home, I was forced to sit with the family and watch them east dinner. When they finished their meal, my foster mother would scrape the meager leftovers onto a paper plate; that was my supper. If I didn't seem appreciative, she would berate me. I felt unwanted and worthless.

Because I moved so frequently, I rarely had friends. I was always the new kid, the stranger, the misfit on the sidelines. I would watch boys in the schoolyard trade baseball cards, but I never had any cards to trade. Never owned any toys. Never had a birthday party. The only consistent thing in my childhood was the black canvas bag I used to carry my few belongings whenever I was sent to another home.

One night, my foster mother's children accused me of breaking something. I tried to defend myself. But she did not believe me and sent me to my room without dinner. I sat on my cot in the dusty, dark attic where I slept (I was not tall enough to reach the light switch) with tears streaming down my face and felt a familiar lump in my throat. It was there so often, I called it Lumpy.

"I don't belong here. I don't belong anywhere," I thought. I opened the attic window, climbed on the ledge, jumped to the closest tree branch and shimmied down to the street below. Scared and alone, I ran to the only place I knew, my school. I sat on the ground and leaned against a green dumpster. "I'm garbage. Just like in this dumpster, I'm nothing but garbage."

A teacher found me the next morning and called social services. I was moved to another foster home.

Perhaps now you will see why these next experiences impacted me so strongly.

When I was about 10 or 11 and being moved from my fourth to my fifth foster home, I was assigned a new caseworker named Mae Morse. A tall, angular woman with a rather hawkish, sculpted face topped with graying blonde hair.

Mae and I were about to walk to the front door of my next home when she stopped, knelt down next to me, took both my hands in hers, looked me in the eyes and said, "Never forget, Bobby. You are worthwhile."

No one had ever said anything like that to me before. For the first time in my life – I felt like a person who mattered. Those words tattooed themselves on my spirit and have remained there ever since.

During the next year whenever Mae came to check on my status, she reinforced her message at the conclusion of each of our meetings. In fact, as time went by she would ask me what she was going to say. I'd take her hand in my own small hand and say, "Never forget, you are worthwhile." Mae Morse was my first guiding light.

After aging out of the system at 17, with no family support or money, I walked into the office of the Albany *Times Union* to apply for a job as an office boy. There was a line of young men waiting to be interviewed for the position. Since there wasn't any urgency to fill the lowest job in the department, the manager, Margaret Mahoney, took applications in between handling other chores. I was last in line.

When it came my turn, she looked at me and said, "I want to ask you a question."

"Yes, ma'am," I replied.

"Why are you wearing that hat?"

I explained that my friend suggested I looked too young and should wear a hat to the interview.

"But," she admonished, "you have been inside this department for over an hour. You are supposed to take your hat off when you walk inside."

I then whisked the hat off and explained that I'd never had a hat before and did not know what to do with it. Her stern stare turned into a warm smile. To this day, I am convinced she gave me the job because I did not know enough to take off my hat.

The paper became my family. I had been working there around four months when Margaret asked me to come to her office. She sat me down in a chair facing her and said, "I was a foster parent myself. When I saw that you came through the foster care system, I felt inspired to take an interest in you. I've been the office manager here for 15 years and have seen office boys come and go. Your positive manner has really impressed me. I have been observing you Bobby, and I believe you are full of promise."

It was magical. In that moment, Margaret Mahoney gave me permission to have ambition and changed my life forever.

Hearing these affirming eight words, "You are worthwhile. You are full of promise," I no longer saw myself as driftwood – but as a person with purpose and possibility.

EDUCATION AT SEA
by Bob Danzig

When I was called to serve in the U.S. Navy during the Korean conflict, I left the Albany *Times Union* to go to radio training school. Upon graduation, I was assigned to the USS Recovery, a rescue and salvage vessel anchored at the Brooklyn Navy yard, just 150 miles from my hometown, Albany, New York. As the ship had not moved in seven years, I was told I could expect a land-based tenure for my remaining naval service. That promise was short lived.

As I set foot on board, the ship foghorn blared out three bursts, the gangplank rose behind me, and the USS Recovery began to pull away from the dock. This startled me. The very last thing I thought might happen in choosing this assignment was that I would leave the cozy safety of the Brooklyn dock and head out to points unknown in a dark and mysterious ocean. All my other shipmates were excited by the prospect of going to sea, but this new sailor felt like a fish out of water. Once again I was adrift.

My duty station was on the bridge of the ship, where the radio shack was located. The shipmate in the bunk above me was also one of the sailors working on the bridge. His name was Bob Myers. As we began to get acquainted, Bob told me that he had joined the Navy after graduating from New York University with an honors degree in English literature.

Bob had negotiated for two lockers near our bunks. The second was filled with all the classics—Blake, Milton, Homer, Shakespeare and just about every other author in the Modern Library series.

With my learning deprived, foster home background and minimal devotion to school, it seemed natural and honest to admit to Bob that I had never read a complete book. Rather than looking down at me, he said that he would adopt me as a student if I were genuinely open to learning. Thus began my education "abroad."

Bob would have me read one of the great novels. Then, we'd follow-up with hours of fascinating discussion about character development, plot nuance and the writing style of each great work's author. I had no idea where I was going with the information Bob gave me. I just knew I enjoyed his teaching. He introduced me to worlds and people far removed from my previous experiences, and I began to see the world in color. He also taught me how to let the author guide my imagination and helped me realize the unique gift an author can provide a reader.

By the time I left the USS Recovery, I had the privilege of a passionate guided tour through a vast collection of many of the world's great books. More importantly, Bob Myers showed me that I had the potential to learn.

A PORT IN THE STORM
by Bob Danzig

After the Navy, I resumed my job as a classified salesman at the Albany *Times Union*. At the time, the retail advertising salesmen were generating greater revenue than the classified salesmen.

My colleagues and I were in direct competition with the Gannett-owned *Knickerbocker News*. I went to our advertising director, Mark Collins, and proposed that I be given an opportunity to handle the retail advertising food category. The competing *Knickerbocker News* had 100 percent of the food advertising because, historically, it was the city newspaper that serviced a more cohesive audience as compared to the wide area distribution of our morning newspaper.

I told Mr. Collins that if he gave me a six-month trial period to manage the food category, I would also continue to handle my classified job. If he felt I was falling down on the job, he could stop the experiment.

Mr. Collins gave me the opportunity, but insisted I give up the classified territory. So, I left my old job and began a new sales position with zero business.

Frank J. Nigro was the leading food merchant in Albany. He owned the Albany Public Markets, which he literally built up from a single corner, outdoor vegetable bin.

I began to call on Frank Nigro every day with a new idea or some piece of research. I would take his ads from the competitive press, add a little spin and show him how much more effective and punchy they could be.

Years later, he told me that my inventiveness and diligence had always intrigued him. In contrast with the others who were working in the business he had built, he said I always represented a fresh new promise for him.

I don't believe I had the food category for 60 days when Frank astonished me by splitting his schedule. Instead of running 10 pages a week exclusively in the *Knickerbocker News*, he ran five pages with each of us. Within one year, the *Times Union* owned the food category; within two years it acquired the *Knickerbocker News*. My job as a retail advertising salesman was secure.

Seeing Frank Nigro every day allowed me to view, firsthand, the integrity of his relationship with every vendor, supplier and employee. I frequently met him at the customer service area of his main store just as a customer arrived with a complaint about an item. He acted immediately and, with great courtesy, gave the customer a replacement item or his money back. In those instances, the customer always went away satisfied.

Every employee was treated with trust. He would chat amicably with each one, underscoring the fact that his grocery empire was built on this simple credo: "If you do the right thing with everyone with whom you come in contact, the majority will do the right thing for you." His character was the cornerstone of his leadership, and it became part of the foundation of those under his influence.

About three years into my relationship with Frank, I applied for the new position of retail advertising manager at the newspaper but was told I was too young. That afternoon, I paid my regular visit to Frank. He took one look at me and he could tell something was going on. "You don't seem to be yourself," he said, "What's the problem?"

I explained what had happened. "That's not a problem. Go down and resign this afternoon."

"Frank," I said, "I have children to support. I can't resign."

"No, no. You resign and come to work for me. You will become my advertising and sales promotion director for the food chain. You can also become the promotion director of the shopping center I'm opening."

I accepted his offer, and we began to plan the opening event. Frankly, I did not have a clue what to do. We were opening the first shopping center in the Albany area in late October. I recalled a conversation I had with one of the copy boys from the newspaper, who had become a sports writer. When we lunched together before his promotion, he talked all the time about how inspired he was by a cousin who was a professional baseball player with the Pittsburgh Pirates. His name was Bill Mazeroski.

It just so happened that the Pittsburgh Pirates were in the World Series, and in the last inning of the seventh game, the very same Bill Mazeroski hit the winning home run.

I called my former copy boy colleague and asked him if he could possibly invite his cousin to be the star guest at the opening of the shopping center. He did, and Bill agreed to come. He threw a pitch to Frank Nigro at a small baseball diamond we set up at the shopping center.

The fact that we had the all-star winning home run hitter created a phenomenon. Thousands and thousands of people showed up. The opening was a smash hit – all because I had paid attention when I was the office boy and he was the copy boy. The shopping center opening was a stunning success.

Within a few weeks, the newspaper management called me up and asked me out to lunch. I told Frank, and he encouraged me to go. At the lunch meeting, the newspaper's senior manager said, "Bob, we have been thinking this over and concluded that you're really not so young. We would like you to come back to the newspaper and take the job of retail advertising manager."

I went back to Frank Nigro after lunch and said, "This is an awkward situation, but...."

"Don't even say anything," he replied. "They now want you to be retail advertising manager of the paper."

"Yes."

"I knew that would happen," he said. "I was only giving you a port in the storm. I just wanted to provide you with a harbor until the newspaper thought things through."

STEPPING UP TO THE PLATE
by Bob Danzig

When I first joined the advertising sales staff at the *Times Union*, Angelo Monaco (Angie to everyone) was the retail advertising sales manager. He had a face that looked as if it was chiseled from a mountainside: deep lines, a permanent frown, a long oval shape, all topping a reluctant shirt and necktie-framed neck.

Angie looked and acted like a "man's man." Although I rarely saw him smoke a cigarette, I never saw him without a long, black, ivory-tipped cigarette holder in his lips. It seemed more prop than habit, and had the desired effect of causing one to look at his lips carefully when his low-pitched voice was whispering some instruction through and around that cigarette holder. Intimidation seemed his ally against any who had a direct reporting relationship to him.

At the time, my sales territory was the grocery stores. A major account was the A&P chain, which favored our *Times Union* only slightly because we had a Sunday newspaper and our competitor did not. A&P was opening their Albany Superstore, and all the national executives were to be in Albany for the Monday morning opening. Kick-off for the event was to be a two-page ad in our Sunday *Times Union*. I handled the account, processed the ad, and was frankly "pumped up" with pride at our coup of having the launch exclusively in our newspaper.

On Sunday morning I raced to get the paper and flipped through the pages looking for the colorful opening ads for the new superstore. No ad! Sinking feeling. Disaster looming in my imagination, I drove to the newspaper plant and talked to the composing room foreman, who then chased down the original copy. The insertion date for the ad to run, in my clear handwriting, was for the following Sunday. I had scheduled the ad for the biggest event in A&P history for the wrong Sunday.

I wandered out of the plant devastated and confused, certain my career was over. Almost without thinking, I drove to the home of Angie Monaco, who was just returning from church with his family. I burst out in a shriek that I had incorrectly scheduled the major opening ad.

Angie leaned against the car, slowly took out his cigarette holder, managed that tight-lipped grin and said, "You cannot be telling me you left the ad out of the paper can you?"

"Yes," I answered.

With that, he waved his arm, beckoning me to follow him into the house. Once inside, he picked up the telephone and asked for the home number and address of Jack Casey, the A&P regional manager. With address in hand, he stormed out of the house, barely giving me enough time to follow, and we drove to Jack Casey's home.

Angie rang the bell, and when Jack answered, told him what I had done. They both stared at me, and then Angie said, "We are here to start over and get four pages of opening announcements in the Monday morning paper – two pages in the first section and two pages in the second section, all without charge to A&P."

Jack agreed with the remedy and the three of us set off to the newspaper to make the arrangements. On the drive down, Angie told Jack that we must keep in mind that the only reason A&P's opening day could be saved by running the double impact ads on Monday was because I had owned up, sought him out, and acted like a partner, rather than a simple employee. Jack agreed. Later that day a fruit basket arrived at my home with a message from Jack: "You Saved the Day Partner. Thank You!"

On Monday I told Angie about the basket. He smiled for the first time I could remember, and said that the life lesson for me was to always step up to the plate when a mistake had occurred. That lesson served me well at all levels of my career.

PROFESSIONAL INHERITANCE
by Bob Danzig

Gene Robb was the publisher of the Albany *Times Union*, a towering figure who left a subtle but permanent imprint on my life, like a watermark on fine paper. He didn't just touch my life; he guided me as well. A gentle man, with movie-star good looks, Gene was both a lawyer and a journalist. He was truly a refined man with an uncommon air of elegance about him. He manifested these qualities of leadership in a subdued but effective way – breathing personal integrity into every aspect of the Albany *Times Union*.

Gene Robb had a great passion for words; he loved the world of writing. That's what first brought us together. I was studying English literature at Siena College nights and had begun to publish small pieces in the college's literary journal, the Beverwyck, under the name R. Danzig.

Mr. Robb was on the Board of Trustees at Siena College, and, therefore, received every publication the college printed, including the literary journal.

One day, we were riding on the elevator at the newspaper when he turned to me and said, "I see an R. Danzig at Siena College writing for the Beverwyck. Is that someone related to you?"

I said, "No, Mr. Robb. That is me. I go to Siena College at night."

Our conversation ended there, but afterwards Gene Robb did something one might not be able to do today. He became intrigued because I was a successful young salesman going to college at night as an English major, a subject dear to his heart.

Without my knowledge, he had my grades sent to him after every semester.

When I graduated from Siena College in 1962, Mr. Robb asked me to join him for breakfast one Saturday morning. He told me that it was his intention to retire from the publisher's position in 1974 and write editorials. That is when I discovered he had been having my grades sent to his office. He said, "I've concluded that I would like you to be an optional candidate to succeed me someday. With that in mind, I am going to put you into a 12-year program where you'll go into the various disciplines of the newspaper. But the deal will be that whatever job you go into, if you can't cut it, you can't go back to the old job. You are not going to be a crown prince. You really must perform every assignment."

Seven years short of completing the program, Gene died suddenly of a heart attack, and I succeeded him as publisher of the *Times Union*. At first, it was bewildering for me to walk into the office that was once Gene's. He was such an unusual human being because he focused so intensely on the spirit and soul of the newspaper. That focus became part of my professional inheritance. He had taught me that we were more than a business institution, more than an employer of people. He taught me that a newspaper has to reflect the essence of its community. It cannot do this unless the person who sits in the publisher's chair constantly nurtures that relationship. Those lessons were extraordinary gifts for him to pass on. They never left me.

NEW DOORS
by Bob Danzig

On an oddly warm January day in 1977, 27 years after I first applied for a job as an office boy and seven years after serving as the publisher of the Albany *Times Union*, I left my beloved paper for the last time.

I was in New York City, about to cross a busy Manhattan street. Ahead of me, I could see the statuesque, bronze doors of the Hearst Corporation Headquarters building. I was about to walk through those doors as the new nationwide president of Hearst Newspapers.

As I stood contemplating those corporate doors, a flood of "door memories" flashed in my mind. I thought of all the strange foster home doors I had walked through during my childhood. None of them deserved my memory because none ever created the warmth of "being home." I thought of the countless times I walked through the doors of the Albany *Times Union* over the years, first as an office boy, then a salesman, and then as the publisher. I could recall the sense of finally feeling like I belonged somewhere. A place that I could call "home." Then too, there were the doors of my own residence. Having married and become a father to five amazing children, I had a real family of my own.

Now, here I was, about to walk through those massive bronze doors to again be humbled by the knowledge of the enormous responsibilities facing me. I knew that in time those corporate doors would afford me a sense of "belonging." Still, I must have stood staring at them for at least a half hour before going in.

Finally, I took a deep breath, crossed the street, walked through those bronze doors and smiled at the fact that this former foster child was about to experience yet another fresh start moment.

OWN IT
by Bob Danzig

In 1987, 10 years after I became President of the Hearst Newspaper Group, preparations were underway for Hearst Corporation's 100-year anniversary. Many events and activities were planned in advance. Among them were preparations for a Silver Centennial book, which would celebrate the talent of the entire corporation.

A well-known graphic design agency was hired. They suggested we fly our newspaper editors to New York City, where each would be interestingly posed in a unique fashion as part of a group photograph for the book. The photo shoot took place about a year before the publication. The idea had a "buzz" to it – the exciting key component needed to celebrate 100 years of great talent.

About four months before the anniversary date, I suddenly realized that several staff changes had occurred since the photograph was taken. Some editors had retired, one had passed away, and new editors had replaced them. I called the graphic design agency. They advised me that local photographers at each newspaper could photograph the new editors, and their agency would insert the replacement pictures.

My problem solved, I forgot all about it, and we began to firm up our other anniversary events. Without my knowing, the Centennial issue went to press.

Someone at the printer producing the anniversary issue knew some of our editors and also knew someone at *Time* magazine. He tipped them off that our Hearst Centennial book was printed with the heads of our newspaper editors on other people's bodies. *Time* went to press with a silhouette outline of the changed photos and the group photo shoot of our centennial book. They asked readers to name the mystery editors.

Our corporate communications director, who was apoplectic as he stumbled over his words, called me to describe the *Time* article. I was numb and convinced this error could end my Hearst corporate career.

The next morning, I had a call from Frank Bennack Jr., our president and corporate CEO, asking me to bring our corporate communications director to his office. Frank had a long oval-shaped table in his conference room with about 50 copies of *Time* magazine all opened to the offending article.

"Have you seen these?" he asked.

"Well yes, but I haven't seen this many copies."

He looked me straight in the eyes and asked, "How could this possibly happen?"

Although I felt my career slipping away, I said, "This is my responsibility. I never checked the proofs after the graphic design agency made the changes. They simply changed the heads of our new editors and inserted them on the former editors' bodies. They took a shortcut, but I did not take the time to check. I own the problem."

The next moment is etched deeply in my psyche, he said, "In a situation like this there is only one thing to do."

I thought, "Here comes the guillotine, off goes my head."

Then he said, "The only thing to do is laugh!" When he said that, I laughed long and hard with relief. He also said, "Thank you, Bob, for taking responsibility. Someone else would have the fault lie at another person's feet. Good for you."

The *Time* magazine article made the *Silver Centennial* book perhaps the most celebrated in any company's 100-year anniversary. It became a collector's item.

ROOM 401
by Bob Danzig

Cream colored walls with a single divider curtain between them were the basic décor of this, one of many, intensive cardiac care hospital rooms. Each room was exactly alike; only the distinction of patients sharing the two-in-one bedroom expressed the difference.

My behind-the-curtain roommate was a glint-in-the-eye, mischievous, gargling-humor-through-the-tubes-in-his-throat, pixie-like chap named Gene Wald. We shared the room and the triggering circumstances of severe heart attacks.

With all the uncertainty, confusion and discomfort of a debilitating heart problem, anyone could experience a permanent downswing in mood, unless his or her roommate was someone like Gene.

Gene's approach to the 32 days we shared room 401 was to focus on the fun. Our room became the hub for our wing of the hospital's ambulatory patients, nurses and off-duty doctors – to congregate for food, good company and good will. "Tubes up" as he was, he managed to be the magnet for all, the spark to ignite that good will. And, he taught me to join in the spirit of the moment.

Some several years before my heart attack, my family and I moved from our upstate New York hometown to our New Jersey home, which offered easy commuter access to my office in New York City and Newark airport. With that move, we left behind all of our life-long friends and business associates. Now, traveling the country overseeing our nationwide group of newspaper companies, I was simply too busy to notice that

I had not developed new pals; my life had become entirely focused on my work and my family.

Gene became my first new friend during that month plus in the hospital. Our meeting was purely due to each of us having had a heart attack, going to the same hospital and randomly being assigned to share the same room. Room 401, my roommate and the atmosphere of good will in the face of adversity were a launching pad for a changed life. Room 401 proved to be the incubator, preparing me to begin a new life phase with an abundance of friends, a focus on my physical well-being and a more balanced attitude about the pressures of business.

Gene graduated from 401 first. I went on to the New York Hospital for open-heart surgery and was told I would need several months of quiet rest before I could expect to take even the smallest baby steps towards a normal life. I could not drive a car or walk more than a block. All I could do was sit and hope my body would mend.

On my first day home, Gene arrived and asked me to join him in building a model airplane. The next day he came with a heart happy picnic from a local deli, and the next day he took me for a ride in the country. In fact, since he was also mending from a less severe heart condition but had not yet been released to return to work, he came to see me with some fresh activity every single day for six weeks.

In the seventh week, with my vigor returning, he drove me to his local exercise club where he had gifted me a trial membership. In the eighth week, with my walks now at three miles a day, Gene had me join his Saturday walking group for their weekly jaunt.

A few years later, with our friendship robust, Gene's heart again suffered from an attack. Sadly, he did not survive. Although his body closed down, his sparkling spirit did not.

Gene's "live life with a smile" attitude and caring way – live on in the lives of all those he touched.

Because Gene introduced me to the hum of good humor, which proved to be the centerpiece of my health club and Saturday walking friends, my life has never returned to the imbalance of earlier days.

Room 401 was different from any other room in the cardiac unit. The difference was the joy filled spirit of my friend, Gene Wald, who chose me to be the happy recipient of his guidance and support.

GUIDING FUTURE FRAMERS
by Bob Danzig

A year before retiring from being President of Hearst Newspapers, a corporate colleague, Gordon Jones, head of our Business Publishing group, asked me to join him in proposing a new internal leadership enhancement program at Hearst. We studied the best such programs in corporate America, reviewed premier executive development programs at key universities, and we outlined a proposal for Hearst CEO Frank Bannack Jr. to consider. He agreed to the idea and endorsed our partnering with Northwestern University, which had a rich media understanding in their program. Thus was the Hearst Management Institute – HMI – launched.

Gordon and I partnered as co-deans in 1999. Unfortunately, he fell ill, and I began my service as Dean of HMI. Since then, I had the privilege of serving as dean for over 15 years. In that time, the program guided more than 600 leader talents, chosen by their group presidents to participate and become what I call "Future Framers" of the Hearst Corporation destiny. An ancillary bonus is the fact that these talents might never have known each other except for the HMI bonding experience.

I handed the mantle over to David Barrett, the former President of Hearst Television, this year and now serve as Dean Emeritus of HMI.

When Gordon Jones first suggested I join hands with him in framing this brand new internal leadership enhancement program, I had no idea it would become another fresh start moment.

MORE THAN A DINNER
by Bob Danzig

My pal, Walter Anderson, the editor or *Parade* Magazine, encouraged me to go forward as I was writing my first book. When it was published, he gave me a PR pop to reach Parade's 37 million readers. The success of *The Leader Within You* launched my speaking career.

One night Walter invited me to join him for dinner at the Waldorf Astoria in NYC. After a bit of chitchat, he told me that he had been teaching The Confidence Course for the past five years at the New School University in Manhattan. He said the course was based on a book he had written, and he wanted to test the principles with live students before going forward with the publication. He added that the tools he had developed really worked, and the book had been published.

I chewed slowly on my supper and wondered where this was leading. Walter then said, "I have agreed to do a series for PBS that is being televised on the same night I am scheduled to teach my course. The students are all signed up and ready to go. This is my academic baby, and you are the only person I would allow to teach it."

I replied, "As a former classified advertising salesman, I can smell when I am being sold. I know nothing about this class or about teaching. Maybe you should start thinking about someone else."

He said, "I will outline what you cover every week, and I know you can inspire these students. What if I give you a copy of my book and we meet next Monday for dinner to decide? And by the way, the course begins next Monday night."

I read the entire book on the plane to Hattiesburg, Mississippi, where I was scheduled to speak. I finished it sitting on a yellow plastic chair at the Hattiesburg airport. I said to myself, "This is a big idea."

When Walter and I met, I told him I was going to teach the class with a larger purpose in mind. That was my "fresh start moment." Seven years later, I had guided hundreds of adult students to live with more confidence; I spoke to several thousand more by including these principles in my talks.

Speaking to audiences around the country about these confidence-enhancing tools, I determined that one day I would film a series for people to access those tools. I am pleased to say that vision has been realized.

The seed Walter planted continues to flower. That meeting was truly more than dinner.

LEARNING FROM THE BEST
by Bob Danzig

One evening, my good friend Rich Ruffalo introduced me by phone to Nancy Vogl, who owned a speakers bureau in Michigan. Nancy was courteous and told me that she only represented speakers whom she saw speak in person. She said if I ever spoke in Michigan she would try to attend. She gave me her contact information and gracefully hung up.

A few weeks later, I was invited to speak to students at the University of Georgia. I called Nancy and asked if she would come for those two days to hear me. She said, "No, but I will come for one day."

After I spoke, a young woman named Kelli Parker (her story appears in Chapter One) asked me a question about success. She said she had grown up in foster care and didn't have the opportunities or support that I did.

Until that day, I had never spoken about my childhood in public. It was a black hole that was better left undisturbed. Yet, there she was right in front of me, and she needed my help. So, I answered her by sharing my hidden past. I spoke about my painful childhood growing up in foster care. I told her that I had no family support and was receptive to learning from others and open to "fresh start" moments. And, recalling the profound impact Mae Morse and Margaret Mahoney had on me, I told her how worthy and capable she was of creating the life she deserved.

That was the day Nancy observed me speaking. On the drive to the airport, she said, "You are the most authentic speaker I have ever heard. But you must focus on the childhood you have overcome, rather than the fact that you have been president of a multi-billion dollar company."

I answered, "No. I will not do that." (I had spoken about my past to that young woman, but talking publicly about my childhood was not something I was prepared to do on a regular basis.)

Nancy said, "Fine, then you have to find someone else to work with you."

A few days went by. I chewed on Nancy's offer, called her and said I was willing to give her way a try.

We arranged to meet at a Chicago airport conference room once a month, and she guided me in all the techniques that draw an audience to a speaker. I learned the magic of pauses, the glue of storytelling and the words that resonate with audience hearts, not just minds.

Then Nancy began to book me as a professional speaker. She introduced me to many of the nation's best speakers bureaus. Within a year I was booked steadily. Six years later I was inducted into the Speaker's Hall of Fame – only five speakers are selected each year from 4,000 candidates. Since then, I have shared my message of hope and possibility with over a million people. Meeting Nancy gave me the privilege of casting a wider light.

A GIFT FOR LIFE
by Bob Danzig

Fresh starts come in all sizes and shapes. I thought I would share one of my inclinations regarding a simple change in language.

Whenever I thank someone for what they have done for me and they answer, "No problem," I say, "Would you like a gift for life?" They are eager to hear what I have to say next.

I look them in the eye and say, "When you use the words, 'No problem,' energetically, it's a double negative. It creates a barrier or distance between you and the person you are speaking with. When you substitute the 'no problem' cliché with the words, 'my pleasure,' it has the opposite effect and draws people to you."

Words have power. Let's choose wisely.

A TRIBUTE TO MAE MORSE
by Bob Danzig

Mae Morse left an indelible impression on me as a child. Half a century later, I asked an investigative reporter if he could take a stab at finding her. He called two weeks later and said, "Good news. She is in a nursing home in Scotia, New York."

The next day, I was sitting in the foyer when the automatic doors whooshed open. A nursing aide wheeled Mae Morse towards me. Her pure white hair was perfectly coiffed, and she had light rouge on her cheeks. I knelt down next to her wheelchair and said, "Miss Morse."

"Call me Mae," she replied sharply.

"Mae, I was called Bobby as a child in foster care, and you were my social worker for a year. Every time you met with me, you said the same thing: 'Never forget, you are worthwhile.' I came here tonight to tell you that I never forgot your words. I held on to them all these years. I want you to know how grateful I am. Your words changed my life."

Mae leaned over in her wheelchair, put her nicely rouged face next to my cheek and said, "I told every foster child that."

In that moment, I realized there was nothing special about me. However, Mae Morse was special to every child she met, which underscores the power of a few words to shape a life.

As I left the nursing home, I turned to wave and smile at Mae Morse. She raised her arm, waved back and said, "Never forget. You are worthwhile."

Reflections

OPEN ARMS
by Bob Danzig

Growing up, I bounced around from one foster home to the next without ever being adopted. Yet today, I have a beautiful wife, five wonderful children and 10 treasured grandchildren. My life is overflowing with a tight family, supportive friends and a fruitful career.

As a young boy sitting with Mae Morse, I never imagined I would have so many champions in my life that inspired "fresh start" moments. Mae offered me my first glimpse of hope by affirming my sense of self. Margaret Mahoney took that a step further by reinforcing my potential and igniting my spirit. Bob Myers helped me realize that I could learn, giving me the confidence to return to school and further my education. Frank Nigro offered me a job he knew would be temporary and in the process, encouraged me to set higher goals. Gene Robb championed the next stage of my life by putting me in a development program towards becoming publisher of the newspaper. Gene Wald literally helped my heart heal. His support and enthusiasm motivated me to pursue a writing career. Walter Anderson's faith in me resulted in my teaching The Confidence Course, an area of interest that continues to flow into my current projects. Nancy Vogl's clarity of vision paved the way for my second career as a professional speaker.

All these individuals saw something in me that I never knew existed. I see that same quality in all of you – the power to meet opportunities with open arms, to invite change and create the life you deserve.

So, what fresh start buttons are my fingers on now that I tiptoe past 80? Let me, as Shakespeare might respond, count the ways: Prior to publishing *Fresh Start Moments,* I recorded four talks entitled *Tools to Enhance Confidence, Becoming An Effective Speaker, Nurturing the Leader Within You* and *Leadership Wisdom.* My wife Dianne and I, along with Michael Rosner and Kira Rosner (a brother and sister writing team) are working on several TV and film treatments. One of my books is being shopped for a reality show by the bubbly talent, Gia Ghadimian, and I have acquired a gifted agent in Los Angeles, Todd Christopher. I am currently writing my memoirs; about to embark on my next *Fresh Start Moments* book; and let's not forget the flyer on my desk about tap dancing lessons for seniors.

Life is so much more joy-filled when we "keep our finger on the start button."